T0385503

DUMBARTON OAKS
MEDIEVAL LIBRARY

Daniel Donoghue, General Editor

WRITINGS ON BODY AND SOUL

AELRED OF RIEVAULX

DOML 71

Writings on Body and Soul

Aelred of Rievaulx

Edited and Translated by

BRUCE L. VENARDE

DUMBARTON OAKS
MEDIEVAL LIBRARY

HARVARD UNIVERSITY PRESS
CAMBRIDGE, MASSACHUSETTS
LONDON, ENGLAND
2021

First Printing

Library of Congress Cataloging-in-Publication Data
Names: Aelred, of Rievaulx, Saint, 1110–1167, author. | Aelred, of Rievaulx,
    Saint, 1110–1167. Oratio pastoralis. | Aelred, of Rievaulx, Saint, 1110–
    1167. Oratio pastoralis. English. | Aelred, of Rievaulx, Saint, 1110–1167.
    De spirituali amicitia. | Aelred, of Rievaulx, Saint, 1110–1167. De
    spirituali amicitia. English. | Aelred, of Rievaulx, Saint, 1110–1167. De
    quodam miraculo mirabili. Latin (Venarde) | Aelred, of Rievaulx, Saint,
    1110–1167. De quodam miraculo mirabili. English (Venarde) | Aelred, of
    Rievaulx, Saint, 1110–1167. De institutione inclusarum. | Aelred, of
    Rievaulx, Saint, 1110–1167. De institutione inclusarum. English. |
    Venarde, Bruce L., 1962– editor, translator.
Title: Writings on body and soul / Aelred of Rievaulx ; edited and
    translated by Bruce L. Venarde.
Other titles: Dumbarton Oaks medieval library ; 71.
Description: Cambridge, Massachusetts : Harvard University Press, 2021. |
    Series: Dumbarton oaks medieval library; DOML 71 | Includes
    bibliographical references and index. | Latin, with English translation
    following; introduction and notes in English.
Identifiers: LCCN 2021007287 | ISBN 9780674261181 (cloth) ·
Subjects: LCSH: Spiritual life—Christianity—Early works to 1800. |
    Prayers, Medieval—Early works to 1800. | Friendship—Religious
    aspects—Christianity—Early works to 1800. | Love—Religious
    aspects—Christianity—Early works to 1800.
Classification: LCC BX891.3 .A3513 2021 | DDC 248—dc23
LC record available at https://lccn.loc.gov/2021007287

Contents

Introduction

Aelred had a practiced understanding of holy scripture. He left for posterity an eternal memorial: splendid books and treatises adorned by lucid style and packed with edifying instruction by the inspired spirit of wisdom and learning that filled him. He was as well a man of perfect integrity, endowed with worldly wisdom, witty, eloquent, genial and charming, generous and discreet. Moreover, he surpassed all contemporary ecclesiastical leaders in his patience and tenderness and was extremely compassionate about the infirmities, both physical and moral, of others.

—Jocelyn of Furness, *Life of Waltheof*

I confess to you, my God, that I am not as contrite or fearful about my past actions as I should be, nor suitably concerned about present ones. And you, sweet Lord, have placed such a one—such a one!—over your household, over the sheep of your pasture. You command me, troubled too little about myself, to be troubled about them. You command me, not in the least adequate to pray for my own sins, to pray for them. And you command me, who have taught myself little, to teach them. Woe is me: what have I done, what have I dared, to what have I agreed?

—Aelred of Rievaulx, *A Pastoral Prayer*

AELRED'S LIFE

Aelred, abbot of Rievaulx from 1147 until his death twenty years later, was born in 1110, the son, grandson, and great-grandson of priests. Most of the details of his biography come from an account of his life and miracles written by Walter Daniel, his scribe and confidant in his last years.[1] His birthplace was Hexham, in northern England. He received his initial education there and perhaps also studied at the school of the cathedral of Durham, in which his grandfather and great-grandfather had served as canons. In 1124, Aelred joined the court of David I, the newly crowned king of Scotland. He probably continued his formal education there alongside the king's son and stepson. Aelred rose to the position of steward, an important official in the royal household. After about a decade in David's service, while traveling on the king's business Aelred chanced to visit the monastery of Rievaulx, deep in the North Yorkshire countryside. He entered the community in 1134. The rest of his life would be spent in the spheres of both ecclesiastical and secular elites.

Rievaulx Abbey was founded in 1132, a daughter house of the Burgundian Cistercian monastery of Clairvaux. The Cistercians, whose origins lay in the late eleventh century, were characterized by their strict adherence to the Rule of Saint Benedict and by their austerity. Cistercian communities included both professed monks, or choir monks, and lay brothers, men who lived in service to the abbey but did not take monastic vows. The most famous Cistercian and the most famous monk of twelfth-century Europe was Abbot Bernard of Clairvaux (1090–1153), who sent the first abbot

and monks to Rievaulx. Aelred, then, joined a new community composed largely of French-born monks. According to his own account in *Spiritual Friendship,* he began intensive study of holy writings after his conversion to monastic life. Aelred's first diplomatic mission came in 1142, when he went to Rome as the representative of his abbot, part of a group of northern English clerics who objected to what they saw as the illegitimate election of the new archbishop of York. Soon after his return from Rome, Aelred was named master of novice monks at Rievaulx and in 1143 became the founding abbot of Rievaulx's new daughter house of Revesby in Lincolnshire. Success in guiding Revesby's first years led him to be elected the third abbot of Rievaulx in 1147.

As Rievaulx's abbot, Aelred was the spiritual and administrative leader of a rapidly growing abbey that had five daughter houses. According to Walter Daniel, the community of Rievaulx grew to include 140 choir monks and another 500 lay brothers and laymen.[2] Under Aelred's direction, Rievaulx amassed a considerable landed patrimony and embarked on a major building program.[3] The abbot continued his activities as a diplomat and advisor to fellow churchmen and secular elites. He also had administrative responsibilities for Rievaulx's daughter houses, which he visited regularly. Finally, he increasingly turned to writing, which he had begun as novice master at Rievaulx or perhaps as abbot of Revesby, but certainly by the early 1140s. In Aelred's time, Rievaulx became the most important Cistercian monastery in England, a haven that Walter Daniel described as "the home of piety and peace, the abode of perfect love of God and neighbor."[4]

Walter Daniel paid little attention to Aelred's public life,

although he noted that the abbot corresponded with popes, kings, bishops, and other highly placed people. Aelred's letters, unfortunately, have survived in only a few fragments. Nonetheless, it is clear that that the abbot was much in demand as advisor and mediator in difficult times.[5] King Henry I of England died without a legitimate male heir in 1135, shortly after Aelred became a monk. Civil war broke out between Henry's nephew Stephen, who took the throne, and Henry's daughter Mathilda, widow of the German emperor Henry V. Peace was restored nearly two decades later with the agreement that Stephen would be succeeded as king by Henry Plantagenet, Mathilda's son and thus the grandson of Henry I. Henry Plantagenet was crowned Henry II of England in late 1154. Aelred was probably among Stephen's councilors, and there is no doubt he performed that role for the young Henry II. A letter of advice to Archbishop Thomas Becket came from Rievaulx; Aelred may well have been its author.[6] The abbot certainly served as peacemaker, mediator, and advisor to other religious figures. Two of the texts in this volume show Aelred in those capacities. He chronicled his participation in and advice concerning the scandalous affair of the nun of Watton in *A Certain Marvelous Miracle* and addressed *Teachings for Recluses,* a guide to solitary religious life for women, to his sister.

Starting in the late 1150s, Aelred was subject to debilitating illnesses, probably both arthritic and digestive. Despite his infirmities, he continued to serve as abbot of Rievaulx. From about 1157 Aelred lived at first in the monastery's infirmary, then finally in a private dwelling on the grounds of Rievaulx. But this private retreat was, according to Walter Daniel, thronged with adoring monks. Even when more or

less bedridden in his last several years, Aelred continued to travel. His last documented trip was to the Scottish Cistercian abbey of Melrose less than a year before his death in early 1167. And most important for posterity, it was in these last years that Aelred wrote or completed many of the writings for which he is best remembered.

AELRED'S WRITINGS

No less a figure than Bernard of Clairvaux commissioned Aelred's first major work, *The Mirror of Charity,* in the early 1140s. In it, Aelred laid out many of the themes that would characterize his writings to the end of his life: love of God, love of neighbor, and the relationship between the two. As befitted one who moved in high political circles, Aelred next turned to historical subjects, starting with an account of the Battle of the Standard (1138) between Scottish forces led by King David I and English forces in the service of King Stephen; David was an ally of his aunt, the empress Mathilda, during the civil war in England. This narrative dates to the early 1150s, around which time Aelred also wrote a *Lamentation for the Death of David of Scotland* and *Genealogy of the Kings of the English.* In the 1150s and early 1160s, Aelred wrote about saints and their relics, most notably a life of England's saint-king Edward the Confessor (d. 1066). He also transcribed sermons delivered to his monks and wrote thirty-one homilies based on the book of Isaiah. In his last years, during which his physical limitations had become very severe, the abbot focused primarily on the themes addressed two decades earlier in *The Mirror of Charity.* They feature in two of the texts that appear here: *Teachings for Recluses*

and *Spiritual Friendship,* a Christian reworking of the treatise *On Friendship* by Cicero (d. 44 BCE), the Roman orator, statesman, and philosopher.

The charming and witty figure, wise man, kind mentor, guru, biblical scholar, and brilliant writer memorialized by Jocelyn of Furness, or the sinful, anxious abbot Aelred portrayed himself to be, was a controversial figure in his lifetime. He remains so today, the object of extensive and sometimes contentious scholarship.[7] Walter Daniel was sometimes defensive in the *Life of Aelred,* completed shortly after its subject's death. Of Aelred's election as abbot of Rievaulx, Walter writes that "there are some who think that he rose to rule this house by willful ambition" and noted that critics accused him of being "a glutton, a drunk, and a friend of publicans who gives up his body to baths and ointments."[8] Walter also notes the abbot's patience with those weak in body and character; he welcomed to Rievaulx men no other monastery would accept. In a subsequent letter aimed at critics of his encomium, Walter explains that by saying the young Aelred lived as a monk in the court of King David, he was referring to his humility, noting almost casually and without elaboration that "Aelred occasionally deflowered his chastity."[9] In his own times, then, Aelred had enemies who regarded him as an ambitious, lax, self-indulgent sensualist.

In his writings, Aelred offered ample material for critics. His recollections of his youth in *A Pastoral Prayer* and *Teachings for Recluses* include what sound like more than occasional sexual sins. The close bonds described in *Spiritual Friendship*

have led some modern scholars to claim that Aelred was gay or that, at very least, he had a circle of intimates in the monastery who incurred resentment from those who were not members of it. Although *Spiritual Friendship* fails to mention the friendship between Scipio and Laelius that was the cornerstone of Cicero's treatise, it cites as models the mythological figures of Orestes and Pylades and, repeatedly, the biblical David and Jonathan, two friendships whose homoerotic overtones are unmistakable. The precise nature of Aelred's sexual interests and history are impossible to determine, but it is easy to imagine his gentle treatment of errant monks and his close friendships arousing malicious gossip.

The monks of Rievaulx revered Aelred, whose accomplishments and reputation could easily have incited jealousy while provoking criticism that he paid too little attention to his responsibilities as a spiritual leader. Again, Aelred himself invited criticism, often voicing his regret that practical affairs demanded so much of his time. He frequently preached away from Rievaulx, and although information about his public life is incomplete, he clearly knew some of the most powerful people of his day.[10] Rievaulx under his guidance became populous, wealthy, and highly regarded. Aelred managed to be many things to many people, and as is usual in such cases, he inspired detractors as well as admirers.

The Contents of This Book

Many of Aelred's writings have autobiographical elements, including all those presented here. *Spiritual Friendship, A Certain Marvelous Miracle,* and *Teachings for Recluses* were

completed in the last years of Aelred's life. *A Pastoral Prayer,* too, has usually been dated to this late period, but it could well be a much earlier work, written on the occasion of his election as abbot of Revesby in 1143 or as abbot of Rievaulx in 1147. It is an excellent introduction to Aelred as a person, an abbot, and a thinker, so it appears first.

A PASTORAL PRAYER

"O good shepherd Jesus," begins Aelred's plea for divine aid in his position as abbot, shepherd of his monastic flock. In straightforward yet passionate language, Aelred asserts his unworthiness for his office and wonders why God has imposed it on him. He proceeds to ask God's help to lead wisely, compassionately, and with attention to the needs of each individual under his care. Aelred then prays for his monks. He hopes he may rule and teach them well and that God will guide them and provide for the spiritual and temporal needs of "your household, your own people." The abbot concludes by commending his flock to God, in the hopes that its members will carry out their vocations joyfully, thereby attaining eternal life. Throughout, Aelred's worry about his unworthiness is balanced by hope and trust as he expresses gratitude for God's many favors. *A Pastoral Prayer* is packed with biblical citations and allusions and draws inspiration from writings on the similar themes by Abbot John of Fécamp (d. 1070), Archbishop Anselm of Canterbury (1033/4–1109), and Aelred's fellow Cistercian abbot William of Saint-Thierry (ca. 1080–1148), behind all of which stands Augustine in his *Confessions.* It is nonetheless highly personal, its presentation elegant and powerful.

Spiritual Friendship

As Aelred explains in a prologue, when young he found comfort and guidance in Cicero's eloquent book on friendship, which he wants to rework on the authority of scripture and other holy writings. It has three books, which he summarizes as covering the definition of friendship, then its rewards, and finally its cultivation and preservation. Each book is framed as a dialogue. The first is between Aelred and Ivo, a young monk of the monastery of Wardon, a daughter house of Rievaulx that Aelred is visiting. Books 2 and 3 are set at Rievaulx, some years later, and recount a conversation between Aelred and two of his monks, Gratian and Walter. Part of the pleasure of *Spiritual Friendship* derives from the character sketches that emerge from the conversations. Ivo is a starry-eyed youngster, timid yet prone to intellectual impetuousness. Gratian is loving, eager, and generous, even to Walter, whose irascibility and self-righteousness show that he is based on none other than Walter Daniel, whose writings also disclose those traits.[11] Presiding over it all is Aelred, modest, patient, learned, and ever so slightly long-winded.

The treatise covers more subjects than Aelred's précis suggests. It includes questions of the origins of friendship; different kinds of friendship, both good and bad; the sort of people among whom friendship exists; who makes the best friend; the stages of friendship and reasons and procedures for dissolving it; the characteristics, pleasures, and duties of friendship; its limits; and its spiritual aspects. In an extended final section, Aelred recalls two of the most important friendships of his life.

Spiritual Friendship was completed sometime between

1164 and Aelred's death in early 1167. As he promises at the beginning, Aelred draws extensively on earlier writings. The foundation is Cicero's *On Friendship,* frequently quoted and alluded to throughout. The second and third books of *Spiritual Friendship* are rich in positive and negative examples of friendship drawn from scripture, especially the historical books of the Hebrew Bible. Aelred frequently quotes or cites Ambrose of Milan's *On Duties* and Augustine's *Confessions,* as well as other pagan and Christian authors. But Aelred does more than pile up quotations, references, and examples. Instead, he creates a work of synthesis on the power of any friendship that has its origins and purpose in Christ.

Aelred's most popular work in the Middle Ages, *Spiritual Friendship* was copied in whole or in part in many manuscripts in England and on the Continent. At least one of the shorter versions was long attributed to Augustine. Around 1200, the scholar and diplomat Peter of Blois wrote an immensely successful treatise entitled *Christian Friendship,* heavily dependent on *Spiritual Friendship* and the *Mirror of Charity. Spiritual Friendship* was first translated into a vernacular language, French, in the thirteenth century. Interest in *Spiritual Friendship* waned in the later Middle Ages but was revived in the twentieth century. In recent decades the text has been translated into Dutch, English, Finnish, French, German, Italian, and Spanish.

A Certain Marvelous Miracle

This brief narrative, closer to Aelred's historical writings than to the other three texts in this book, recounts events

that took place around 1160 and were recorded two or three years later. It is a shocking story of sex and violence. A four-year-old orphan girl was sent to Watton, an East Yorkshire monastery of the Gilbertine Order that housed both men and women, canons and nuns, as well as lay brothers and sisters. As a teenager, she begins a torrid affair with a lay brother of the community. She becomes pregnant, her fellow nuns bind her with chains and imprison her, and her fleeing lover is captured through trickery and handed over to the nuns of the community. The nuns take their revenge on him in a gruesome fashion, and he vanishes from the narrative. When it is clear that the teenage nun is about to give birth in her cell, she has two visions, during the second of which she sees two beautiful women in white carrying away what appears to be an infant. The next morning, she is no longer pregnant and soon her fetters begin to come loose. Aelred, invited to Watton to investigate and consult, concludes that God was behind this second miracle and the matter should be left to God. The account ends as Aelred, back at Rievaulx, hears that the last of her bonds has fallen away.

Readers have been hard pressed to interpret the narrative, which fails to tell us things like who the girl's parents were, what happened to her and her lover subsequently, or even her name. It is likely that Aelred wanted to keep her identity, and that of her family, private. However, two things stand out. First, as his title and prologue make clear, Aelred saw this as a miracle story, not a tawdry tale but a manifestation of God's power and grace. Second, Aelred's treatment of the protagonist is gentle, even compassionate. He makes it clear that the nun, however great a sinner, was tempera-

mentally unsuited to monastic life. He notes that although her seducer had only sex on his mind, she thought of love, and Aelred shows her stoically accepting her brutal treatment, saying she deserved worse. When Aelred visits after some of her fetters have unaccountably fallen off, the nuns suggest she be chained up again. He forbids it as presumptuous and faithless.

TEACHINGS FOR RECLUSES

Aelred's guide for women leading a solitary religious life also dates to the abbot's last years. Recluses, also known as anchoresses, were enclosed in their ordinarily doorless cells in a formal religious ceremony. *Teachings for Recluses* is addressed to the abbot's sister, who has had long experience as a recluse, and she is urged to share its contents with young women aspiring to this way of life. At the end, Aelred notes that the text is divided into three parts: one about the outer self, one about the inner self, and finally a guide to meditation designed to increase devotion to God. After a brief account of the origins of this way of life, complete with a satirical portrait of women who carry it out in an unholy fashion, Aelred begins in earnest to describe how the recluse should organize her life in matters like food, drink, clothing, contact with others, silence, and daily routine. He moves on to consideration of the merits of solitude and virginity, the practice of chastity, the cultivation of humility and simplicity, how to serve fellow humans while avoiding them, and how to love God. This last subject opens the third section, a three-part guide to meditation on Christ's favors past, pres-

ent, and future. The past here is the life of Christ. Aelred outlines a mental pilgrimage in which the recluse becomes an emotion-filled participant-observer at events from the Annunciation to Christ's crucifixion and resurrection. Meditation on the present is to include reflection on the blessings of this life; here Aelred contrasts his sister's lifelong purity to his own youthful sins. The meditation on the future concerns what comes after the death of the body, and Aelred places his sister at the seat of Christ's judgment to observe the fate of the wicked and the good. The meditation, and the treatise, ends with a description of the joys of eternal blessedness.

Although the recluse was to be solitary, she was hardly alone; in fact, many English recluses lived in cells built on the outside of a church wall. Aelred prescribes two servants to perform domestic duties and an elderly and reputable local priest to serve as spiritual advisor or confessor. Anyone wanting to speak with the recluse can do so only with a third party present and with her priest's permission. Still, that leaves three people with whom the recluse has regular interactions, and although other visitors are in general discouraged, Aelred expects her to receive some, including bishops and monastic officials. This is in keeping with the setting of this solitary life; many recluses, both male and female, lived not isolated in the countryside but in or near villages and towns.[12]

Teachings for Recluses is a highly inventive work, combining several elements into a harmonious whole. Some of the first section reads like a monastic rule, and the remarks on the inner life and youthful transgressions are in keeping

with both traditional and more novel themes in Christian spirituality. At the same time, the description of the failings of some recluses is excellent satire. The prescription for a "threefold meditation" contains nothing new in itself; calls to contemplate the life of Christ, one's own life and behavior, and life after death are found in the works of other twelfth-century writers, including Bernard of Clairvaux. But the length and the passionate tone of the meditations are noteworthy. *Ancrene Wisse,* a Middle English guide for female solitaries written in the early thirteenth century, drew heavily on *Teachings for Recluses,* and the imaginative participation in the life of Christ Aelred recommends was much in vogue in the late medieval and early modern eras.

TRANSLATING AELRED

Translating Aelred's Latin into faithful yet idiomatic English is a demanding task. I have sometimes divided long periodic sentences into two or even three parts to enhance clarity and readability, changed passive voice to active, and reduced the frequency of both asyndeton (absence of conjunctions) and polysyndeton (multiple successive conjunctions). The main difficulty, however, is with individual words, and the reader should be aware of some choices I have made, especially where nuance or consistency proves impossible.

Aelred often uses, more or less interchangeably, words that denote sweetness, pleasure, charm, enjoyment, and delight: the nouns *suavitas, dulcedo,* and *iocunditas* and the adjectives *suavis, dulcis,* and *iocundus.* In the absence of any clear pattern, I have used several English words to translate each

set of nouns and adjectives, preferring "sweetness" or "sweet" for *suavitas/suavis* and *dulcedo/dulcis*. The demands of idiomatic English, however, do not permit complete consistency, for example when Aelred refers to something as both *suavis* and *dulcis*. In a similar vein, Aelred draws on Latin's rich vocabulary for nouns and verbs to express tenderness or devotion: *amor* and *amare, dilectio* and *diligere,* and *caritas*. *Amor* and *amare* usually have positive connotations and refer to the feelings of God or humankind, but they can also be associated with carnality and wickedness, which context makes clear. *Dilectio* and *diligere,* which also signify traits or capacities of God and people alike, are unambiguously positive. In the texts translated here, Aelred uses *caritas* to refer almost exclusively to feelings of humans toward one another.[13] For the most part, I have translated all these words simply as "love." *Caritas* is sometimes "loving-kindness," but to render it so in all instances would be clumsy in English.

Most vexing of all is *affectus,* a word rarely used in classical Latin that features prominently in Aelred's writings. In his first major work, *The Mirror of Charity,* Aelred writes that *affectus* is "a certain spontaneous and sweet inclination of the very spirit toward someone" *(est igitur affectus spontanea quadam ac dulcis ipsius animi ad aliquem inclinatio)*. That definition is less helpful than modern scholars and translators would like, especially since Aelred locates *affectus* variously in the *mens* (mind), *anima,* (soul), *animus* or *spiritus* (spirit), and *cor* (heart). In any case, it is unlike the capacity of reason, which can be accounted for and is not spontaneous. Here again consistency proves impossible, in part because Aelred was not consistent in his usage of the term. I have

translated *affectus* variously as "affect," "affection," "attachment," "emotion," and "feeling," according to context and the demands of English idiom. *Caveat lector.*

Biblical translations are my own, although I have consulted the Douay-Rheims Vulgate.

Manuscript reproductions were made available courtesy of the British Library Board (MS Cotton Nero A III, fols. 2r–43v, for *De institutis reclusarum,* presented in this volume as *Teachings for Recluses*) and by permission of the Master and Fellows of Jesus College, Cambridge (for *De quodam miraculo mirabili,* presented in this volume as *A Certain Marvelous Miracle*). I thank also the Columbia University Rare Book and Manuscript Library for permission to inspect its manuscript of *De spiritali amicitia,* presented in this volume as *Spiritual Friendship.*

This book has two supremely skilled midwives. Joshua Hanley (BPhil, University of Pittsburgh, 2018) worked alongside me on Aelred for almost his entire undergraduate career, sharing his ideas about Aelred's writings and commenting on draft translations in great detail. David Townsend of the University of Toronto has reviewed both texts and translations with a sympathy for both Aelred and me that I am unable to describe or acknowledge adequately. I am grateful to Professors Tyler Sergent and Brian Patrick McGuire for sharing their thoughts on translation. At the editorial stage, Danuta Shanzer and Julia Barrow provided painstaking and extremely useful commentary. Nicole Eddy took superb care of the manuscript. For other help, I am grateful to

the libraries and librarians of Harvard University, especially Jack Eckert.

It has become a leitmotif in books of this series to express gratitude for the extraordinary kindness and generosity of Jan Ziolkowski. Just because it's a cliché doesn't mean it's not true. *Tibi gratias ago, magister, nunc et in perpetuum.*

With this volume, I hope to honor my coworkers at the University of Pittsburgh, 1996–2016, living and dead. Of the latter, I remember with special fondness Bob Doherty, Orysia Karapinka, and Hugh Kearney. I dedicate the book to Patty Landon, Grace Tomcho, and Kathy Gibson. What a privilege that was—and so much fun.

Notes

1 Walter Daniel, *The Life of Aelred of Rievaulx,* ed. and trans. Maurice Powicke (London, 1950). What follows is a very brief summary of Aelred's life and activities. Modern biographical studies on which I draw are included in the second section of the Bibliography below; sources besides Walter Daniel's account permit us to be more specific about some dates and extra-ecclesiastical activities.

2 Walter Daniel, *Life of Aelred,* 38.

3 Emilia Jamroziak, *Rievaulx Abbey and Its Social Context, 1132–1300: Memory, Locality, and Networks* (Turnhout, 2005); Peter Fergusson and Stuart Harrison, *Rievaulx Abbey: Community, Architecture, Memory* (New Haven, CT, 2000).

4 Walter Daniel, *Life of Aelred,* 37.

5 For a thorough account, see Jean Truax, *Aelred the Peacemaker: The Public Life of a Cistercian Abbot* (Collegeville, MN, 2017).

6 See Truax, *Aelred the Peacemaker,* 196–213.

7 The bibliography on Aelred's life and writings is vast. For a complete list of publications dated 1996 to 2015, see Marsha Dutton, ed., *A Companion to Aelred of Rievaulx (1110–1167)* (Leiden, 2017), 296–324. Two earlier

bibliographies (cited in the same volume, p. 325) compiled publications before 1996.

8 Walter Daniel, *Life of Aelred,* 33–34.

9 Walter Daniel, *Life of Aelred,* 76.

10 Truax, *Aelred the Peacemaker.*

11 Walter Daniel identified himself as the Walter of *Spiritual Friendship* in his *Life of Aelred.*

12 See Tom Licence, *Hermits and Recluses in English Society, 950–1200* (Oxford, 2011).

13 Underpinning human *caritas* in Cistercian thought, however, is the biblical statement that God is love (*Deus caritas est,* 1 John 4:8) and demonstrates love toward humanity.

A PASTORAL PRAYER

O bone pastor Iesu, pastor bone, pastor clemens, pastor pie: ad te clamat miser et miserabilis quidam pastor, etsi infirmus, etsi imperitus, etsi inutilis, ovium tamen tuarum qualiscumque pastor. Ad te, inquam, clamat, O bone pastor, iste non bonus pastor ad te clamat, anxius pro se, anxius pro ovibus tuis.

2. Recogitans enim pristinos annos meos in amaritudine animae meae, pavesco et contremisco ad nomen pastoris, cui me indignissimum si non sentio, certe desipio. Sed etsi misericordia tua sancta est super me ut erueres de inferno inferiori miseram animam meam, qui misereris cui volueris et misericordiam praestas in quem tibi placuerit, ita peccata condonans ut nec damnes ulciscendo, nec confundas improperando, nec minus diligas imputando, nihilominus tamen confundor et conturbor, memor quidem bonitatis tuae sed non immemor ingratitudinis meae. Ecce enim, ecce est ante te confessio cordis mei, confessio innumerabilium criminum meorum, a quorum dominatu sicut placuit misericordiae tuae liberasti infelicem animam meam. Pro quibus omnibus, quantum conari possunt, grates et laudes exsolvunt tibi omnia viscera mea.

2 Sed non minus debitor tibi sum etiam et pro illis malis quaecumque non feci, quoniam certe quidquid mali non feci, te utique gubernante non feci, cum vel subtraheres facultatem, vel voluntatem corrigeres, vel resistendi dares virtutem.

3 Sed quid faciam, Domine Deus meus, et pro his quibus adhuc iusto iudicio tuo aut fatigari aut prosterni pateris

O good shepherd Jesus, good, gentle, loving shepherd: a poor and wretched shepherd cries out to you—however weak, unpracticed, and useless, but for what he is worth still a shepherd of your sheep. He cries out to you, I say, O good shepherd, this shepherd who is not good cries out to you, worried about himself, worried about your sheep.

2. For as I ponder my early years in my soul's bitterness, I fear and tremble at the title of shepherd. If I do not realize I am most unworthy of it, I am surely a fool. But although your holy mercy is upon me to rescue my poor soul from the depths of hell—you who are merciful to whomever you want and take pity on whomever you please, pardoning sins so as not to condemn in vengeance, nor to shame in reproach, nor to love less in accusation—nonetheless I am ashamed and disturbed, mindful as I am of your goodness but not unmindful of my ingratitude. For here, here before you is my heart's confession, a confession of the countless sins from whose domination you have freed my unhappy soul as it pleased your mercy. My whole being, to the best of its ability, in return offers thanks and praise for all of this.

But I am likewise no less in your debt also concerning 2 those evils I did not do, since surely any evil I left undone was according to your guidance: either you removed the capacity for evil, or corrected my will, or gave me the strength to resist.

But what in addition should I do, my Lord God, about 3 those evils with which you, in your just judgment, still allow

servum tuum, filium ancillae tuae? Innumerabilia enim sunt, Domine, pro quibus sollicita est in oculis tuis peccatrix anima mea, quamvis non ea contritione, nec tanta cautione, quantam exigeret necessitas mea vel affectaret voluntas mea.

3. Confiteor itaque tibi, Iesus meus, salvator meus, spes mea, consolatio mea. Tibi confiteor, Deus meus, me nec pro praeteritis esse adeo contritum vel timidum ut deberem, nec pro praesentibus adeo sollicitum ut oporteret. Et tu, dulcis Domine, talem—talem!—constituisti super familiam tuam, super oves pascuae tuae, et qui parum sollicitus sum pro meipso, iubes ut sollicitus sim pro illis, et qui pro meis peccatis, orare nequaquam sufficio, iubes me orare pro illis, et qui meipsum parum docui, iubes ut doceam illos. Miser ego, quid feci, quid praesumpsi, quid consensi? Immo tu, dulcis Domine: quid de hoc misero consensisti? Obsecro, dulcis Domine: nonne haec est familia tua, populus tuus peculiaris, quem secundo eduxisti de Aegypto, quem creasti, quem redemisti? Denique de regionibus congregasti eos et habitare facis unius moris in domo.

2   Cur ego, fons misericordiae, tales tali, tam caros tibi tam proiecto ab oculis tuis commendare voluisti? An ut responderes affectionibus meis et traderes me desideriis meis, essemque quem artius accusares, districtius damnares, nec pro meis tantum peccatis sed etiam pro alienis punires? Itane, O piissime, ut esset causa manifestior cur unus peccator acrius puniretur, dignum fuit ut tot et tales periculo exponerentur? Quod enim maius periculum subditis quam stultus praelatus et peccator?

your servant and your handmaid's son to be worn down and debased? For there are countless things in your sight, Lord, that trouble my sinful soul, although it lacks the measure of contrition and vigilance my need demands and my will desires.

3. And so I confess to you, my Jesus, my savior, my hope, my consolation. I confess to you, my God, that I am not as contrite or fearful about my past actions as I should be, nor suitably concerned about present ones. And you, sweet Lord, have placed such a one—such a one!—over your household, over the sheep of your pasture. You command me, troubled too little about myself, to be troubled about them. You command me, not in any way adequate to pray for my own sins, to pray for them. And you command me, who have taught myself little, to teach them. Woe is me: what have I done, what have I dared, to what have I agreed? And you, sweet Lord: to what did you agree regarding this wretch? I implore you, sweet Lord: is this not your household, your own people whom you led out of Egypt a second time, whom you created, whom you redeemed? At last you have gathered them together from various places and made them live in common under one roof.

Why then, source of mercy, did you want to entrust such people to such a man, those so dear to you to one banished from your sight? Was it to respond to my feelings and surrender me to my desires, to be the one you reproach more sharply and condemn more harshly, to punish me not only for my own sins but also for the sins of others? Truly, most loving one, was it fitting that so many such people be exposed to danger in order to make it quite clear why one sinner should be punished more harshly? What greater danger is there for those under him than a foolish, sinful superior?

2

3   An—quod de tanta bonitate dignius creditur, suavius experitur—ideo talem constituisti super familiam tuam, ut manifesta fieret misericordia tua et notam faceres sapientiam tuam, ut sublimitas sit virtutis tuae, non ex homine, ut si forte placuerit benignitati tuae per talem bene regere familiam tuam, *non glorietur sapiens in sapientia sua,* nec iustus in iustitia sua, *nec fortis in fortitudine sua,* quoniam cum bene regunt populum tuum illi, tu potius regis quam illi? Sic, sic: *Non nobis, Domine, non nobis sed nomini tuo da gloriam.*

4. Verum qualicumque iudicio me indignum et peccatorem in hoc officio posuisti (vel poni permisisti), quamdiu tamen pateris me praeesse illis, iubes me sollicitum esse pro illis et attentius orare pro illis. Ergo, Domine, non in iustificationibus meis prosterno preces ante faciem tuam, sed in miserationibus tuis multis, et ubi tacet meritum, clamat officium.

2   Sint igitur oculi tui super me et aures tuae ad preces meas. Sed quoniam, ut sanxit lex divina, officium sacerdotis est pro se primo, deinde pro populo sacrificium offere, qualecumque hoc orationis sacrificium pro peccatis meis primum tuae immolo maiestati.

5. Ecce vulnera animae meae, Domine: omnia videt oculus tuus vivus et efficax, *et pertingens usque ad divisionem animae et spiritus.* Vides certe, Domine mi, vides in anima mea et praeteritorum peccatorum meorum vestigia et praesentium pericula, causas etiam et materias futurorum. Vides haec, Domine, et sic volo ut videas. Tu enim scis, O inspector cordis mei, quia nihil est in anima mea quod vellem latere oculos tuos, etiam si eorum possem cavere conspectum.

Or perhaps—something more worthily believed, more ₃ sweetly experienced—you chose to place such a man at the head of your household so that your mercy might be made clear and your wisdom known, that the excellence of your virtue might not derive from man, and so that if it happens to please your kindness to rule your household well through the likes of me, *a wise man might not boast of his wisdom,* nor a just man of his justice, *nor a strong man of his strength.* For when they rule your people well, is it not really you who rule rather than they? Yes, yes: *Give glory not to us, Lord, not to us, but to your name.*

4. But by whatever judgment you placed this unworthy sinner in this office (or permitted me to be placed), as long as you allow me to lead them, you command me to be concerned about them and pray more attentively for them. Therefore, Lord, I do not lay my prayers before you in my own righteousness, but according to your many mercies, and where merit is silent, duty cries out.

So let your eyes be upon me and your ears open to my ₂ prayers. But because divine law has ordained that it is a priest's duty first to offer sacrifice for himself, then for his people, I first offer your majesty this sacrifice of prayer, whatever it is worth, for my sins.

5. Lord, behold my soul's wounds. Your keen, living eye sees all *and reaches all the way to the division of soul and spirit.* Surely you see, my Lord, you see in my soul both the traces of my past sins and the dangers of present ones and even the causes and substance of those to come. You see them, Lord, and so I want you to see them. For you, in your scrutiny of my heart, know there is nothing in my soul I want hidden from your eyes, even if I could avoid your gaze.

2   Vae illis quorum voluntas est ut abscondantur a te. Non enim efficiunt ut non videantur a te, sed potius ut non sanentur et puniantur a te. Vide me, dulcis Domine, vide me. Spero enim in pietate tua, O misericordissime, quia aut pius medicus videbis ut sanes, aut benignissimus magister ut corrigas, aut indulgentissimus pater ut ignoscas.

3   Hoc est igitur quod rogo, O fons pietatis, confidens de illa omnipotentissima misericordia tua et misericordissima omnipotentia tua, ut in virtute suavissimi nominis tui et mysterii sacrosanctae humanitatis tuae, dimittas mihi peccata mea et sanes languores animae meae, memor bonitatis tuae, immemor ingratitudinis meae. Et contra vitia et passiones malas quae adhuc impugnant eam—sive ex antiqua consuetudine mea pessima, sive ex cottidianis et infinitis negligentiis meis, sive ex infirmitate corruptae et vitiatae naturae meae, sive ex occulta malignorum spirituum tentatione—virtutem et fortitudinem administret mihi dulcis gratia tua, ut non consentiam neque regnent in meo mortali corpore, neque praebeam eis membra mea arma iniquitatis, donec perfecte sanes infirmitates meas et cures vulnera mea et deformia mea formes.

4   Descendat spiritus tuus bonus et dulcis in cor meum, et praeparet in eo habitaculum sibi, mundans illud *ab omni inquinamento carnis et spiritus* et infundens ei fidei, spei, et caritatis augmentum, compunctionis, pietatis et humanitatis affectum; aestus concupiscentiarum rore suae benedictionis extinguat, libidinosas commotiones et carnales affectiones sua virtute mortificet; praestet mihi in laboribus, in vigiliis, in abstinentia fervorem et discretionem ad te amandum, laudandum, orandum, meditandum, et omnem secundum te

Woe to those who desire to be hidden from you! They 2 cannot make themselves invisible to you but rather cause themselves not to be healed but to be punished by you. Look at me, sweet Lord, look at me. My hope is in your love, O most merciful one, for you will see to it that you heal like a loving physician, correct like the kindest teacher, and forgive like the most tender father.

So this is what I ask, O source of love, confident in your 3 most omnipotent mercy and your most merciful omnipotence: by the power of your sweetest name and the mystery of your most hallowed humanity, forgive my sins and heal the sickness of my soul, remembering your goodness and forgetting my ingratitude. Let your sweet grace guide me in virtue and strength to combat the vices and wicked passions that still assail my soul—whether they arise from my worst, longstanding habits, from my infinite, daily carelessness, from the weakness of my broken and corrupted nature, or from the hidden temptation of evil spirits—so that I do not give in to them, nor that they rule my mortal body, nor that I offer them my limbs as weapons of wickedness until you completely heal my weaknesses, tend to my wounds, and remedy my deformities.

Let your good, sweet spirit come down into my heart and 4 prepare a home there, cleansing the heart *of all filth of flesh and spirit* and filling it with the increase of faith, hope, and love and the inclination to compunction, loving-kindness, and humane compassion. Let that spirit extinguish the fire of my desires with the dew of blessing. Let it kill lustful agitation and carnal urges with its power. Let it provide me, in my labors, vigils, and fasting, with the fervor and discretion to love, praise, supplicate, and contemplate you, all the

actum et cogitatum, devotionem et efficaciam, et in his omnibus usque ad finem vitae meae perseverantiam.

6. Et haec quidem necessaria mihi sunt propter me, O spes mea. Sunt alia quibus indigeo non solum propter me, sed et pro illis quibus me iubes prodesse magis quam prae-esse. Postulavit aliquando quidem antiquorum sapientiam dari sibi ut sciret regere populum tuum; rex enim erat et pla-cuit sermo in oculis tuis et exaudisti vocem eius et necdum in cruce obieras, necdum illam miram caritatem ostenderas populo tuo.

2 Ecce, dulcis Domine, ecce in conspectu tuo populus tuus peculiaris ante quorum oculos crux tua et signa passionis tuae in eis. Hos regendos commisisti huic peccatori servulo tuo. Deus meus, *tu scis insipientiam meam* et infirmitas mea *a te non* est *abscondita.* Peto itaque, dulcis Domine, non aurum, non argentum, non lapides pretiosos dari mihi, sed sapien-tiam ut sciam regere populum tuum. Emitte eam, O fons sapientiae, de *sede magnitudinis tuae ut mecum sit, mecum labo-ret,* mecum operetur, in me loquatur, disponat cogitationes, sermones, et omnia opera mea et consilia mea secundum beneplacitum tuum, ad honorem nominis tui, ad eorum profectum et meam salutem.

7. Tu scis, Domine, cor meum, quia quidquid dederis servo tuo, voluntas mea est ut totum impendatur illis et to-tum expendatur pro illis, insuper et ipse libenter impendar pro illis. Sic fiat, Domine mi, sic fiat. Sensus meus, sermo meus, otium meum et occupatio mea, actus meus et cogita-tio mea, prosperitas mea et adversitas mea, mors mea et vita mea, sanitas et infirmitas mea, quidquid omnino sum, quod vivo, quod sentio, quod discerno—totum impendatur illis et

devotion and capacity to act and think in accordance with you, and perseverance in all these things until the end of my life.

6. And these things, O my hope, are surely necessary for my own sake. There are other things I need not only for me but also for the sake of those whom you command me to help rather than rule. One of the ancients once asked that he be allowed to know how to rule your people. He was a king, and his words were pleasing in your eyes and you listened to his voice when you had not yet died on the cross, not yet shown that wonderful love to your people.

Here, sweet Lord, here in your sight are your own people. 2
Before their eyes are your cross and the signs of your suffering are in them. You have committed them to be ruled by this sinner, your lowly servant. My God, *you know my foolishness* and my weakness is *not a secret from you.* Therefore, sweet Lord, I ask to be given not gold, silver, or precious stones, but the wisdom to know how to rule your people. Send wisdom, O font of wisdom, from *the throne of your greatness, to be with me, labor with me,* work with me, speak in me, and shape my thoughts, words, and all my actions and decisions according to your will, to the honor of your name, for their spiritual progress and my salvation.

7. Lord, you know my heart: it is my will that whatever you give to your servant be devoted entirely to them, spent entirely for them, and moreover that I myself should be devoted gladly to them. May it so happen, my Lord, may it so happen. My feelings, my speech, my rest and my work, my action and my thought, my success and my adversity, my death and my life, my health and my sickness, all that I am, what I live, what I feel, what I discern—let it all be paid out

totum expendatur pro illis pro quibus tu ipse non de-
dignabaris expendi.

2   Doce me itaque servum tuum, Domine, doce me, quaeso,
per spiritum sanctum tuum quomodo me impendam illis et
quomodo me expendam pro illis. Da mihi, Domine, per
ineffabilem gratiam tuam ut patienter sustineam infirmitates eorum, pie compatiar, discrete subveniam. Discam
magisterio spiritus tui maestos consolari, pusillanimes robo-
rare, lapsos erigere, infirmari cum infirmis, uri cum scandalizatis, omnibus omnia fieri, ut omnes lucrifaciam. Da verum sermonem et rectum et bene sonantem in os meum,
quo aedificentur in fide, spe, et caritate, in castitate et humilitate, in patientia et oboedientia, in spiritus fervore et mentis devotione.

3   Et quoniam tu dedisti illis hunc caecum ductorem, indoc-
tum doctorem, nescium rectorem, et—si non propter me,
propter illos—tamen doce quem doctorem posuisti, duc
quem alios ducere praecepisti, rege quem rectorem statuisti.
Doce me itaque, dulcis Domine, corripere inquietos, consolari pusillanimes, suscipere infirmos, et uniquique pro
natura, pro moribus, pro affectione, pro capacitate, pro
simplicitate, pro loco et tempore, sicut tu videris expedire,
memetipsum conformare. Et quoniam, vel propter infirmitatem carnis meae vel propter pusillanimitatem spiritus mei
vel propter vitium cordis mei, parum vel certe nihil aedifi-
cant eos labor aut vigiliae aut abstinentia mea, aedificet eos,
rogo, largiente misericordia tua, humilitas mea, caritas mea,
patientia mea, et misericordia mea. Aedificet illos sermo
meus et doctrina mea et prosit illis semper oratio mea.

entirely to them and spent entirely for them, for the good of those for whom you yourself did not scorn to be spent.

Therefore, Lord, teach me your servant, teach me, I be- 2 seech you, through your holy spirit, how to devote myself to them and how to spend myself for them. Grant me through your indescribable grace the ability to endure their weaknesses patiently, to suffer with them lovingly, to help them discerningly. Let me learn from your spirit's instruction how to comfort the sorrowful, strengthen the fainthearted, raise the fallen, be weak with the weak, share resentment with the offended, become all things to all people so to gain them all. Give me truthful and righteous words, eloquent on my tongue, so that they may be built up in faith, hope, and love, in chastity and humility, in patience and obedience, in fervor of spirit and devotion of mind.

And because you have given them this blind leader, this 3 untaught teacher, this ignorant guide, teach one you have made a teacher, lead him you have ordered to lead, rule him you have appointed to rule—if not for my sake, then for theirs. Teach me, therefore, sweet Lord, to rebuke the restless, to comfort the fainthearted, to support the weak, and to adapt my own self to each one according to his nature, habits, disposition, capacity or simplicity, according to place and time, just as you see fit. Owing to the weakness of my flesh, the faintheartedness of my spirit, and the corruption of my heart, my labor, vigils, and fasting can strengthen them little or indeed not at all, so I beg that through the gift of your mercy, my humility, my love, my patience, and my mercy may do so. Let my words and my teaching strengthen them and my prayer always be to their benefit.

8. Tu autem, misericors Deus noster, exaudi me pro illis, quem ad orandum te pro illis et officium compellit et invitat affectus: animat autem consideratio tuae benignitatis. Tu scis, dulcis Domine, quantum diligam eos, quomodo effusa sint in illos viscera mea, quomodo liquescat super illos affectus meus. Tu scis, mi Domine, quod non in austeritate neque in potentia spiritus mei imperem illis, quomodo optem in caritate prodesse magis quam praeesse illis, in humilitate substerni illis, affectu autem esse in illis quasi unus ex illis.

2   Exaudi me itaque, exaudi me, Domine Deus meus, ut sint oculi tui aperti super illos die ac nocte. Expande piissimas alas tuas et protege eos, extende dexteram tuam sanctam et benedic eos, infunde in corda eorum spiritum tuum sanctum, qui servet eos in unitate spiritus et vinculo pacis, in carnis castitate et mentis humilitate.

3   Ipse adsit orantibus et adipe et pinguedine dilectionis tuae repleat viscera eorum, et suavitate compunctionis reficiat mentes eorum, et lumine gratiae tuae illustret corda eorum, spe erigat, timore humiliet, caritate inflammet. Ipse eis preces suggerat, quas tu velis propitius exaudire. Ipse dulcis spiritus tuus insit meditantibus ut ab eo illuminati cognoscant te et memoriae suae imprimant quem in adversis invocent et consulant in dubiis. In tentatione laborantibus ipse pius consolator occurrat et succurrat et in angustiis et tribulationibus vitae huius adiuvet infirmitatem eorum.

4   Sint, dulcis Domine, ipso spiritu tuo operante—et in se ipsis et ad invicem et ad me—pacati, modesti, benevoli,

8. Hear me further, our merciful God, on behalf of those for whom duty compels me and affection invites me to pray to you: contemplation of your kindness encourages me. Sweet Lord, you know how much I love them, how my heart is poured out to them, how my affection flows over them. My Lord, you know that I would not command them in harshness or haughtiness, how I hope to benefit them in love rather than rule over them, to be subject to them in humility, and to be in their affections as if I were one of them.

Hear me, then, hear me, my Lord God, so that your eyes 2 may be upon them day and night. Spread out your most loving wings and protect them, stretch out your holy right hand and bless them, pour out your holy spirit into their hearts to keep them in unity of spirit and the bond of peace, in chastity of flesh and humility of mind.

Let your spirit be with them in prayer and fill their hearts 3 with the ample richness of your love, and refresh their minds with the sweetness of compunction, and brighten their hearts with the light of your grace, lift them with hope, humble them with fear, inflame them with love. Let it supply them with the prayers you would wish to hear. Let that same sweet spirit be with them in meditation so that, enlightened by it, they come to know you and impress on their memory the one they call on in adversity and consult in perplexity. May this same loving comforter rush to the aid of those laboring in temptation and help their weakness in the trials and tribulations of this life.

Through the action of your same spirit, sweet Lord, let 4 them be—with themselves, toward each other, and toward me—peaceful, modest, and kind, obedient, dutiful to one

invicem oboedientes, invicem servientes, et supportantes invicem. Sint spiritu ferventes, spe gaudentes, in paupertate, in abstinentia, in laboribus et vigiliis, in silentio et quiete, per omnia patientes. Repelle ab eis, Domine, spiritum superbiae et vanae gloriae, invidiae et tristitiae, acediae et blasphemiae, desperationis et diffidentiae, fornicationis et immunditiae, praesumptionis et discordiae. Esto secundum fidelem promissionem tuam in medio eorum, et quoniam tu scis quid cuique opus est obsecro ut quod infirmum est in illis tu consolides, quod debile non proicias, quod morbidum sanes, quod maestum laetifices, quod tepidum accendas, quod instabile confirmes, ut singuli in suis necessitatibus et tentationibus tuam sibi gratiam sentiant non deesse.

9. Porro de his temporalibus quibus in hac vita miseri huius corpusculi sustentatur infirmitas sicut videris et volueris provide servis tuis. Hoc unum peto a dulcissima pietate tua, Domine mi, ut quidquid illud fuerit, sive parvum sive multum, facias me servum tuum omnium quae dederis fidelem dispensatorem, discretum distributorem, prudentem provisorem. Inspira et illis, Deus meus, ut patienter sustineant quando non dederis, moderate utantur quando dederis, et ut de me servo tuo et propter te etiam illorum, semper hoc credant et sentiant quod utile sit illis; tantum diligant et timeant me, quantum videris expedire illis.

10. Ego autem commendo eos sanctis manibus tuis et piae providentiae tuae ut non rapiant eos quisquam de manu tua nec de manu servi tui cui commendasti eos, sed in sancto proposito feliciter perseverent. Perseverantes autem vitam aeternam obtineant, te praestante dulcissimo Domino nostro, qui vivis et regnas per omnia saecula saeculorum. Amen.

another, and supportive of one another. May they be fervent in spirit, joyous in hope, ever patient in poverty, in fasting, in work and vigils, in silence and rest. Drive from them, Lord, the spirit of pride and vainglory, envy and sadness, spiritual weariness and blasphemy, despair and distrust, fornication and uncleanness, presumption and discord. Be in their midst, according to your faithful promise, and, because you know what each one needs, I pray that you strengthen what is weak in them, not disdain what is feeble, heal what is sick, gladden what is sad, kindle what is lukewarm, and make steady what is unstable, so that each one knows that your grace is with him in his needs and temptations.

9. Furthermore, as you see fit, provide your servants in this wretched life with worldly goods that support the weakness of this frail body. I ask this one thing of your sweetest love, my Lord: make me, your servant, a faithful steward, judicious distributor, and prudent provider of what you give, be it little or much. And inspire them, my God, to endure patiently when you give nothing, exercise moderation when you give something, and as regards me, your servant and because of you theirs, let them always believe and sense what is good for them. Let them love and fear me as much as you think benefits them.

10. I, moreover, entrust them to your sacred hands and your loving providence, so that none should snatch them from your hand nor from the hand of your servant to whom you have entrusted them, but that instead they persevere joyfully in their holy purpose. And may they in their perseverance gain eternal life with your help, our sweetest Lord, who live and reign for ever and ever. Amen.

SPIRITUAL FRIENDSHIP

Cum *adhuc puer* essem in scholis, et sociorum meorum me gratia plurimum delectaret, inter mores et vitia quibus aetas illa periclitari solet, tota se mens mea dedit affectui et devovit amori, ita ut nihil mihi dulcius, nihil iucundius, nihil utilius quam *amari* et *amare* videretur. 2. Itaque inter diversos amores et amicitias fluctuans, rapiebatur animus huc atque illuc et verae amicitiae legem ignorans, eius saepe similitudine fallebatur. Tandem aliquando mihi venit in manus ille liber quem de amicitia Tullius scripsit et qui statim mihi et sententiarum gravitate utilis et eloquentiae suavitate dulcis apparebat. 3. Et licet nec illud amicitiae genus me viderem idoneum, gratulabar tamen quamdam amicitiae formulam reperisse, ad quam amorum meorum et affectionum valerem revocare discursus.

Cum vero placuit bono Domino meo corrigere devium, elisum erigere, salubri contactu mundare leprosum, *relicta spe saeculi,* ingressus sum monasterium. 4. Et statim legendis sacris litteris operam dedi, cum prius nec ad ipsam earum superficiem oculus lippiens et carnalibus tenebris assuetus sufficeret. Igitur cum sacra scriptura dulcesceret, et parum illud scientiae quod mihi mundus tradiderat earum comparatione vilesceret, occurrebant animo quae de amicitia in

When I was *still a boy* in school, the favor of my class-
mates gave me the greatest pleasure, and among the habits
and vices that usually endanger youth, my mind gave itself
over completely to affection and devoted itself to love to
the extent that nothing seemed sweeter to me, nothing
more delightful, nothing more useful, than *to be loved* and *to
love*. 2. Therefore my spirit, wavering among different loves
and friendships, was tossed this way and that, and not knowing the law of true friendship, was often deceived by something that resembled it. At long last there came into my
hands the book Cicero wrote about friendship, which immediately struck me as useful for the seriousness of its ideas
and sweet for the charm of its eloquence. 3. Although I did
not think myself suited to that kind of friendship, still I rejoiced to have discovered a guide to friendship according to
which I might be able to ground my wandering loves and affections.

But when it pleased my good Lord to reform one gone
astray, restore one ruined, and cleanse the leper with his
healing touch, I entered a monastery, *worldly prospects abandoned.* 4. I devoted myself at once to the study of holy writings, although previously my eyes, bleary and accustomed to
carnal darkness, were not capable of even a superficial understanding of them. Therefore, while holy scripture was
growing sweet, and what little knowledge the world had
given me was becoming worthless by comparison, what I

praefato libello legeram, et iam mirabar quod non mihi more solito sapiebant. 5. Iam tunc enim nihil quod non dulcissimi nominis Iesu fuisset melle mellitum, nihil quod non scripturarum fuisset sale conditum, meum sibi ex toto rapiebat affectum. Et iterum atque iterum ea ipsa revolvens quaerebam, si forte possent scripturarum auctoritate fulciri. 6. Cum autem in sanctorum patrum litteris de amicitia plura legissem, volens spiritualiter amare nec valens, institui de spiritali amicitia scribere et regulas mihi castae sanctaeque dilectionis praescribere.

7. Opusculum igitur istud in tribus distinximus libellis: in primo, quid sit amicitia, et quis eius fuerit ortus vel causa commendantes; in secundo, eius fructum excellentiamque proponentes; in tertio, quomodo et inter quos possit usque in finem indirupta servari prout potuimus enodantes. 8. In huius igitur lectione si quis profecerit, Deo gratias agat et pro peccatis meis apud Christi misericordiam intercedat. Si quis autem superfluum aut inutile putat esse quod scripsimus, parcat infelicitati meae, quae fluxum cogitationum mearum huius meditationis me compulit occupatione restringere.

INCIPIT TRACTATUS EIUSDEM
DE SPIRITALI AMICITIA.

[*Aelredus:*] Ecce ego et tu, et spero quod tertius inter nos Christus sit. Non est modo qui obstrepat et non est, qui intercidat amica colloquia, grataeque huic solitudini nullius

had read in the aforementioned book kept pressing on my mind, and I now found it strange that I had lost my taste for it. 5. Already by then nothing that was not flavored with the honey of the sweetest name of Jesus, nothing that was not seasoned with the salt of the scriptures, completely captivated me. Mulling over Cicero's ideas, I wondered if perhaps they might be supported by the authority of the scriptures. 6. Since I had read a great deal about friendship in the writings of the holy fathers and wanted to love spiritually but could not, I resolved to write about spiritual friendship and dictate for myself the rules of chaste and holy love.

7. We have therefore divided this little work into three books. The first describes what friendship is, and what the origin and cause of friendship are. The second lays out its reward and excellence. The third explains to the best of our ability how and between whom it can be kept unbroken to the very end. 8. Therefore, if someone profits from reading this treatise, let him thank God and plead for Christ's mercy on my sins. If someone thinks what I have written unnecessary or unhelpful, let him pardon the misfortune of the preoccupation that has forced me to dam the flood of my thoughts in this meditation.

HERE BEGINS THE SAME AUTHOR'S TREATISE
ON SPIRITUAL FRIENDSHIP.

*A*elred: Here we are, you and I, and I hope that Christ is the third among us. Now there is no one to disturb us, no one to interrupt our friendly conversation, and nobody's voice or noise to interrupt this pleasant solitude. Come now,

vox vel tumultus irrepit. Age nunc, carissime, aperi pectus tuum, et amicis auribus quidquid placet instilla; nec ingrate accipiamus locum, tempus et otium. 2. Nam paulo ante in turba fratrum me residente, cum omnes undique circumstreperent—et alius quaereret, et alius disputaret, et iste de scripturis, ille de moribus, alter de vitiis, de virtutibus alter quaestiones ingererent—tu solus tacebas, et nunc caput erigens, parabas aliquid proferre in medium; sed quasi vox in ipsis interciperetur faucibus, iterum demisso capite tacebas; nunc parvo intervallo secedens a nobis et iterum rediens tristem vultum praeferebas, quibus omnibus mihi dumtaxat dabatur intelligi, te ad proferendum tuae mentis conceptum, et horrere multitudinem et optare secretum.

3. *Ivo:* Profecto ita est, et gratulor plurimum, intelligens quod cura tibi est de puero tuo, cuius tibi mentem mentisque propositum non alius quam spiritus caritatis aperuit. Et utinam hoc mihi tua concedat dignatio, ut quotiescumque filios tuos qui hic sunt visitaveris, vel semel mihi liceat, caeteris remotis tui habere copiam, et aestus pectoris mei sine perturbatione proferre.

4. *Aelredus:* Faciam quidem et libens. Delector enim plurimum, quod te pronum ad haec vana et otiosa non video, sed semper aliquid utile et profectui tuo necessarium proloqui. Loquere ergo secure et cum amico omnes curas tuas cogitationesque commisce, ut vel discas aliquid vel doceas, des et accipias, profundas et haurias.

5. *Ivo:* Ego quidem discere paratus sum, non docere, non dare, sed accipere, haurire non profundere, sicut mihi aetas praescribit, imperitia cogit, hortatur professio. Sed ne in his

dearest one, open your heart, and pour whatever you like into friendly ears. Let us accept the place, time, and leisure gratefully. 2. A little while ago, when I was sitting with the crowd of brothers and they all assaulted us with noise from every corner—one questioning, another arguing, this one tossing out claims about scripture, that one about conduct, another about vices, still another about virtues—you alone were silent. At one point, lifting your head, you were on the verge of joining the fray, but as if your voice were caught in your throat you were silent and again bowed your head. Then, withdrawing from us and after a brief pause returning again, you revealed a gloomy face. I simply took all this to mean that you had the idea of speaking your mind, but shuddered at the throng and wanted privacy.

3. *Ivo:* That's exactly right, and I'm most grateful to realize how much you care for your son, whose mind and state of mind nothing other than the spirit of loving-kindness has revealed to you. And how I wish your esteemed self would grant me this: however often you visit your sons here, that I be allowed, at least once, to enjoy your abundant gift when all others are elsewhere, and to reveal the glowing heat of my heart without being disturbed.

4. *Aelred:* I will do so, and happily. I am glad to see that you are not prone to this empty and idle talk, but always give voice to something useful and necessary for your spiritual progress. Therefore, speak freely and discuss concerns and thoughts with a friend, so that you learn or teach something, give and receive, pour out and drink in.

5. *Ivo:* I'm perfectly ready to learn, not to teach, not to give, but to receive, to drink in, not to pour out. So my youth prescribes, my inexperience compels, my religious vow

tempus ad alia necessarium insipienter insumam: volo me aliquid de spirituali amicitia doceas, videlicet, quid sit, quid pariat utilitatis, quod eius principium, quis finis, utrum inter omnes esse possit, et si non inter omnes, inter quos, quomodo etiam possit indirupta servari, et sine aliqua dissensionis molestia sancto fine concludi?

6. *Aelredus:* Miror, cur a me haec aestimas esse quaerenda, cum satis superque ab antiquissimis, excellentissimisque doctoribus de his omnibus constet esse tractatum, maxime cum pueritiam tuam in huiusmodi studiis triveris et Tullii Ciceronis librum *De amicitia* legeris, ubi copiosissime de his omnibus quae ad eam spectare videntur iucundo stylo disseruit, et quasdam, ut ita dicam, leges ac praecepta descripserit.

7. *Ivo:* Non usquequaque ipse mihi ignotus est liber, utpote qui in eo aliquando plurimum delectabar, sed ex quo mihi de sanctarum scripturarum favis aliquid coepit emanare dulcedinis, et mellifluum Christi nomen sibi meum vindicavit affectum, quidquid sine caelestium litterarum sale, ac dulcissimi illius nominis condimento, quamvis subtiliter et eloquenter disputatum legero vel audiero, nec sapidum mihi potest esse nec lucidum. 8. Eapropter vel ea ipsa quae dicta sunt—si tamen sunt consona rationi—vel certe alia quae disputationis istius poscit utilitas, velim mihi scripturarum auctoritate probari, et quemadmodum ea ipsa, quam inter nos oportet esse amicitia, et in Christo inchoetur, et secundum Christum servetur, et ad Christum finis eius et utilitas referatur plenius edoceri. Constat enim Tullium verae amicitiae ignorasse virtutem, cum eius principium finemque, Christum videlicet, penitus ignoraverit.

exhorts. But so that I don't foolishly squander time needed for other matters, I want you to teach me something about spiritual friendship, namely: What it is? What is its usefulness? What are its beginning and end? Can it exist among all, and if not among all, among whom? How can it be kept unbroken, and how it can come to a holy end without any harmful disagreements?

6. *Aelred:* I am amazed you think I should be asked these questions, since everyone knows they have all have been more than adequately discussed by the most ancient and excellent teachers, and especially since you spent your youth studying the matter and have read Cicero's book *On Friendship,* in which he fully addressed everything that seems to pertain to the subject in charming style. He also sketched out, so to speak, some laws and teachings about friendship.

7. *Ivo:* That book is far from unknown to me, since at one time I took great pleasure in it. But since the honeycomb of holy scriptures began to drip some of its sweetness on me and the mellifluous name of Christ made its claim on my affection, anything I read or hear that lacks the salt of heavenly writings and the seasoning of his sweetest name, however subtle and eloquent, is neither delicious nor clear. 8. So—assuming it is in harmony with reason—I'd like what's been said, and of course other matters as the usefulness of this discussion require, to be tested by the authority of scripture and to be taught how the friendship that ought to exist among us should begin in Christ, be preserved according to Christ, and have purpose and usefulness with reference to Christ. Obviously, Cicero did not know the virtue of true friendship, since he was completely ignorant of its beginning and end, namely Christ.

9. *Aelredus:* Victus sum fateor ut quasi meipsum nesciens nec vires proprias metiens, de his non quidem te doceam, sed tecum potius conferam, cum tu ipse viam utrisque aperueris, lumenque illud splendidissimum, in ipsa inquisitionis nostrae ianua accenderis, quod nos non sinat errare per devia, sed certo tramite ad certum finem propositae quaestionis perducat. 10. Quid enim sublimius de amicitia dici potest, quid verius, quid utilius, quam quod in Christo inchoari, et secundum Christum produci, et a Christo perfici debeat, probetur? Age nunc, et quid primum de amicitia videatur esse quaerendum, edicito.

Ivo: Primum quid sit amicitia, arbitror disserendum—ne videamur in inani pingere; si nesciamus quid sit illud—de quo debeat disputationis nostrae series tenorque procedere.

11. *Aelredus:* Nonne satis tibi est hinc, quod ait Tullius: "Amicitia est rerum humanarum et divinarum, *cum benevolentia et caritate consensio*"?

12. *Ivo:* Si tibi sufficit ista definitio, mihi iudico satisfactum.

13. *Aelredus:* Ergo quibuscumque fuerit de rebus humanis atque divinis sententia eadem eademque voluntas cum benevolentia et caritate—ad amicitiae perfectionem eos pervenisse fatebimur?

14. *Ivo:* Quidni? Verumtamen caritatis vel benevolentiae nomine quid ethnicus ille significare voluerit non video.

15. *Aelredus:* Forte nomine caritatis mentis affectum, benevolentiae vero operum expressit effectum. Nam ipsa in

9. *Aelred:* I confess myself persuaded that not knowing myself, as it were, nor accurately assessing the extent of my own abilities, I may not in fact teach you anything about these matters, but will instead discuss them with you, since you yourself have shown us the way forward at the very beginning of our investigation and lit a most brilliant lamp which will not allow us to wander into blind alleys but instead lead us on a sure path to the certain conclusion of the investigation we have proposed. 10. For what can be called more sublime about friendship, truer, more useful, than that it may be proven to begin in Christ, advance according to Christ, and be perfected by Christ? Come now, and say what it seems to you should be considered first on the subject of friendship.

Ivo: I think we should discuss first what friendship is—so we don't seem to write on the wind, not knowing what we're doing—and then the order and direction of our discussion should proceed from there.

11. *Aelred:* Are you not satisfied to start with what Cicero says: "Friendship is *agreement* about matters human and divine *along with goodwill and love*"?

12. *Ivo:* If that definition is good enough for you, it's good enough for me.

13. *Aelred:* So those who were of the same opinion, of the same will concerning matters human and divine, along with goodwill and love—will we grant that they attained the perfection of friendship?

14. *Ivo:* Why not? Still, I don't see what that pagan meant by "love" or "goodwill."

15. *Aelred:* Perhaps by the term "love" he expressed attachment of the mind but by "goodwill" the effect of

rebus humanis atque divinis, mentibus utriusque cara, id est suavis et pretiosa debet esse consensio; benevola etiam et iucunda in rebus exterioribus operum exhibitio.

16. *Ivo:* Fateor placet mihi satis ista definitio, nisi et ethnicis et Judaeis, iniquis insuper Christianis eam convenire putarem. Quod autem vera amicitia inter eos qui sunt sine Christo esse non possit, mihi fateor esse persuasum.

17. *Aelredus:* Satis nobis in consequentibus elucescet, utrum definitio minus aliquid habeat, vel superabundet in aliquo, ut vel a nobis reprobetur vel quasi sufficiens, et extra nihil recipiens admittatur. Ex ipsa tamen definitione, quamvis forte tibi minus videatur esse perfecta, intelligere utcumque poteris quid sit amicitia.

18. *Ivo:* Non sim tibi oneri, rogo te, si non ista sufficiant, nisi ipsius vocabuli rationem mihi enucleaveris?

19. *Aelredus:* Geram tibi morem, si tamen parcas inscitiae meae, ut me non cogas docere quod nescio. Ab "amore," ut mihi videtur, "amicus" dicitur, ab "amico," "amicitia." Est autem amor quidam animae rationalis affectus per quem ipsa aliquid cum desiderio quaerit et appetit ad fruendum, per quem et fruitur eo cum quadam interiori suavitate, amplectitur et conservat adeptum. Cuius affectus et motus in *Speculo* nostro, quod satis cognitum habes, quam lucide potuimus ac diligenter, expressimus.

actions. For that very agreement concerning matters human and divine must be dear to the minds of both, that is, delightful and precious, and the actual practice of good works should be both benevolent and pleasant.

16. *Ivo:* I admit that this definition pleases me well enough, except that I think it also suits pagans and Jews, not to mention wicked Christians. I admit I'm convinced that there can't be true friendship between those who live without Christ.

17. *Aelred:* It will become clear enough to us as we go along whether the definition lacks something, or has too much of something, and hence whether we ought to reject it or approve it as more or less adequate and containing nothing superfluous. However, from the definition as it stands, even if it seems less than perfect to you, you can still have some idea of what friendship is.

18. *Ivo:* Would I be a nuisance, I ask you, if I say this definition is not adequate unless you explain to me the meaning of the word?

19. *Aelred:* I will humor you provided you pardon my lack of knowledge and do not force me to teach what I do not know. As I see it, "friend" *(amicus)* derives from "love" *(amor)* and "friendship" *(amicitia)* derives from "friend" *(amicus)*. Love is a certain affection of the rational soul through which it ardently seeks some goal and strives to enjoy it. Through love, the soul enjoys the goal's attainment, embraces it, and preserves it with a kind of inner pleasure. We have described the soul's affections and development as clearly and carefully as we could in our *Mirror of Charity,* which you know quite well.

20. Porro amicus quasi amoris, vel ut quibusdam placet, ipsius animi custos dicitur, quoniam amicum meum amoris mutui, vel ipsius animi mei oportet esse custodem, ut omnia eius secreta fideli silentio servet, quidquid in eo vitiosum viderit, pro viribus curet et toleret, cui et gaudenti congaudeat, et dolenti condoleat, et omnia sua esse sentiat, quae amici sunt. 21. Amicitia igitur ipsa virtus est, qua talis dilectionis ac dulcedinis foedere ipsi animi copulantur, et efficiuntur unum de pluribus. Unde ipsam amicitiam non inter fortuita vel caduca, sed inter ipsas virtutes, quae aeternae sunt, etiam mundi huius philosophi collocaverunt. Quibus Salomon in Proverbiis consentire videtur *"Omni,"* inquiens, *"tempore diligit, qui amicus est,"* manifeste declarans amicitiam aeternam esse, si vera est. Si vero desierit esse, nec veram fuisse, cum videretur existere.

22. *Ivo:* Quid est igitur quod inter amicissimos graves ortas inimicitias legimus?

23. *Aelredus:* De his suo loco uberius, si Deus voluerit, disputabimus. Haec volo interim credas, numquam fuisse amicum, qui laedere potuit eum quem in amicitia semel recepit. Sed nec eum verae amicitiae gustasse delicias qui vel laesus desiit diligere semel amavit. *Omni* enim *tempore diligit qui amicus est.* 24. Etsi arguatur, etsi laedatur, etsi tradatur flammis, etsi cruci affigatur, *omni tempore diligit qui amicus est* et, ut ait noster Hieronymus, *"Amicitia quae desinere potest numquam vera fuit."*

25. *Ivo:* Cum tanta sit in amicitia vera perfectio, non est mirum quod tam rari fuerunt quos veros amicos antiquitas commendavit. "Vix enim," ut ait Tullius, "tria vel quatuor

20. Next, a friend is in some sense called a guardian of love, or as some prefer, a guardian of the spirit itself. For my friend should be the guardian of mutual love and my own spirit, keep all its secrets in faithful silence, and to the best of his ability heal and endure whatever he sees is corrupt in them. Let him rejoice with his friend when he rejoices, grieve with him when he grieves, and think all his friend's feelings are his own. 21. Friendship, then, is the very virtue in which spirits themselves are joined by the bond of such love and sweetness that one is made from many. Hence even philosophers of this world place friendship not among accidental or fleeting concerns, but among the eternal virtues themselves. In Proverbs, Solomon seems to agree with them, saying, *"He is a friend who loves at all times,"* stating clearly that if true, friendship is eternal, but if it ends, it was not true friendship even though it seemed to be.

22. *Ivo:* So why is it that we read about intense hostility arising among dearest friends?

23. *Aelred:* God willing, we will discuss that question more fully in its place. For the moment, I want you to remember that there has never been a friend capable of hurting anyone he had once taken into friendship. By extension, he who has, even if hurt, ceased to cherish one he once loved has not tasted the delights of true friendship. *He is a friend who loves at all times.* 24. Even if he is accused, even if he is hurt, even if he is thrown into a fire, even if he is nailed to a cross, *he is a friend who loves at all times.* As our Jerome says, *"Friendship that can end was never true friendship."*

25. *Ivo:* Since there is such perfection in true friendship, it's no wonder ancient writers designated people as true friends so rarely. As Cicero says, "Tradition going back a very

amicorum paria in tot retro saeculis fama concelebrat."
Quod si nostris, id est Christianis temporibus, tanta est ra-
ritas amicorum, frustra, ut mihi videtur, in huius virtutis
inquisitione desudo, quam me adepturum, eius mirabili sub-
limitate territus, iam pene despero.

26. *Aelredus:* "Magnarum rerum," ut ait quidam, "ipse
conatus magnus est." Unde virtuosae mentis est sublimia
semper et ardua meditari, ut vel adipiscatur optata, vel lucidius intelligat et cognoscat optanda, cum non parum credendus sit profecisse, qui virtutis cognitione didicit quam
longe sit a virtute. 27. Quamvis de nullius virtutis acquisi-
tione desperandum sit Christiano, cum quotidie ex Evangelio vox divina resultat, *"Petite et accipietis,"* et caetera. Nec
mirum si inter ethnicos verae virtutis rari fuerunt secta-
tores, qui virtutum largitorem et Dominum nesciebant,
de quo scriptum est, *"Dominus virtutum ipse est rex gloriae."*
28. In cuius profecto fide, non dico tria vel quatuor, sed mille
tibi proferam paria amicorum, qui quod illi de Pylade et
Oreste pro magno miraculo dicunt vel fingunt, parati erant
pro invicem mori. Nonne, secundum Tullianam definitionem, verae amicitiae virtute pollebant, de quibus scriptum
est: *"Multitudinis credentium erat cor unum et anima una; nec
quisquam aliquid suum esse dicebat, sed erant illis omnia communia"*? 29. Quomodo non inter eos *rerum divinarum et humanarum, cum caritate et benevolentia fuit* summa *consensio,*
quibus cor unum et anima una erat? Quot martyres pro fratribus animas posuerunt! Quot non pepercerunt expensis,
non laboribus, non ipsius corporis cruciatibus! Credo te

long time honors scarcely three or four pairs of friends." But if in our own, that is, Christian times, friendship is such a rarity, it seems to me that it's wasted effort to seek a virtue that terrifies me with its sublimity, one I now almost despair of ever attaining.

26. *Aelred:* "Striving for great achievements is itself great," as someone says. Hence it is characteristic of a virtuous mind to meditate ceaselessly on sublime and difficult subjects. The mind may either attain what it hoped for, or know and see more clearly what it ought to hope for. We should staunchly believe that someone has succeeded when he has learned, by recognizing virtue, how far from it he is. 27. A Christian should not despair of acquiring any particular virtue since the divine voice from the Gospel resounds daily, "*Ask and you will receive,*" and so on. No wonder that among the pagans the devotees of true virtue were rare, since they did not know the Lord and dispenser of virtues of whom it is written, "*The Lord of virtues is the king of glory himself.*" 28. The pagans discussed or imagined the friendship of Pylades and Orestes as a great marvel, but I say emphatically that I could offer you not just three or four pairs of friends, but thousands ready to die for one other in their faith. Those of whom it is written, "*There was one heart and one soul among the multitude of believers; none of them called anything his own, but they had all things in common*"—were they not strong in the virtue of true friendship according to Cicero's definition? 29. How could there not have been complete *agreement about matters human and divine along with goodwill and love* among those whose heart and soul were one? How many martyrs laid down their lives for their brothers! How many spared no expense or trouble, even suffering the torture of their

multoties, non sine lacrymis, legisse puellam illam Antiochenam, pulcherrima cuiusdam militis fraude ereptam lupanaribus, ipsum postmodum socium habuisse martyrii, quem custodem pudicitiae invenerat in lupanari. 30. Multa tibi huius rei proferrem exempla, nisi et prolixitas prohiberet, et silentium nobis ipsa copia indixisset. Annuntiavit enim Christus Jesus, et locutus est, et *"Multiplicati sunt super numerum. Majorem,"* inquit, *"hac dilectionem nemo habet, quam ut animam suam ponat quis pro amicis suis."*

31. *Ivo:* Ergone inter amicitiam et caritatem nihil distare arbitrabimur?

32. *Aelredus:* Immo plurimum. Multo enim plures gremio caritatis quam amicitiae amplexibus recipiendos divina sanxit auctoritas. Non enim amicos solum, sed et inimicos sinu dilectionis excipere, caritatis lege compellimur. Amicos autem eos solos dicimus, quibus cor nostrum et quidquid in illo est committere non formidamus, illis vicissim nobis eadem fidei lege et securitate constrictis.

33. *Ivo:* Quam multi saeculariter viventes et sibi in quibuslibet vitiis consentientes simili sibi foedere copulantur, et prae cunctis mundi deliciis gratum et dulce etiam talis amicitiae vinculum experiuntur! 34. Non sit tibi molestum inter tot amicitias illam quam spiritalem ad differentiam aliarum credimus nominandam, quae illis quodammodo involvitur et obscuratur, et illam quaerentibus et desiderantibus occurrunt et obstrepunt ab earum, ut ita dixerim, communione secernere, ut illarum comparatione clariorem

own bodies! I believe you have read often, and not without tears, about the girl of Antioch, rescued from a brothel by a certain soldier's most honorable trickery, and that later the same man who had served as a guardian of her chastity in the brothel was her companion in martyrdom. 30. I could offer you many examples of this sort, except that fear of wordiness forbids it and their very abundance imposes silence on us. For Jesus Christ announced it when he said, *"They multiplied beyond number. No man,"* he said, *"has greater love than this: to lay down his life for his friends."*

31. *Ivo:* So do we think there's no difference between love and friendship?

32. *Aelred:* There is an enormous difference. Divine authority decreed that many more are to be received into the clasp of love than the embraces of friendship. In fact, we are obliged by the law of loving-kindness to receive not only our friends but also our enemies into the bosom of love. We call friends only those to whom we do not fear to entrust our heart and whatever is in it, they having been bound to us in turn by the same law and security of loyalty.

33. *Ivo:* Yet how many people living a worldly life and sharing certain vices are united to one another in a similar alliance and find the bond with a friend of that ilk pleasanter and sweeter than all the world's delights! 34. I hope it's not too much trouble for you to distinguish, among so many friendships, the one we believe should be called spiritual, as opposed to other kinds with which it is in a sense entangled and obscured, and which rush in and drown out, if I might put it that way, those who seek and desire spiritual friendship. By making spiritual friendship more distinct for us and

eam nobis ac proinde optabiliorem faciens, ad eius nos acquisitionem vehementius excites et accendas.

35. *Aelredus:* Falso sibi praeclarum amicitiae nomen assumunt inter quos est coniventia vitiorum, quoniam qui non amat, amicus non est; non autem amat hominem, qui amat iniquitatem; qui enim diligit iniquitatem non amat sed odit animam suam, qui vero suam non diligit, animam utique alterius amare non poterit. 36. Unde colligitur eos amicitiae solo nomine gloriari, fallique eius similitudine, non veritate fulciri. Verumtamen cum in hac tali amicitia, quam vel libido commaculat, vel avaritia foedat, vel incestat luxuria, tanta ac talis experiatur dulcedo, libet conicere quantum habeat suavitatis illa quae quanto honestior est, tanto est securior, quanto castior, tanto et iucundior, quanto liberior, tanto et felicior. 37. Patiamur tamen ut propter quamdam quae in affectibus sentitur similitudinem, etiam illae amicitiae quae verae non sunt, amicitiae nuncupentur; dum tamen ab illa quae spiritalis est, et ideo vera, certis indiciis distinguantur. 38. Dicatur itaque amicitia alia carnalis, alia mundialis, alia spiritalis. Et carnalem quidem creat vitiorum consensus, mundialem spes quaestus accendit, spiritalem inter bonos vitae morum studiorumque similitudo conglutinat.

39. Verum amicitiae carnalis exordium ab affectione procedit quae instar meretricis divaricat pedes suos omni transeunti, sequens aures et oculos suos per varia fornicantes, per quorum aditus usque ad ipsam mentem pulchrorum corporum vel rerum voluptuosarum infertur imago, quibus ad libitum frui putat esse beatum, sed sine socio frui minus

consequently more desirable by comparison with the other kinds, you will more forcefully excite us and set us on fire to acquire it.

35. *Aelred:* Those who are complicit in vice manufacture a false claim to the honorable name of friendship, since one who does not love is not a friend and furthermore, he who does not love his fellow man loves wickedness; for he who loves wickedness does not love his soul but hates it, and he who does not love his own soul can by no means love another's. 36. It follows that they glory in friendship in name only; they are deceived by something resembling friendship, not supported by its truth. But since such great sweetness is experienced in a type of friendship stained by lust, or fouled by greed, or polluted by extravagance, we can imagine how much sweetness friendship has when the more honorable, chaste, and free it is, the more secure, delightful, and happy it is. 37. Yet let us concede that, because of a certain similarity in how emotions are felt, even those friendships that are not true should be called friendships, provided that they are distinguished by certain attributes from spiritual and thus true friendship. 38. And so one friendship is called carnal, a second worldly, a third spiritual. For example, complicity in vice creates the carnal, hope for material gain kindles the worldly, and shared perspective about way of life and interests among good people melds the spiritual.

39. The origin of carnal friendship proceeds from a state of mind that follows its whoring eyes and ears this way and that like a prostitute spreading her legs for all who pass by. Through these entries to the senses the image of beautiful bodies or pleasure-giving objects comes to a mind that considers itself blessed to enjoy them as it likes, but thinks it

aestimat esse iucundum. 40. Tunc, motu, nutu, verbis, obsequiis, animus ab animo captivatur, et accenditur unus ab
altero, et conflantur in unum, ut inito foedere miserabili,
quidquid sceleris, quidquid sacrilegii est, agat alter et patiatur pro altero nihilque hac amicitia dulcius arbitrantur, nihil
iudicant iustius, *idem velle* et *idem nolle,* sibi existimantes
amicitiae legibus imperari. 41. Haec itaque amicitia nec
deliberatione suscipitur, nec iudicio probatur, nec regitur
ratione; sed secundum impetum affectionis per diversa rap-
tatur, non modum servans, non honesta procurans, non
commoda incommodave prospiciens, sed ad omnia incon-
siderate, indiscrete, leviter, immoderateque progrediens.
Idcirco vel quasi quibusdam Furiis agitata a semetipsa con-
sumitur vel eadem levitate resolvitur qua contrahitur.

42. At amicitia mundialis, quae rerum vel bonorum temporalium cupiditate partitur, semper est plena fraudis atque
fallaciae; nihil in ea certum, nihil constans, nihil securum;
quippe quae semper cum fortuna mutatur et sequitur marsupium. 43. Unde scriptum est: "*Est amicus secundum tempus,
et non permanebit in die tribulationis.*" Tolle spem quaestus et
statim desinet esse amicus. Quam amicitiam quidam ele-
ganti versu ita derisit:

Non est personae sed prosperitatis amicus,
quem fortuna tenet dulcis, acerba fugat.

44. Attamen huius amicitiae vitiosae principium quosdam plerumque ad quamdam verae amicitiae provehit

less delightful to enjoy them without company. 40. Next, spirit is captured by spirit through a gesture, a nod, words, or services rendered; one fires up another and they are fused into one. As a result, once the lamentable pact has been made, each performs and endures any crime or sacrilege for the other. They decide there is nothing sweeter than their friendship, judge nothing more just, thinking that *wishing* and *not wishing the same things* is thrust on them by the laws of friendship. 41. Therefore this friendship is neither begun with thoughtfulness, nor tested by good judgment, nor governed by reason, but is instead dragged off in every direction according to the force of inclination. It has no limit, pays no attention to what is honorable, looks to no profit or loss, carrying on instead thoughtlessly, recklessly, casually, and without restraint in all matters. For that reason, either it is devoured, as if driven by the Furies, as it were, or it dissolves in the same frivolity with which it was founded.

42. Now worldly friendship, which is born of desire for earthly goods or wealth, is always full of fraud and trickery. Nothing about it is settled, nothing consistent, nothing secure, since worldly friendship changes according to fortune and pursues profit. 43. Hence it is written: *"He is a friend only for the moment and will not remain so in hard times."* Take away the hope of profit and immediately he ceases to be a friend. Someone mocked this kind of friendship thus, in elegant verse:

He is not a friend of the person but his prosperity,
whom sweet fortune maintains but bitter drives away.

44. And yet the beginning of this depraved friendship often leads many to a certain measure of true friendship. That

portionem; eos scilicet qui primum spe lucri communis foedus ineuntes dum sibi in iniquo mammona fidem servant, in rebus dumtaxat humanis, ad maximum perveniunt gratumque consensum. Attamen vera amicitia nullo modo dicenda est quae commodi temporalis causa suscipitur et reservatur.

45. Amicitia enim spiritalis quam veram dicimus non utilitatis cuiusque mundialis intuitu, non qualibet extra nascente causa, sed propria naturae dignitate, et humani pectoris sensu desideratur, ita ut fructus eius praemiumque non sit aliud quam ipsa. 46. Unde Dominus in Evangelio: "*Posui vos,*" inquit, "*ut eatis et fructum afferatis,*" id est, "*ut invicem diligatis.*" In ipsa namque vera amicitia itur proficiendo, et fructus capitur perfectionis illius dulcedinem sentiendo. Amicitia itaque spiritalis inter bonos vitae, morum, studiorumque similitudine parturitur, quae est in rebus humanis atque divinis *cum benevolentia et caritate consensio.*

47. Quae quidem definitio ad amicitiam exprimendam satis mihi videtur esse sufficiens, si tamen more nostro "caritas" nuncupetur, ut ab amicitia omne vitium excludatur, "benevolentia" autem ipse sensus amandi qui cum quadam dulcedine movetur interius exprimatur. 48. Ubi talis est amicitia, ibi profecto est *idem velle* et *idem nolle,* tanto utique dulcius, quanto sincerius, tanto suavius, quanto sacratius; ubi sic amantes nihil possunt velle quod dedeceat, nihil quod expediat nolle. 49. Hanc nempe amicitiam prudentia dirigit, iustitia regit, fortitudo custodit, temperantia moderator. De quibus suo loco disputabimus. Nunc autem si de

is, there are those who, first entering into friendship in hope of common profit as they remain loyal to themselves in their wicked Mammon, reach the peak of pleasurable agreement as far as human affairs are concerned. Nevertheless, in no way should something that begins and continues for the sake of worldly profit be called true friendship.

45. The spiritual friendship we call true is desired not for consideration of worldly benefit or for any outward cause, but for its own natural dignity and the sentiment of the human heart, so that its fruit and reward is nothing but friendship itself. 46. Hence the Lord in the Gospel: "*I have proposed that you go forth and bear fruit,*" that is, "*that you love one another.*" There is an ongoing process of improvement in friendship itself; the fruit is harvested by savoring the sweetness of its perfection. Therefore, spiritual friendship among good people is born of shared perspective on life, habits, and interests, which is *agreement along with goodwill and love* in matters human and divine.

47. Indeed, this definition seems to me adequate to describe friendship, provided that "love" is meant according to our usage, so that all vice is excluded from friendship, and that by "goodwill" is expressed the instinct to love roused with a measure of interior sweetness. 48. Where there is such love, there is certainly *wishing* and *not wishing the same things,* and the more sweet and delightful it is, the more sincere and holy it is. Those who love in this way can wish for nothing that is dishonorable and reject anything that is unfitting. 49. Of course, prudence guides this friendship, justice rules it, strength protects it, and discretion moderates it. We shall discuss these four virtues in their place. But for now, tell me if you judge that the question you thought

eo quod primum quaerendum putasti, videlicet, "Quid sit amicitia?" satis datum aestimas, edicito.

50. *Ivo:* Sufficiunt plane ea quae dicta sunt, nec mihi suggeritur aliquid ultra quod quaeram. Sed antequam ad alia transeamus, scire desidero unde primum amicitia inter mortales orta est. Natura an casu, an necessitate aliqua, vel certe praecepto, aut lege humano generi imposita, in usum venerit, usus vero eam commendabilem fecerit?

51. *Aelredus:* Amicitiae, ut mihi videtur, primum ipsa natura humanis mentibus expressit affectum, deinde experientia auxit, postremo legis auctoritas ordinavit. Deus enim summe potens et summe bonus, sibi ipsi sufficiens bonum est; quoniam bonum suum, gaudium suum, gloria sua, beatitudo sua, ipse est. 52. Nec est aliquid extra ipsum quo egeat, non homo, non angelus, non caelum, non terra, nec aliquid quod in ipsis est, cui omnis creatura proclamat: *"Deus meus es, quoniam bonorum meorum non eges."* Nec tantum sibi sufficit ipse, sed et omnium rerum sufficientia ipse est, dans aliis esse, aliis et sentire, aliis insuper et sapere, ipse omnium existentium causa, omnium sentientium vita, omnium intellegentium sapientia. 53. Ipse itaque summa natura omnes naturas instituit, omnia suis locis ordinavit, omnia suis temporibus discrete distribuit. Voluit autem, nam et ita ratio eius aeterna praescripsit, ut omnes creaturas pax componeret, et uniret societas, et ita omnia ab ipso qui summe et pure unus est quoddam unitatis vestigium sortirentur. Hinc est quod nullum genus rerum solitarium reliquit, sed ex multis quadam societate connexuit.

54. Nam ut ab insensibilibus ordiamur: quae humus vel

should be discussed first, that is, "What is friendship?" has been answered satisfactorily.

50. *Ivo:* Clearly, what has been said will suffice and nothing occurs to me that I would discuss further. But before we move along to other topics, I desire to know how friendship first arose among mortals. Was it from nature, chance, or some necessity? Or did it actually come into use through teaching or law imposed on humankind, after which its practice made it praiseworthy?

51. *Aelred:* It seems to me that nature itself first stamped the feeling of friendship on human minds, which experience then increased, and finally the authority of law sanctioned. For God, supreme in power and goodness, is a good sufficient unto himself, since he himself is his own good, joy, glory, and blessedness. 52. There is nothing outside himself that he could need, no human, angel, heaven, earth, or anything that is in them, since all he has created cries out to him, *"You are my God, for you have no need of my goods."* Not only is he sufficient unto himself, but he is sufficiency for all other things, giving some existence, others sensation, still others thought. He is the cause of everything that exists, the life of everything with sensation, the wisdom of all who think. 53. So the supreme nature himself made all natures, arranged all things in their place, and wisely apportioned all things in their time. As his eternal reason dictated, he wanted all his creatures to be ordered by peace and united by affinity. Thus they would all receive from him, who is supremely and purely one, a mark of unity. For this reason, he left no type of being by itself, but from the many he joined each in a kind of society.

54. Let us start with creatures that lack sensation. What

quod flumen unum unius generis gignit lapidem, aut quae silva unam unius generis arborem producit? Ita inter ipsa insensibilia quasi amor quidam societatis elucet, cum nihil eorum solum sit sed cum quadam sui generis societate et creetur et persistat. Verum inter ipsa sensibilia quanta amicitiae species et societatis amorisque fulgeat imago, quis facile dixerit? 55. Certe cum in caeteris omnibus irrationabilia deprehendantur, in hac tantum parte ita humanum animum imitantur, ut pene ratione agi aestimentur. Ita se sequuntur, ita colludunt sibi, ita motibus simul et vocibus suum exprimunt et produnt affectum tam avide et iucunde mutua societate fruuntur, ut nihil magis quam ea quae amicitiae sunt curare videantur. 56. Sic etiam in angelis divina sapientia providit, ut non unus videlicet crearetur, sed plures; inter quos grata societas et amor suavissimus eamdem voluntatem, eumdem crearet affectum, ne cum alter superior, inferior alter videretur, locus pateret invidiae, si non obstitisset caritas amicitiae, et ita solitudinem excluderet multitudo, iucunditatem augeret in pluribus caritatis communio.

57. Postremo cum hominem condidisset, ut bonum societatis altius commendaret, "*Non est bonum,*" inquit, "*esse hominem solum; faciamus ei adiutorium simile sibi.*" Nec certe de simili, vel saltem de eadem materia hoc adiutorium virtus divina formavit, sed ad expressius caritatis et amicitiae incentivum, de ipsius substantia masculi feminam procreavit. Pulchre autem de latere primi hominis secundus assumitur, ut natura doceret omnes aequales, quasi "collaterales," nec

soil or river produces only one kind of stone, or what forest produces only one species of tree? Thus among insentient beings, it is as if love of company manifests itself, since none of them exists alone, but each is created and endures in a sort of society with its own kind. But concerning sentient beings, who could say easily how brightly gleam the appearance of friendship and the image of society and love? 55. Granted that in all other respects animals are considered irrational, in this one respect they imitate the human spirit with the result that they are thought to act almost according to reason. Animals follow one another, play with each other, express and disclose their affections in movement and sound alike, enjoy each other's company so eagerly and delightedly that in these ways that they seem to care for nothing more than what are elements of friendship. 56. Divine wisdom provided for the angels in the same way, namely, not one but many were created, among whom pleasant companionship and the most delightful love created one and the same will and affection. Although one might seem superior and another inferior, giving rise to envy, the love of friendship prevented it, and in the same manner, the multitude of angels warded off loneliness while the sharing of love among many increased their delight.

57. When at last God had created man, in order to recommend most highly the goodness of companionship, he said, "*It is not good for man to be alone; let us make him a helper like himself.*" Divine virtue formed the helper not from similar or even the same material, but created woman from the very substance of man as an explicit incentive to love and friendship. Beautifully, the second human was taken from the side (*latus*) of the first, so nature would teach that all are equals,

esset in rebus humanis superior vel inferior, quod est amicitiae proprium. 58. Ita natura mentibus humanis ab ipso
exordio amicitiae et caritatis impressit affectum, quem interior mox sensus amandi quodam gustu suavitatis adauxit.
At post lapsum primi hominis, cum refrigescente caritate
cupiditas subintrasset fecissetque bono communi privata
praeponi amicitiae caritatisque splendorem avaritia invidia-
que corrupit, contentiones, aemulationes, odia, suspiciones
corruptis hominum moribus invehens. 59. Tunc boni quique
inter caritatem et amicitiam distinxerunt, animadvertentes
quod etiam inimicis atque perversis sit impendenda dilectio, cum inter bonos et pessimos esse non possit voluntatum
vel consiliorum ulla communio. Amicitia itaque quae sicut
caritas inter omnes primum et ab omnibus servabatur, inter
paucos bonos naturali lege resedit qui, videntes a multis sacra fidei ac societatis iura violari, arctiori se dilectionis et
amicitiae foedere constrinxerunt, inter mala quae videbant
et sentiebant in mutuae caritatis gratia quiescentes.

60. Verum his in quibus omnem virtutis sensum oblitte-
ravit impietas, ratio quae in eis exstingui non potuit ipsum
amicitiae et societatis affectum non reliquit, adeo ut sine
sociis, nec avaro divitiae, nec ambitioso gloria, nec voluptas
posset placere luxurioso. Compacta sunt itaque etiam inter
pessimos quaedam societatis foedera detestanda, quae amicitiae pulcherrimo nomine palliata, lege et praeceptis a vera
amicitia fuerant distinguenda; ne cum ista appeteretur, in

"collateral," as it were, and that in human affairs there is no superior or inferior, which is a characteristic of friendship. 58. Thus from the very beginning, nature impressed on human minds an attachment to friendship and love, which an interior disposition toward loving promptly increased by a taste of sweetness. But after the fall of the first man, when greed had crept in as love grew cold and private gain took precedence over common good, avarice and envy corrupted the brilliance of friendship and love and brought strife, rivalry, hatred, and suspicion into the corrupted habits of humankind. 59. Then all good people made a distinction between love and friendship, noting that love should be extended even to enemies and the perverse, whereas there can be no community of will or purpose between the good and the wicked. Therefore friendship, which just like love was at first maintained among all and by all, persisted between a few good people by natural law. Seeing the sacred laws of loyalty and association were being violated by many, they bound themselves more tightly in a pact of love and friendship and found respite in the gift of mutual love amid the evils they saw and experienced.

60. But for those in whom wickedness obliterated all sense of virtue, the force of reason in them that could not be extinguished held onto the inclination toward love and fellowship at least to the extent that without companions, wealth could not please the greedy, nor glory the ambitious, nor gratification the lustful. Therefore, cursed pacts of fellowship were struck between even the worst people. Disguised under the most lovely name of friendship, these agreements had to be distinguished from true friendship by law and teaching, so that when real friendship was sought,

illa propter quamdam eius similitudinem incaute incidere-
tur. 61. Sic amicitiam quam natura instituit, quam robora-
vit usus, legis auctoritas ordinavit. Manifestum proinde est
amicitiam naturalem esse sicut virtutem, sicut sapientiam,
et caetera quae propter se, quasi bona naturalia, et appe-
tenda sunt et servanda, quibus omnis qui ea habet bene
utitur, quibus nullus prorsus abutitur.

62. *Ivo:* Nonne, quaeso te, sapientia multi abutuntur, qui
ex ea hominibus placere cupiunt, vel in seipsis pro collata
sibi sapientia superbiunt, vel certe hi qui eam venalem habent, et quaestum existimant pietatem?

63. *Aelredus:* Hinc tibi satisfaciet noster Augustinus, cuius
verba sunt haec: "*Qui sibi placet, stulto homini placet, quia profecto stultus est, qui sibi placet.*" Qui vero stultus est sapiens
non est et qui sapiens non est, non habendo utique sapientiam, sapiens non est. Quomodo igitur sapientia male utitur,
qui sapientiam non habet? Sic et superba castitas virtus non
est, quia superbia ipsa quae vitium est, eam quae virtus putabatur, sibi conformem facit, et ideo iam non virtus sed
vitium est.

64. *Ivo:* Sed pace tua dico, incongruum mihi videtur, quod
amicitiae sapientiam adiunxisti, cum inter illas nulla sit
comparatio.

65. *Aelredus:* Saepe minora maioribus, bona melioribus,
infirmiora fortioribus, etsi non coaequantur, coniunguntur
tamen maxime in virtutibus, quae licet a se graduum diversi-
tate discrepent, quadam tamen sibi similitudine vicinantur.
Vicina est enim virginitati viduitas, viduitati coniugalis

false friendship was not carelessly entered into because of a certain similarity. 61. Thus the authority of law ordained the friendship that nature established and practice strengthened. Accordingly it is clear that friendship is natural, like virtue and wisdom and other things that are, like natural goods, both to be sought and preserved for their own sake. Everyone who has them uses them well and nobody abuses them altogether.

62. *Ivo:* I have to ask: aren't there plenty of people who abuse wisdom, who desire to please others with it, or brag to themselves regarding the wisdom they have acquired, or of course those who think it can be bought and sold and reckon the pursuit of profit is goodness?

63. *Aelred:* Our Augustine will satisfy you on this point. His exact words are, *"He who pleases himself pleases a fool, because obviously one who pleases himself is a fool."* But a fool is not wise, and one who is not wise is not wise because he lacks wisdom. How, therefore, does one who lacks wisdom misuse it? In just the same way that proud chastity is not a virtue, because pride itself is a vice, conforming itself to what is considered a virtue. Therefore, it is then not a virtue but a vice.

64. *Ivo:* But I've got to say, with your permission, that to me it seems incongruous that you linked wisdom with friendship, since there's no comparing the two.

65. *Aelred:* Especially where virtues are concerned, often the lesser is connected to, albeit not quite equal to, the greater, the good to the better, and the weaker to the stronger. Although virtues may differ from one another in degree, they still may be neighbors through a certain likeness. Widowhood is close to virginity, conjugal chastity close to

castitas, et quamvis inter has virtutes magna sit differentia, in eo tamen quod virtutes sunt, nonnulla est convenientia. 66. Neque enim ideo pudicitia coniugalis virtus non est, quia praecellit continentia vidualis, quibus licet sancta praeferatur virginitas, earum tamen gratiam non oblitterat. Quamvis si ea quae de amicitia dicta sunt diligenter advertas, invenies eam sapientiae sic vicinam vel infertam ut pene dixerim amicitiam nihil aliud esse quam sapientiam.

67. *Ivo:* Obstupesco fateor, nec facile id mihi persuaderi posse existimo.

68. *Aelredus:* Exciditne tibi dixisse scripturam, "*Omni tempore diligit qui amicus est*"? Ait etiam, sicut meministi, noster Hieronymus, "*Amicitia quae desinere potest numquam vera fuit.*" Amicitiam etiam nec subsistere quidem sine caritate, satis superque monstratum est. Cum igitur in amicitia et aeternitas vigeat, et veritas luceat, et caritas dulcescat, utrum nomen sapientiae tribus his debeas abrogare, tu videris.

69. *Ivo:* O quid est hoc? Dicamne de amicitia quod amicus Iesu Ioannes de caritate commemorat: "Deus amicitia est"?

70. *Aelredus:* Inusitatum quidem hoc, nec ex scripturis habet auctoritatem. Quod tamen sequitur de caritate, amicitiae profecto dare non dubito, quoniam *qui manet in amicitia, in Deo manet, et Deus in eo.* Quod cum de ipsius fructu vel utilitate coeperimus disputare, nos manifestius pervidebimus. Nunc si quid sit amicitia pro simplicitate ingenioli mei satis diximus, caetera quae enucleanda proposuisti alio tempori reservemus.

widowhood, and although there is a great difference between these virtues, there is some connection in that they are all virtues. 66. For that reason, conjugal chastity is no less a virtue because a widow's continence surpasses it, and even if holy virginity is preferable to both, it does not obliterate the grace of chastity and continence. Although if you pay close attention to what has been said about friendship, you will find it so close to wisdom and so filled with it that I would almost say that friendship is nothing other than wisdom.

67. *Ivo:* I admit that I'm dumbfounded, and I don't think I can be easily persuaded on that point.

68. *Aelred:* Has it escaped you that scripture says, "*He is a friend who loves at all times*"? And, as you recall, our Jerome said, "*Friendship that can end was never true friendship.*" It has been more than satisfactorily shown, too, that friendship cannot exist without love. Since in friendship eternity flourishes, truth shines forth, and love becomes sweet, whether you should deny these three the name of wisdom is up to you.

69. *Ivo:* Oh, what is this? Should I say of friendship what Jesus's friend John said of love, that "God is friendship"?

70. *Aelred:* That is quite unusual and has no scriptural authority. Yet what follows from John's statement about love I do not hesitate in the least to apply to friendship, since *he who abides in love abides in God, and God in him*. We will see this more clearly when we begin to discuss the reward and usefulness of friendship. If, in the simplicity of my limited understanding, we have said enough for now about what friendship is, let us reserve for another time the other matters you have proposed to discuss in detail.

71. *Ivo:* Licet aviditati meae nimis ista sit molesta dilatio, ad hoc tamen non solum tempus cenae, cui deesse non permittimur, sed etiam multorum, quibus debitor tu es, exspectatio satis onorosa compellit.

LIBER SECUNDUS

DE SPIRITALI AMICITIA.

[*Aelredus:*] Iam nunc, frater, accede, et quidnam causae fuerit quod paulo ante cum carnalibus illis carnalia compararem solus sedebas, modicum semotus a nobis, et nunc oculos huc illucque vertebas, nunc frontem confricabas manu, nunc capillos digitis attrectabas, nunc iram ipsa facie praeferens, aliquid tibi praeter votum accessisse, crebra vultus mutatione querebaris, edicito.

2. *Galterus:* Profecto ita est. Quis enim patienter sustineat tota die nescio quos exactores Pharaonis tui habere copiam; nos autem quibus specialiter debitor es, nec rarum tecum habere posse colloquium?

3. *Aelredus:* Et illis quoque gerendus est mos, quorum vel optamus beneficia, vel maleficia formidamus. Quibus vel nunc tandem exclusis, tanto mihi gratior est solitudo, quanto molestior inquietudo praecessit. Nam optimum cibi condimentum fames est; nec mel aliave species vinum sic sapidum reddit, ut sitis vehemens aquam. Quocirca erit tibi forte haec nostra collatio quasi cibus vel potus quidam spiritalis, eo iucundior quo aestus praecessit ardentior.

71. *Ivo:* Although putting it off annoys me greatly in my eagerness, it must be so since it's time for supper, which we are not allowed to miss, and also because the many others to whom you have obligations are forced to endure a very tiresome wait for your attention.

THE SECOND BOOK
OF SPIRITUAL FRIENDSHIP.

Aelred: Now then, brother, come here and tell me why, a little while ago, when you were sitting alone at some distance from us while I was doing worldly business with worldly men, you first cast your glance this way and that, then rubbed your forehead with your hand, then ran your fingers through your hair, then showed anger on your face, complaining in your frequent changes of expression that something contrary to your wishes had happened to you.

2. *Walter:* That's exactly right. Who would sit around patiently all day while some unknown overseers of Pharaoh have your complete attention while we, to whom you are especially indebted, can't even enjoy an occasional conversation with you?

3. *Aelred:* That is the way we have to behave, just as well with those whose favor we hope for as with those whose ill favor we fear. They are gone at last, and the more annoying the preceding disruption, the more gratifying solitude is to me now. Hunger is food's best seasoning; neither honey nor any spice gives wine such flavor as a powerful thirst lends to water. So perhaps our discussion will be a kind of spiritual food and drink for you, just as delicious as the preceding

Age iam, et quod anxio pectore paulo ante parabas evolvere, in medium proferre non differas.

4. *Galterus:* Faciam quidem. Nam si velim de hora causari quam isti nobis reliquere brevissimam, videbor ipse eam mihi facere breviorem. Dic nunc, rogo te, utrum elapsum animo sit, an adhuc memoria teneas, quid inter te quondam et tuum Ivonem de amicitia spiritali convenerit, quas tibi ipse proposuerit quaestiones, quantum in earum enuclea-tione processeris, quid de his quoque stilo tradideris.

5. *Aelredus:* Equidem carissimi mei recordatio, immo continuus amplexus et affectus, ita mihi semper recens est ut, licet ex humanis exemptus conditioni satis dederit, in meo tamen animo numquam videatur obiisse. Ibi semper mecum est, ibi mihi religiosus eius vultus elucet; ibi mihi dulces eius arrident oculi, ibi eius iucunda mihi verba sic sapiunt, ut vel ego videar cum eo ad meliora transisse, vel ipse mecum adhuc in his inferioribus conversari. Scis autem quia plures praeterierunt anni ex quo schedula ipsa cui de spiritali amicitia eius interrogationes measque responsiones impresseram nobis elapsa est.

6. *Galterus:* Non me latent ista. Sed, ut verum fatear, hinc tota ista aviditas et impatientia tota descendit, quod sche-dulam ipsam ante hoc triduum repertam et tibi traditam, a quibusdam accepi. Ostende, quaeso, eam puero tuo; non enim requiescit spiritus meus donec conspectis omnibus et quid illi disputationi desit advertens, ea quae mihi vel mens propria, vel inspiratio occulta suggesserit esse quaerenda, ad tuae paternitatis examen proferam, aut reprobanda, aut ad-mittenda, aut exponenda.

hunger was fierce. Come now, do not put off laying out what you were anxiously preparing to tell me a little while ago.

4. *Walter:* I'll do exactly that. If I wanted to complain about the very short time together those people have left us, I'd seem myself to be making it even shorter. Tell me now, please, whether it has slipped your mind or if you still remember what you and your Ivo once agreed upon concerning spiritual friendship, what questions he asked you, how far you got in answering them, and in addition what of it you wrote down.

5. *Aelred:* Indeed the memory of my dearest brother, or rather his never-ending embrace and affection, is always so fresh in my mind that although being removed from human affairs he has paid his debt to the mortal condition, nevertheless it seems in my heart that he never died. There he is always with me, there his devout face shines on me, there his sweet eyes smile on me, there his charming words have such savor for me that either I seem to have gone to a better world with him or that he still lives with me in this lower realm. You know that many years have passed since the pages on which I had written down his questions about spiritual friendship and my replies were lost to me.

6. *Walter:* I know all that. But to tell the truth, all my eagerness and impatience come from having heard from certain people that the pages were discovered and returned to you three days ago. I beg you to show them to your son. My spirit will not rest until, after inspecting them and making note of what's missing from the discussion, I present for your fatherly consideration—for rejection, approval, or explanation—what either my own mind or unseen inspiration suggests should be investigated further.

7. *Aelredus:* Geram tibi morem, sed solus volo legas quod scriptum est, nec efferatur in publicum, ne forte aliqua resecanda, addenda nonnulla, plurima vero corrigenda aestimaverim.

8. *Galterus:* Ecce adsum, habens aures ad tua verba suspensas, tanto certe avidius, quanto id quod de amicitia legi dulcius sapuit. Quoniam igitur, quid sit amicitia, legi magnifice disputatum, quid cultoribus suis pariat utilitatis, velim mihi insinues. Cum enim res tanta sit, ut certis rationibus visus es comprobasse; tunc primum vehementius appetitur, cum finis eius fructusque cognoscitur.

9. *Aelredus:* Non id pro tantae rei dignitate a me explicari posse praesumo, cum in rebus humanis nihil sanctius appetatur, nihil quaeratur utilius, nihil difficilius inveniatur, nihil experiatur dulcius, nihil fructuosius teneatur. Habet enim fructum vitae praesentis quae nunc est et futurae. 10. Ipsa enim omnes virtutes sua condit suavitate, vitia sua virtute confodit; adversa temperat, componit prospera, ita ut sine amico inter mortales nihil fere possit esse iucundum. Homo bestiae comparetur, non habens qui sibi collaetetur in rebus secundis, in tristibus contristetur, cui evaporet si quid molestum mens conceperit, cui communicet si quid praeter solitum sublime vel luminosum accesserit.

11. *Vae soli, quia cum ceciderit, non habet sublevantem se.* Solus omnino est, qui sine amico est. At quae felicitas, quae securitas, quae iucunditas habere cum quo aeque audeas loqui ut

7. *Aelred:* I will humor you, but I want you to read what is written alone and not share it, in case I think that any material ought to be pruned, or some added, or a great deal be corrected.

8. *Walter:* Here I am, ears pricked up for your words, in fact all the more eager now because what I have read about friendship had such a very sweet taste. So since I have read a splendid discussion of what friendship is, I would like you to convey to me the benefit it offers to those who cultivate it. For although it is such a great thing, as you seem to have proven by sure arguments, it will then first be pursued more eagerly once its purpose and reward are known.

9. *Aelred:* I do not presume, given the enormous importance of this subject, to be able to explain it, since in human affairs nothing is desired with more holiness, nothing is sought more usefully, nothing is found with more difficulty, nothing is experienced with more sweetness, nothing is possessed with greater profit. For friendship bears fruit in this life now as well as in the next. 10. In its very sweetness it seasons all virtues, and by its virtue it transfixes vices. It tempers adversity and stabilizes prosperity to the point that among mortals, almost nothing can give delight without a friend. A man should be likened to an animal if he lacks someone to rejoice with in good fortune and grieve with in sadness, to whom he can vent if his mind conceives of something harmful, and with whom he can share something unusually sublime or remarkable that happens.

11. *Woe to the solitary man, who has no one to lift him up when he falls.* He who is without a friend is completely alone. But what happiness, what security, what delight to have someone to whom you may dare to speak as you do to yourself, to

tibi cui confiteri non timeas si quid deliqueris, cui non
erubescas revelare in spiritalibus si quid profeceris, cui cordis tui omnia secreta committas, et commendes consilia!
Quid igitur iucundius quam ita unire animum animo, et
unum efficere de duobus, ut nulla iactantia timeatur, nulla
formidetur suspicio, nec correptus alter ab altero doleat,
nec laudantem alter alterum adulationis notet vel arguat? 12.
"*Amicus,*" ait sapiens, "*medicamentum vitae est.*" Praeclare quidem id. Non enim validior vel efficacior vel praestantior est
vulneribus nostris in omnibus temporalibus medicina quam
habere qui omni incommodo occurrat compatiens, omni
commodo occurrat congratulans ut, secundum Apostolum,
iunctis humeris, onera sua invicem tolerant nisi quod unusquisque propriam levius quam amici portat iniuriam.

13. *Amicitia* ergo *secundas res splendidiores facit, adversas par-
tiens communicansque leviores.* Optimum ergo vitae medicamentum amicus. Nam ut ethnicis etiam placuit: "*Non aqua,
non igni pluribus locis utimur quam amico.*" In omni actu, in
omni studio, in certis, in dubiis, in quolibet eventu, in fortuna qualibet, in secreto, in publico, in omni consultatione,
domi forisque, ubique amicitia grata, amicus necessarius,
utilis gratia reperitur. Quocirca amici, ut ait Tullius, "*et absentes adsunt sibi, et egentes abundant, et imbecilles valent, et, quod
difficilius dictu est, mortui vivunt.*" 14. Igitur amicitia divitibus
pro gloria, exsulibus pro patria, pauperibus pro censu, ae-
grotis pro medicina, mortuis pro vita, sanis pro gratia, imbe-
cillibus pro virtute, robustis est pro praemio. Tantus enim
amicos honos, memoria, laus desideriumque prosequitur ut

whom you may not fear to confess your failings, to whom you may reveal your spiritual progress without blushing, to whom you may entrust all your heart's secrets and confide your plans! What, then, is more delightful than to join spirit to spirit, to make one out of two, in such a manner that no boasting is to be feared nor suspicion dreaded, when one does not suffer when corrected by the other, nor blame or accuse the other of flattery when he offers praise? 12. A wise man says, "*A friend is medicine for life.*" That is excellent. There is no medicine for our ills in worldly matters that is stronger, more effective, or more outstanding than to have someone to meet every loss with compassion and every success with congratulations, so that, according to the Apostle, they bear each other's burdens shoulder to shoulder—except that each puts up with harm to himself more easily than that to his friend.

13. Thus *friendship makes good times more brilliant and makes bad times easier by dividing and sharing them.* Therefore, a friend really is the best medicine for life. This pleased even the pagans: "*We do not use water or fire in more situations than we use a friend.*" In every action or undertaking, in certainties and uncertainties, in any event or situation, in private and public, in every deliberation, at home or abroad, friendship is welcome everywhere, a friend is a necessity, his usefulness a blessing. Hence friends, as Cicero says, "*are present for one when absent, rich when poor, strong when weak and, more difficult to say, living when dead.*" 14. Consequently, friendship is glory for the rich, a fatherland for exiles, property for the poor, medicine for the sick, life for the dead, a blessing for the healthy, strength for the weak, a reward for the robust. Such great honor, remembrance, praise, and desire accompany

et eorum vita laudabilis, et mors pretiosa iudicetur. Et quod his omnibus excellit, quidam gradus est amicitia vicinus perfectioni, quae in Dei dilectione et cognitione consistit, ut homo ex amico hominis Dei efficiatur amicus, secundum illud salvatoris in Evangelio: "*Iam non dicam vos servos sed amicos meos.*"

15. *Galterus:* Ita, fateor, tua me movit oratio, ita in amicitiae desiderium totum animi mei succendit appetitum, ut nec vivere me crediderim, quamdiu huius tanti boni tam multiplici fructu caruero. Sed hoc quod ultimum posuisti, quod me totum rapuit et pene abripuit a terrenis, plenius mihi enodari desidero: quod scilicet amicitia optimus ad perfectionem gradus existit. 16. Et opportune satis nunc hic noster Gratianus intravit, quem ipsius amicitiae alumnum iure dixerim, cuius totum studium est *amari* et *amare,* ne forte amicitiae nimium avidus, eiusque similitudine deceptus, falsam pro vera, fictam pro solida, pro spiritali carnalem recipiat.

17. *Gratianus:* Ago gratias humanitati tuae, frater, quod non vocato, sed se impudentius ingerenti, nunc tandem ad spiritale convivium concedis accessum. Nam si me serio, non ludo, alumnum amicitiae appellandum putasti, debueram in sermonis principio accersiri, nec aviditatem meam posita verecundia prodidissem. At tu, pater, perge quo coeperas, et causa mei aliquid mensis appone, ut si non satiari ut iste, qui nescio quot ferculis devoratis, nunc me quasi ad reliquias suas fastidiosus ascivit, saltem modicum valeam refocillari.

friends that their lives should be thought praiseworthy and their deaths precious. And what is more than all that, friendship consisting of love and knowledge of God is a step near perfection, so from being a friend of a person, one is made a friend of God, according to the Savior in the Gospel: *"From now on I will call you not servants but my friends."*

15. *Walter:* I confess that your words so move me, so light up the longing of my entire soul with desire for friendship, that I would not believe myself alive as long as I was without the various rewards of so great a good. But I want more fully explained to me the last thing you said, which enraptured me and almost took me away from earthly matters, namely, that friendship is the best step toward perfection. 16. And now, most fittingly, our Gratian has come in, whom I could rightly have called a child of friendship, whose whole desire is *to be loved* and *to love* with the result that in his perhaps excessive eagerness for friendship, deceived by something resembling it, he might mistake false friendship for true, imagined friendship for real, carnal friendship for spiritual.

17. *Gratian:* Thank you for your kindness, brother, for now at last admitting to a spiritual banquet one who was not invited but barges in rather shamelessly. If you thought I should be called a child of friendship seriously, not as a joke, I should have been summoned at the beginning of the conversation and not had to reveal my eagerness, modesty set aside. But you, father, continue what you started and put something on the table for my sake, so that I may at least be somewhat refreshed, if not filled up like Walter who, having dined on I don't know how many courses, has now haughtily offered me his leftovers, so to speak.

18. *Aelredus:* Non verearis, fili, quoniam tanta restant adhuc de amicitiae bono dicenda, quae si quislibet sapiens prosequeretur, nos nihil dixisse putares. Verum quomodo ad Dei dilectionem et cognitionem gradus quidam sit amicitia paucis adverte. In amicitia quippe nihil inhonestum est, nihil fictum, nihil simulatum, et quidquid est, id sanctum et voluntarium et verum est. Et hoc ipsum caritatis quoque proprium est. 19. In hoc vero amicitia spiritali et speciali praerogativa praelucet, quod inter eos qui sibi amicitiae glutino copulantur, omnia iucunda, omnia secura, omnia dulcia, omnia suavia sentiuntur. Ex caritatis igitur perfectione plerosque diligimus, qui nobis oneri sunt et dolori, quibus licet honeste, non ficte, non simulate, sed vere voluntarieque consulimus, ad secreta tamen eos amicitiae nostrae non admittimus. 20. Quocirca in amicitia coniunguntur honestas et suavitas, veritas et iucunditas, dulcedo et voluntas, affectus et actus. Quae omnia a Christo inchoantur, per Christum promoventur, in Christo perficiuntur. Non igitur videtur nimium gravis vel innaturalis ascensus, de Christo amorem inspirante quo amicum diligimus, ad Christum semetipsum amicum nobis praebentem, quem diligamus ut suavitas suavitati, dulcedo dulcedini, affectus succedat affectui. 21. Itaque amicus in spiritu Christi adhaerens amico efficitur cum eo *cor unum et anima una,* et sic per amoris gradus ad Christi conscendens amicitiam, unus cum eo spiritus efficitur in osculo uno. Ad quod osculum anima quaedam sancta suspirans: "*Osculetur me,*" inquit, "*osculo oris sui.*"

22. Consideremus istius osculi carnalis proprietatem ut

18. *Aelred:* Fear not, my son: there is still so much left to say on the goodness of friendship. If any wise man were continuing the discussion, you would think we had said nothing. But pay attention to a few words about how friendship is a sort of step toward the love and knowledge of God. In friendship, of course, there is nothing dishonorable, nothing contrived, nothing pretended. What is present is holy and willing and true. This is also a characteristic of charity. 19. But in this, friendship shines forth with this special and spiritual claim: among those who are attached to each other by the bond of friendship, all things are experienced as pleasant, secure, sweet, and delightful. Therefore, in the perfection of charity, we cherish many people who are a burden and a grief to us and although we have authentic regard for them and not in a contrived or pretended manner, still we do not admit them to the intimacy of our friendship. 20. Accordingly, friendship joins honor and delight, truth and pleasure, sweetness and goodwill, affection and action. All of these are begun with Christ, advanced through Christ, and perfected in Christ. Thus it does not seem too steep or unnatural an ascent from the love Christ inspires in us to cherish a friend, to Christ offering himself to us as a friend whom we may cherish in turn, so that delight succeeds delight, sweetness succeeds sweetness, affection succeeds affection. 21. Therefore a friend attached to a friend in the spirit of Christ is made *one heart and one soul* with him, and ascending the steps of love to friendship with Christ in this fashion, he is made one spirit with him in one kiss. Sighing for this kiss, one holy soul said, "*Let him kiss me with the kiss of his mouth.*"

22. Let us consider the nature of this carnal kiss so that

de carnalibus ad spiritalia, de humanis ad divina transeamus. Duobus alimentis vita hominis sustentatur, cibo et aere, et sine cibo subsistere potest quidem aliquamdiu, at sine aere ne una quidem hora. Itaque ut vivamus, ore haurimus aerem et remittimus. Et ipsum quidem quod emittitur vel recipitur spiritus nomen obtinuit. 23. Quocirca in osculo duo sibi spiritus obviant, et miscentur sibi et uniuntur. Ex quibus quaedam mentis suavitas nascens, osculantium movet et perstringit affectum.

24. Est igitur osculum corporale, osculum spiritale, osculum intellectuale. Osculum corporale impressione fit labiorum, osculum spiritale coniunctione animorum, osculum intellectuale per Dei spiritum infusione gratiarum. Osculum proinde corporale non nisi certis et honestis causis aut offerendum est aut recipiendum. Verbi gratia, in signum reconciliationis, quando fiunt amici qui prius inimici fuerant ad invicem, in signum pacis, sicut communicaturi in ecclesia interiorem pacem exteriori osculo demonstrant, in signum dilectionis, sicut inter sponsum et sponsam fieri permittitur vel sicut ab amicis post diuturnam absentiam et porrigitur et suscipitur, in signum catholicae unitatis, sicut fit cum hospes suscipitur. 25. Sed sicut plerique aqua, igni, ferro, cibo et aere, quae naturaliter bona sunt, in suae crudelitatis vel voluptatis satellitium abutuntur, ita perversi et turpes, etiam hoc bono quod ad ea significanda quae diximus, lex naturalis instituit, sua quodammodo flagitia condire nituntur, ipsum osculum turpitudine tanta foedantes ut sic osculari nihil sit aliud quam adulterari. Quod quam sit detestandum, quam abominandum, quam fugiendum, quam adversandum, quilibet honestus intellegit.

we may proceed from the carnal to the spiritual, from the human to the divine. Human life is sustained by two nourishments, food and air. One can last a while without food, but not even an hour without air. In order to live, then, we inhale and exhale air through our mouths. What is inhaled or exhaled is called breath. 23. So in a kiss two breaths meet, are blended, and are joined. From them, a certain sweetness of mind is born, arousing and binding tightly the affection of those who kiss.

24. There is a bodily kiss, a spiritual kiss, and a kiss of understanding. A bodily kiss is made by the pressing together of lips, a spiritual kiss by the joining of spirits, a kiss of understanding through the spirit of God by the infusion of grace. Accordingly, a bodily kiss should not be given or received except for particular and honorable reasons. For example, it could be a sign of reconciliation, when those who had been each other's enemies become friends; or a sign of peace, when those about to receive communion in church demonstrate their inner peace with an outward kiss; or a sign of love, as is permitted between husband and wife or given and received by friends after a long absence; or a sign of catholic unity, as when a guest is received. 25. But just as many people abuse water, fire, iron, food, and air, which are naturally good, and make them accomplices in their cruelty and sensual pleasure, so too the perverse and lustful strive to season their crimes with a bodily kiss, even with this good that natural law established to signify the things we just mentioned, sullying the kiss itself with such lust that to be kissed that way is to be defiled. Any respectable person understands how much this sort of kiss should be detested, abominated, shunned, and resisted.

26. Porro osculum spiritale proprie amicorum est, qui sub una amicitiae lege tenentur. Non enim fit oris attactu, sed mentis affectu, non coniunctione labiorum, sed commixtione spirituum, castificante omnia Dei spiritu, et ex sui participatione caelestem immitente saporem. Hoc osculum non inconvenienter osculum dixerim Christi, quod ipse tamen porrigit non ex ore proprio sed alieno, illum sacratissimum amantibus inspirans affectum, ut videatur illis quasi unam animam in diversis esse corporibus, dicantque cum propheta, *"Ecce quam bonum et quam iucundum habitare fratres in unum."* 27. Huic ergo osculo assuefacta mens et a Christo totam hanc dulcedinem adesse non ambigens, quasi secum reputans et dicens, "O si ipsemet accessisset!" ad illud intellectuale suspirat et cum maximo desiderio clamans, *"Osculetur me,"* dicit, *"osculo oris sui,"* ut iam terrenis affectibus mitigatis et omnibus quae de mundo sunt cogitationibus desideriisque sopitis, in solius Christi delectetur osculo et quiescat amplexu, exultans et dicens, *"Laeva eius sub capite meo, et dextera illius amplexabitur me."*

28. *Gratianus:* Amicitia haec, ut video, non est popularis, nec qualem eam somniare consuevimus. Nescio quid hic Galterus hactenus senserit, ego aliud nihil amicitiam esse credidi quam inter duos tantam voluntatum identitatem, ut nihil velit unus quod alter nolit, sed tanta sit inter utrosque in bonis malisque consensio, ut non spiritus, non census, non honor, nec quidquam quod alterius sit, alteri denegetur, ad fruendum pro voto et abutendum.

26. Next, the spiritual kiss is characteristic of friends who are bound by one and the same law of friendship. It is made not with a touch of the mouth but a feeling of the mind, not by joining the lips but mingling spirits, while the spirit of God makes all things pure and imparts heavenly flavor by sharing in it. I would fittingly call this the kiss of Christ that he offers, however, not with his own mouth but another's, inspiring the most sacred affection in those who love, so that it seems to them that there is, so to speak, one soul in different bodies, and they say with the prophet, "*See how good and pleasant it is for brothers to live in unity.*" 27. Therefore the soul grows accustomed to this kiss, having no doubt that all its sweetness comes from Christ, as if reflecting on itself and saying to itself, "Oh, if only he himself had come!" The soul then sighs for the kiss of understanding, crying out with the greatest desire, "*Let him kiss me with the kiss of his mouth,*" so that, once earthly attachments are assuaged and all worldly thoughts and affections stilled, the soul may delight in the kiss of Christ alone and rest in his embrace as it exults and says, "*His left hand is under my head and his right hand will embrace me.*"

28. *Gratian:* As I see it, this is no ordinary friendship, nor the sort we are accustomed to dream about. I don't know what Walter here may have gathered so far. I believed friendship was nothing other than such great sameness of wills between two people that the one wants nothing that the other does not, and the agreement between them in good things and evil is so great that neither life, nor wealth, nor honor, nor any possession of the one would be denied the other for him to enjoy or abuse as he pleases.

29. *Galterus:* Longe aliud in priori dialogo memini me didicisse, ubi ipsa definitio amicitiae posita et exposita, merito ad eius fructum altius inspiciendum me vehementius animavit. De qua sufficienter instructi, certam nobis metam, quatenus debeat amicitia progredi, cum diversorum diversa sententia sit, petimus praefigi. Sunt namque quidam qui contra fidem, contra honestatem, contra commune bonum vel privatum favendum putant amico. Quidam solam fidem detrahendam iudicant, caetera non cavenda. 30. Alii pro amico contemnendam pecuniam, exspuendos honores, maiorum inimicitias subeundas, exilium etiam censent non fugiendum, seipsum, in quibus non obsit patriae, nec contra fas alium laedat, etiam in inhonestis et turpibus exponendum. Sunt et qui hanc metam in amicitia constituunt, ut unusquisque, sicut erga seipsum, sic et afficiatur erga amicum. 31. Quidam amico in omni beneficio vel obsequio vicem rependere, satis dare amicitiae credunt.

Mihi sane nulli horum esse cedendum, hac nostra collatione satis persuasum est. Unde aliquam certam mihi in amicitia metam a te opto constitui, maxime propter hunc Gratianum, ne forte secundum nomen suum ita velit esse gratiosus, ut incaute fiat vitiosus.

32. *Gratianus:* Haud ingrate hanc tuam pro me accipio sollicitudinem, nisi tamen sitis audiendi praepediret, forte iam nunc tibi redderem talionem. Sed quid potius ad tuas inquisitiones respondere velit, pariter audiamus.

33. *Aelredus:* Certam in amicitia metam Christus ipse praefixit, *"Maiorem hac,"* inquiens, *"dilectionem nemo habet,*

29. *Walter:* I remember learning something quite different in the first dialogue, where the very definition of friendship as proposed and explained inspired me to consider its rewards in greater depth. Now sufficiently informed on that subject, we ask that a definite limit be set for us as to how far friendship should go, since different people have different opinions. For instance, there are some who think that a friend should be favored over loyalty, honesty, and both public and private good. Others judge that loyalty should be excluded from that list, but not the rest. 30. Still others are of the opinion that for a friend, money should be scorned, worldly honors rejected, the ill will of elders endured, even that exile should not be avoided, and that a friend should expose himself to dishonor and disgrace as long as he does no harm to the fatherland nor injures another unrightfully. And there are those who fix the limit of friendship at this: everyone should behave toward a friend as toward himself. 31. Some believe that to pay back every service or allegiance in turn is to satisfy the demands of friendship.

I am sufficiently persuaded by our discussion that none of these opinions is in fact acceptable. So I wish that you would establish a fixed limit for me, and especially for the benefit of Gratian here, so he should not, in accordance with his name, so want to be gracious that he carelessly becomes wicked.

32. *Gratian:* I gratefully accept your concern on my behalf. If thirst for listening did not get in the way, I'd reply in kind right now. Instead, let's listen together to what he wishes to say in response to your questions.

33. *Aelred:* Christ himself set a fixed limit for friendship, saying, "*No man has greater love than this: to lay down his life for*

quam ut animam suam ponat quis pro amicis suis." Ecce quousque tendi debet amor inter amicos, ut scilicet velint pro invicem mori. Satis ne vobis istud?

34. *Gratianus:* Cum maior esse non possit amicitia, cur non satis sit?

35. *Galterus:* Quid si pessimi quique vel ethnici in consensu facinorum et flagitiorum sic se diligant, ut velint pro invicem mori? Eosne ad summam amicitiae conscendisse fatebimur?

36. *Aelredus:* Absit, cum inter pessimos amicitia esse non possit.

37. *Gratianus:* Describe nobis, quaeso, inter quos vel oriri potest vel servari.

38. *Aelredus:* Breviter dico. Inter bonos oriri potest, inter meliores proficere, consummari autem inter perfectos. Quamdiu enim quemquam ex studio malum delectat, quamdiu honestis inhonesta praeponit, quamdiu voluptas ei gratior est puritate, temeritas moderatione, adulatio correptione, quomodo ad amicitiam vel aspirare eum fas est, cum ortus eius ex virtutis opinione procedat? Difficile igitur, immo impossibile tibi est, vel initia eius degustare, si fontem de quo oriri potest nescieris. 39. Foedus est enim amor, nec amicitiae nomine dignus, quo turpe aliquid exigitur ab amico, quod necesse est eum facere qui, necdum vitiis aut sopitis aut depressis, ad quaelibet illicita vel illicitur vel impellitur. Unde illorum detestanda sententia est, qui contra fidem et honestatem pro amico aestimant faciendum.

his friends." That is how far love among friends should go: they should be willing to die for each other. Is that good enough for you?

34. *Gratian:* Since no friendship can be greater, why shouldn't that be good enough?

35. *Walter:* What if wicked people or pagans, as they plot evil and sin, so love one another that they would die for each other? Will we say that they have climbed to the summit of friendship?

36. *Aelred:* Absolutely not, since there can be no friendship among the wicked.

37. *Gratian:* Then tell us, please, among whom friendship can arise and be preserved.

38. *Aelred:* To put it briefly, friendship can arise among the good, advance among the better, and be completed among the perfect. As long as someone is determined to revel in evil, as long as he prefers the dishonorable to the honorable, as long as sensual pleasure is more pleasing to him than purity, rashness than moderation, and flattery than correction, how can he rightly aspire to friendship when its origins proceed from esteem for virtue? Therefore it is difficult, in fact impossible, for you to sample even its beginnings if you don't know the source from which it springs. 39. Love is vile and unworthy of the name of friendship if on its account something disgraceful is demanded of a friend. That is inevitable for someone who, his vices not yet suppressed and stilled, is tricked or forced into forbidden behavior. Hence we must deplore the opinion of those who hold that something contrary to loyalty and honesty should be done for a friend.

40. Nulla enim excusatio peccati est, si amici causa peccaveris. Protoplastus Adam salubrius praesumptionis arguisset uxorem quam, gerendo ei morem, vetitum usurpasset. Multo etiam melius servi regis Saul fidem domino servaverunt, contra eius imperium manum sanguinum subtrahentes, quam Doech Idumaeus, qui regiae crudelitatis minister, Domini sacerdotes sacrilegis manibus interfecit. Ionadab quoque amicus Amon, laudabilius amici prohibuisset incestum, quam quo potiretur optato consilium praebuisset. 41. Sed nec amicos Absalon amicitiae virtus excusat, qui perduellioni praebentes assensum, contra patriam arma tulerunt. Et ut ad haec nostra tempora veniamus, multo certe felicius, Otto Romanae cardinalis ecclesiae, ab amicissimo suo recessit Guidone, quam Iohannes suo adhaesit in tali schismate Octoviano! Cernitis igitur, nisi inter bonos amicitiam stare non posse.

42. *Galterus:* Quid igitur nobis cum amicitia, qui boni non sumus?

43. [*Aelredus:*] Ego "bonum" non ita ad vivum reseco, ut quidam qui neminem volunt esse bonum, nisi eum cui ad perfectionem nihil desit. Nos hominem bonum dicimus, qui secundum modum nostrae mortalitatis, *sobrie et iuste et pie* vivens *in hoc saeculo,* nihil a quolibet inhonestum petere, nec rogatus velit praestare. Inter tales profecto amicitiam oriri, a talibus conservari, in talibus perfici posse non ambigimus. 44. Nam qui vel fidem, vel patriae periculum, vel alterius contra ius et fas laesionem excipientes, semetipsos amicorum exponunt libidini, eos non tam stultos dixerim quam

40. Sinning for the sake of a friend is no excuse for sin. The first man, Adam, would have done better had he denounced his wife's presumption rather than, in humoring her, enjoying what was forbidden. King Saul's servants, refusing to bloody their hands at his command, kept faith with their master much better than Doeg the Edomite, who as a servant of royal cruelty killed the Lord's priests with sacrilegious hands. Jonadab's friend Ammon would have acted more laudably had he prevented his friend's incest rather than offering a plan for him to get what he wanted. 41. Nor does the virtue of friendship excuse Absalom's friends who consented to rebellion, making war on their fatherland. Coming to our own times, how much more fortunate it was that Otto, cardinal of the Roman Church, withdrew from his dearest friend Guido than that John held to his friend Octavian in such a schism! You see, then, that friendship can exist only among the good.

42. *Walter:* What has friendship to do with us, then, who are not good?

43. *Aelred:* I do not prune "good" quite so far down to the quick as do those who would have it that nobody is good except one in whom no element of perfection is lacking. We say a man is good who, given the limits of our mortal condition, lives *soberly, justly, and piously in this life,* does not wish to seek anything dishonorable from anyone, nor to supply anything dishonorable if asked. I am absolutely sure that friendship can arise among such people, be maintained by them, and be perfected in them. 44. Those who expose themselves to the desires of their friends—making exceptions for disloyalty, danger to the fatherland, or some other injury against justice and law—I would not call so much foolish as

insanos, qui parcentes aliis, sibimet non aestimant esse parcendum et aliorum providentes honestati, suam infeliciter produnt.

45. *Galterus:* Fere in illorum cado sententiam qui amicitiam dicunt esse cavendam, rem videlicet plenam sollicitudinis atque curarum, nec timoris vacuam, multis etiam obnoxiam doloribus. Nam cum unicuique satis superque sit sui curam gerere, incautum dicunt se sic aliis obligare, ut necesse sit eum multis implicari curis et affligi molestiis. 46. Nihil praeterea difficilius aestimant quam amicitiam usque ad diem vitae extremum permanere, turpeque nimis sit post initam amicitiam rem in contrarium verti. Unde tutius iudicant sic quemquam amare ut possit odire cum velit, sic amicitiae laxandas habenas, quas vel astringat cum velit vel remittat.

47. *Gratianus:* Frustra igitur tu in loquendo, nos in audiendo laboravimus, si tam facile ab amicitiae tenuerimus appetitu, cuius nobis fructum tam utilem, tam sanctum, tam acceptum Deo, perfectioni tam vicinum, tam multipliciter commendasti. Sit illi ista sententia, cui placet sic amare hodie ut cras oderit, sic amicus omnibus esse, ut nulli sit fidus, hodie laudans, cras vituperans, hodie blandiens, crastino mordens, hodie paratus ad oscula, cras ad opprobria promptus, cuius amor vili pretio comparatur, levissima recedit offensa.

48. *Galterus:* Felle putabam carere columbas! Verumtamen haec istorum sententia, quae sic displicet Gratiano, qualiter refelli possit, edicito.

insane; sparing others, they do not think that they themselves should be spared, and looking after the honor of others, they unhappily betray their own.

45. *Walter:* I almost come down on the side of those who
say friendship should be avoided as a matter full of care and
anxiety, not devoid of fear, and even liable to great anguish.
Since it is enough and more than enough for each man to
take care of himself, it is reckless, they say, for him to so ob-
ligate himself to others that he is necessarily caught up in
many cares and afflicted with much distress. 46. They think
nothing is more difficult than maintaining a friendship until
the last day of life and that it would be a great disgrace for
a friendship, once begun, to be turned into its opposite.
Therefore, they judge it safer to love someone in a way that
allows one to hate at will, and that the reins of friendship
should be relaxed enough that they can been tightened or
loosened at will.

47. *Gratian:* So we have been laboring in vain, you in
speaking, we in listening, if our longing for that friendship
whose reward you have recommended to us several times as
so useful, so holy, so acceptable to God, and so near to perfection may so easily be checked. Let that opinion stand for
him whom it pleases to love in just such a way today as he
may hate tomorrow, be such a friend to all that he is loyal to
none, praising today and vilifying tomorrow, flattering today
and biting tomorrow, prepared for a kiss today and ready for
an insult tomorrow, one whose love comes cheap and vanishes at the slightest offense.

48. *Walter:* And here I thought doves had no bile! But tell
us how this opinion of those that so displeases Gratian can
be refuted.

49. *Aelredus:* Pulchre de his Tullius: "*Solem,*" inquit, "*e mundo tollere videntur, qui amicitiam e vita tollunt, quia nihil a* Deo *melius habemus, nihil iucundius.*" Qualis sapientia amicitiam detestari, ut sollicitudinem caveas, curis careas, exuaris timore, quasi virtus ulla sine sollicitudine, vel acquiri possit vel servari? Itane in te, sine tua magna sollicitudine, aut prudentia contra errores, aut temperantia contra libidines, aut iustitia contra malitiam, aut fortitudo contra ignaviam pugnat? 50. Quis, rogo, hominum, maxime adolescentium, sine dolore maximo vel timore tueri pudicitiam vel lascivientem refrenare valet affectum? Stultus Paulus qui noluit sine aliorum cura et sollicitudine vivere, sed intuitu caritatis, quam virtutem maximam credidit, infirmabatur cum infirmis, urebatur cum scandalizatis? Sed et tristitia illi magna erat et continuus dolor cordi eius pro fratribus suis secundum carnem. 51. Deserenda igitur illi caritas erat, ne sub tot timoribus ac doloribus viveret, nunc quos genuerat, iterum parturiens, nunc fovens ut nutrix, nunc ut magister corripiens, nunc timens, ne sensus illorum a fide corrumperentur, nunc cum multo dolore multisque lacrimis ad paenitentiam provocans, nunc eos qui non egerunt paenitentiam lugens? Videtis quomodo virtutes auferre nituntur e mundo, qui comitem illarum sollicitudinem e medio tollere non formidant.

52. Stulte Chusi Arachites amicitiam quae erat ei cum David tanta fide servavit, ut sollicitudinem securitati praeferret malletque amici participari doloribus quam parricidae gaudiis honoribusque dissolvi? Ego eos non tam homines

49. *Aelred:* Cicero wrote beautifully about those who hold that view: "*Those who remove friendship from their lives seem to remove the sun from the world, because we have nothing from* God *that is better or more delightful.*" What kind of wisdom is it to hate friendship in order to be wary of anxiety, be carefree, divest yourself of fear, as if any virtue can be acquired or preserved without anxiety? Is it not the case that within yourself, prudence battles against error, self-control against lust, justice against spite, and courage against cowardice without any great anxiety on your part? 50. Who, I ask, especially among the young, can maintain chastity or rein in lustful feelings without the greatest grief or fear? Was it foolish of Paul to not want to live without concern and anxiety for others, but instead, with his regard for the loving-kindness he thought the greatest virtue, to be weak with the weak and be burned with the scandalized? But he had both great sadness and constant grief in his heart for his brothers, according to the flesh. 51. Should he have renounced loving-kindness, then, so as not to live in such fear and pain, at one moment in labor again for those to whom he had given birth, at another fostering them like a nurse, at another scolding them like a master, at another fearing that their understanding would be seduced away from faith and calling them to repentance with great pain and many tears, at another mourning those who did not repent? You see how those strive to take virtue out of the world who do not fear to take anxiety, the partner of virtue, from our midst.

52. Did Hushai the Archite act foolishly when he maintained his friendship with David so loyally that he chose anxiety over security and preferred to share his friend's sorrows rather than let himself go in a parricide's joys and honors? I would call those not men but beasts who say one

quam bestias dixerim, qui sic dicunt esse vivendum, ut nulli consolationi sint, nulli etiam oneri vel dolori, qui nihil delectationis ex alterius bono concipiant, nihil amaritudinis sua aliis perversitate inferant, amare nullum, amari a nullo curantes. 53. Absit enim ut eorum quemquam amare concesserim, qui amicitiam quaestum putant, tunc se solis labiis profitentes amicos, cum spes alicuius commodi temporalis arriserit vel cum amicum cuiuslibet turpitudinis ministrum facere temptaverit.

54. *Galterus:* Cum igitur certum sit multos amicitiae similitudine falli, expone, quaeso, cuiusmodi amicitias cavere, quas appetere, colere et conservare debeamus.

55. *Aelredus:* Cum dictum sit eam nisi inter bonos non posse subsistere, facile tibi est pervidere nullam amicitiam quae bonos dedeceat recipiendam.

56. *Gratianus:* Sed nos fortasse in hac discretione, quid deceat vel non deceat, caligamus.

57. *Aelredus:* Geram vobis morem, et quae nobis occurrerint fugiendae breviter annotabo. Est amicitia puerilis, quam vagus et lasciviens creat affectus, divaricans pedes suos omni transeunti, sine ratione, sine pondere, sine mensura, sine alicuius commodi vel incommodi consideratione. Haec ad tempus vehementius afficit, arctius stringit, blandius allicit. Sed affectus sine ratione motus bestialis est, ad quaeque illicita pronus, immo inter licita et illicita discernere non valens. Licet autem plerumque amicitiam affectus praeveniat, numquam tamen sequendus est, nisi eum et ratio ducat, et honestas temperet, et regat iustitia. 58. Igitur

should live in such a way that they are no comfort to anyone, nor even a burden or grief to anyone, who take no pleasure in another's good fortune and in their wrongheadedness express no bitterness to others, making sure to love nobody and be loved by nobody. 53. Far be it from me to concede that someone who thinks friendship is profit actually loves. Such people profess friendship only as lip service when the hope of some temporal gain smiles on them or when they try to make a friend an accomplice in some disgraceful act.

54. *Walter:* Since it is certain, then, that many are deceived by something resembling friendship, explain, please, what sort of friendships we should avoid and which kinds we should seek, cultivate, and maintain.

55. *Aelred:* Since we have said that friendship cannot exist except among the good, it is easy for you to discern that no friendship that disgraces good people should be entertained.

56. *Gratian:* But perhaps we are hazy about the distinction between what is honorable and what is dishonorable.

57. *Aelred:* I will humor you and point out briefly what friendships it occurs to us should be avoided. There is immature friendship, which aimless and licentious feelings create. It spreads its legs for all who pass by and it is irrational, frivolous, and unchecked, lacking any consideration for anyone's loss or gain. For a time this friendship has a very violent effect, a very tight grip, a very seductive attraction. But affection without reason is an animal impulse, prone to illicit behavior, in fact incapable of distinguishing between what is licit and what is illicit. Although feeling often precedes friendship, still it should not be followed unless reason guides it, honor tempers it, and justice rules it. 58. Since

haec amicitia quam diximus puerilem, eo quod in pueris magis regnat affectus, ut infida, et instabilis, et impuris mixta
semper amoribus, ab his quos spiritalis amicitiae dulcedo
delectat, omnimodis caveatur, quam non tam amicitiam,
quam amicitiae dicimus esse venenum, cum illius amoris
numquam modus possit servari legitimus, qui est ab animo
ad animum, sed honestam eius venam, ex carnis concupiscentia fumus quidam emergens, obnubilet et corrumpat,
et neglecto spiritu, ad carnis desideria trahat. 59. Eapropter
primordia amicitiae spiritalis primum intentionis habeant
puritatem, rationis magisterium, temperantiae frenum et
sic suavissimus accedens affectus, ita profecto sentietur dulcis, ut esse numquam desinat ordinatus.

Est et amicitia quam pessimorum similitudo morum
conciliat, de qua dicere supersedeo, cum nec amicitiae nomine digna, ut superius diximus, habeatur. 60. Est praeterea
amicitia quam consideratio alicuius utilitatis accendit, quam
multi ob hanc causam et appetendam et colendam et con-
servandam existimant. Quod si admittimus, quam multos
omni amore dignissimos excludemus; qui cum nihil habeant,
nihil possideant, profecto nihil commodi temporalis ab eis
vel adipisci poterit quis vel sperare.

61. Si vero inter commoda duxeris consilium in dubiis,
consolationem in adversis, et caetera huiusmodi, haec utique ab amico exspectanda sunt, sed sequi debent ista amicitiam, non praecedere. Necdum enim quid sit amicitia didicit, qui aliam vult eius esse mercedem quam ipsam. Quae
tunc plena merces erit colentibus eam, cum tota translata in

it is disloyal, unreliable, and always mingled with impure love, this friendship we have called immature (because feelings rule children more) should be avoided in every way by those who take delight in the sweetness of spiritual friendship. We call that not friendship so much as poison to friendship, since a proper measure of such love, which is between soul and soul, can never be maintained. Rather, a kind of smoke rising from carnal craving clouds and corrupts friendship's pure nature and, as the spirit is neglected, it attracts carnal desires. 59. Therefore, the origins of spiritual friendship should have first of all purity of intention, the instruction of reason, and the restraint of moderation and thus the sweetest initial feeling will surely be experienced with such delight to the extent that it never ceases to be well ordered.

There is also friendship procured by sharing the worst behavior, which I refrain from discussing, since it should not be considered worthy of the name of friendship, as we explained before. 60. Further, there is friendship sparked by consideration of some advantage, which many think should be sought, cultivated, and maintained for that very reason. If we enter into it, we will exclude so many who are most worthy of all love; since these have nothing and possess nothing, surely no one can either obtain nor even hope for any material benefit from them.

61. But if you consider among its benefits advice while in doubt, comfort in adversity, and other things along those lines, certainly these are to be expected of a friend, but they should follow friendship, not precede it. He who wants friendship to have a reward other than itself has still not learned what it is. Its reward will then be complete for those who cultivate it, when, completely transferred to God, it

Deum, in eius contemplatione sepelit quos univit. 62. Nam cum multas et magnas utilitates pariat amicitia fida bonorum, non illam tamen ab istis, sed ab illa istas procedere non ambigimus. Neque enim a beneficiis, quibus Berzellai Galaadites David parricidam filium fugientem et suscepit, et fovit, et numeravit amicum, inter tantos viros partam credimus amicitiam, sed ab ipsa potius tantam gratiam profecisse non dubitamus. Nam quod rex viri illius prius eguerit nemo qui cogitet. 63. Verum quod ipse vir magnarum opum nihil pro his mercedis a rege speraverit, hinc advertere perspicuum est, quod omnes delicias divitiasque civitatis pronius offerenti, nihil suscipere acquievit, suis volens esse contentus. Sic et foedus illud venerabile, quod inter David et Ionathan, non spes futurae utilitatis, sed virtutis contemplatio consecravit, multum utrisque novimus contulisse, cum istius industria vita sit alterius reservata, illius beneficio, huius non sit posteritas deleta. 64. Cum igitur in bonis semper praecedat amicitia, sequatur utilitas, profecto non tam utilitas parta per amicum, quam amici amor ipse delectat.

Utrum igitur de fructu amicitiae satis dixerimus, utrum etiam certas personas inter quas et oriri et servari possit et perfici lucide distinxerimus, utrum praeterea assentationes quae falso amicitiae nomine palliantur, manifeste prodiderimus, utrum quoque certas metas quousque tendi debeat amor inter amicos ostenderimus, vos iudicate.

buries those it has united in the contemplation of him. 62. Although loyal friendship among good people may produce many and considerable benefits, nevertheless we are in no doubt that friendship does not ensue upon favors, but that the favors stem from it. We do not believe that the friendship between such great men was born from the good offices with which Barzillai the Gileadite received David in flight from his parricide son, and supported him and counted him as a friend, but rather we have no doubt that such a great favor grew from the friendship itself. Nobody would think that the king needed Barzillai previously. 63. That the man of great wealth hoped for no reward from the king is clear from the following: Barzillai was satisfied to take nothing from him—although David was quite disposed to offer all the delights and wealth of his city—wanting to be content with what was his. Likewise, it was not hope of future reward but contemplation of virtue that consecrated the revered bond between David and Jonathan, and we know that it bestowed much upon each, since through Jonathan's diligence David's life was preserved and through David's kindness, Jonathan's posterity was not obliterated. 64. Since, therefore, among good people friendship always precedes and reward follows, truly what delights is not so much the reward gained through a friend as the friend's love itself.

Judge for yourselves, then, whether we have spoken enough about the rewards of friendship, whether we also clearly indicated the appropriate people among whom it may arise, be maintained, and be perfected, whether furthermore we have plainly revealed the flatteries clothed in the false name of friendship and finally whether we have shown the fixed limits that love between friends should reach.

65. *Galterus:* Hoc ultimum non satis recordor enodatum.

66. *Aelredus:* Recolitis, ut credo, eorum me refellisse sententiam, qui metas amicitiae in flagitiorum et facinorum consensu constituent, illorum quoque, qui usque ad exilium progrediendum putant, et sine alterius laesione, quamlibet turpitudinem. 67. Nihilominus et illorum, qui secundum speratae utilitatis modum, quantitatem amicitiae metiuntur. Nam duas earum, quas proposuit Galterus, nec mentione dignas existimavi. Quid enim ineptius esse potest quam amicitiam hactenus extendi ut in officiis vel obsequiis vicem quis rependat amico, cum omnia illis debeant esse communia, quibus nimirum esse debet et *cor unum et anima una?* Quam turpe et illud, ut non aliter afficiatur quis erga amicum, quam erga se ipsum, cum unusquisque de se humilia, sublimia sentire debeat de amico.

68. His igitur falsis amicitiae finibus explosis, finem amicitiae ex verbis Domini proferendum putavimus, qui mortem ipsam pro amicis sanxit non esse fugiendam. Verum ne forte, si quilibet turpes sic affecti vellent pro invicem mori, ad amicitiae summam crederentur evecti, diximus inter quas personas oriri possit et perfici amicitia. Deinde illos qui ob multas sollicitudines et curas quas generat cavendam eam existimant ineptiae credidimus arguendos, postremo quae amicitiae bonis omnibus sunt cavendae quam breviter potuimus enodavimus.

65. *Walter:* I don't recall the last point being sufficiently explained.

66. *Aelred:* You remember, I believe, that I refuted the opinion of those who extend the limits of friendship to include the plotting of evil and sin, and of those who think that they should go as far as exile or any vile act that does not involve harming another. 67. I likewise refuted the opinion of those who measure the extent of friendship according to the degree of advantage anticipated. Two of these friendships that Walter put forth I thought unworthy of mention. What could be more absurd than to extend friendship as far as the duty to repay a friend with services and favors, since friends should have all things in common and they should have both *one heart and one soul?* How disgraceful, too, it would be for a friend to regard a friend just as he does himself, since each one of them should have the lowest opinion of himself and the highest of his friend.

68. Thus, having vociferously rejected false aims of friendship, we thought that its true aim should be explained through the words of the Lord, who declared that for the sake of friends, death itself should not be avoided. We specified among which people friendship can arise and be perfected to ensure that if certain disgraceful people were of such a mind as to be willing to die for one another they should not be considered to have risen to the summit of friendship. Then, we shared our belief that those who think that friendship is to be avoided because of the many anxieties and cares it generates should be accused of absurdity. Finally, we explained as briefly as we could which friendships should be avoided by all good people.

69. Patet proinde ex his omnibus certa et vera spiritalis amicitiae meta, nihil videlicet negandum amico, nihil pro amico non sustinendum, quod minus sit quam ipsa pretiosa corporis vita, quam ponendam pro amico divina sanxit auctoritas. Quocirca cum vita animae corporis sit multo praestantior, hoc omnino negandum censemus amico, quod mortem inferat animae—quod nihil aliud est quam peccatum, quod Deum separat ab anima, animam a vita. Verum in his quae vel exhibenda sunt amico, vel pro amico toleranda, quis servandus sit modus, quae cautio adhibenda, non est temporis huius evolvere.

70. *Gratianus:* Non parum mihi Galterum nostrum fateor contulisse; cuius interrogatione provocatus, summam omnium quae disputata sunt brevi comprehendens epilogo, quasi prae oculis in ipsa memoria depinxisti. Age iam, precor, et in ipsis officiis amicorum quis servandus sit modus, quae cautio adhibenda, nobis expone.

71. *Aelredus:* Et haec et alia quaedam de amicitia restant dicenda. Sed hora iam praeteriit, et ad aliud nos negotium isti qui modo venerunt, sua, ut cernitis, importunitate compellunt.

72. *Galterus:* Invitus certe recedo, cras profecto cum se tempus obtulerit rediturus. Videat autem Gratianus ut praesto sit mane, ne ipse nos incuriae, aut nos eum tarditatis arguamus.

69. From all that, then, the fixed and true limit of spiritual friendship is clear: nothing of course should be denied a friend, nothing not endured for a friend that is any less than laying down one's body's precious life for a friend, as divine authority decreed. Therefore, since the soul's life is greatly superior to the body's, we think it entirely necessary to refuse that a friend bring death to his soul—which is nothing other than sin, since it separates God from the soul and the soul from life. But regarding what things should either be offered to a friend or endured for a friend, now is not the time to discuss what moderation should be observed, what caution applied.

70. *Gratian:* I admit that our Walter has done me a real service; prompted by his questioning, in a brief epilogue you have sketched as if before our eyes, in memory itself, a summary of everything that has been discussed. Come now, I beg you, and explain to us what moderation should be observed and what caution applied in the service of friends.

71. *Aelred:* Both these and other matters concerning friendship remain to be discussed. But it is already late, and as you see, those people who have just arrived force us, by their unwelcome insistence, to attend to other business.

72. *Walter:* I'm certainly unwilling to go, but I'll definitely return tomorrow when the opportunity presents itself. Let Gratian see to it that he's there in the morning so he does not accuse us of neglect, nor we accuse him of being late.

LIBER TERTIUS

DE SPIRITALI AMICITIA.

[*Aelredus:*] Unde et quo?

Gratianus: Non latet adventus mei causa.

Aelredus: Num adest Galterus?

Gratianus: Videat ipse. Certe tarditatis non potest arguere nos hodie.

Aelredus: Vis ea quae proposita sunt prosequamur?

Gratianus: Habeo ei fidem. Nam et praesentiam eius mihi reor necessariam, cui et sensus est acutior ad intellegendum, et lingua eruditior ad interrogandum, et memoria tenacior ad retinendum.

Aelredus: Audisti, Galtere? Amicitior tibi Gratianus quam putabas.

Galterus: Quomodo mihi amicus non esset, qui nullius non est? Sed quia utrique adsumus, promissi tui non immemores, otio huic non simus ingrati.

2. *Aelredus:* Fons et origo amicitiae amor est, nam amor sine amicitia esse potest, amicitia sine amore numquam. Amor autem aut ex natura, aut ex officio, aut ex ratione sola, aut ex solo affectu, aut ex utroque simul procedit. Ex natura, sicut mater diligit filium. Ex officio, quando ex ratione dati et accepti quodam speciali affectu coniungimur. Ex sola ratione, sicut inimicos, non ex spontanea mentis inclinatione, sed ex praecepti necessitate diligimus. Ex solo affectu, quando aliquis ob ea quae sola corporis sunt, verbi gratia pulchritudinem, fortitudinem, facundiam, sibi quorumdam inclinat affectum. 3. Ex ratione simul et affectu, quando is

THE THIRD BOOK
OF SPIRITUAL FRIENDSHIP.

Aelred: Where have you come from and why?

Gratian: The reason I've come is no secret from you.

Aelred: Walter is not here, is he?

Gratian: Let him see to that. Surely he can't accuse us of being late today.

Aelred: Do you want us to pursue the subjects proposed?

Gratian: I will rely on Walter, for I think his presence is necessary for me. His faculty for understanding is more acute, his tongue more trained for questioning, and his memory more persistent in retaining.

Aelred: Did you hear, Walter? Gratian is friendlier to you than you thought.

Walter: How could he not be my friend when he's everyone's? But since we are both here, and not forgetting your promise, let's be grateful for this moment of leisure.

2. *Aelred:* The source and origin of friendship is love, for there can be love without friendship, but never friendship without love. Love proceeds from nature, or duty, or reason alone, or affection alone, or from both of the latter together. From nature, just as a mother loves her child. From duty, when in accordance with reason given and received, we are joined by a special affection. From reason alone, as we love our enemies not from spontaneous mental inclination, but in accordance with the command imposed by precept. From affection alone, when someone because of merely corporeal attributes, for example, beauty, strength, or eloquence, bends the affection of certain people to himself. 3. From reason and affection together, when one whom reason urges

quem ob virtutis meritum ratio suadet amandum, morum suavitate, et vitae lautioris dulcedine, in alterius influit animum, et sic ratio iungitur affectui ut amor ex ratione castus sit, dulcis ex affectu. Quis horum vobis amicitiae videtur commodatior?

4. *Galterus:* Hic ultimus sane, quem et virtutis contemplatio format et morum suavitas ornat. Sed utrum omnes quos sic diligimus ad illud amicitiae admittendi sint dulce secretum, scire desidero.

5. *Aelredus:* Primo ponendum est solidum quoddam ipsius spiritalis amoris fundamentum, in quo eius sunt collocanda principia, ut sic recta quis linea ad eius altiora conscendens, ne fundamentum neglegat vel excedat, maximam cautelam adhibeat. Fundamentum illud Dei amor est, ad quem omnia quae vel amor suggerit vel affectus, omnia quae vel occulte aliquis spiritus, vel palam quilibet suadet amicus referenda sunt, diligenterque inspiciendum, ut quidquid astruitur fundamento conveniat, et quidquid illud excedere deprehenditur, ad eius formam revocandum, et secundum eius qualitatem omnimodis corrigendum non dubites. 6. Non omnes tamen quos diligimus in amicitiam sunt recipiendi, quia nec omnes ad hoc reperiuntur idonei. Nam cum amicus tui consors sit animi, cuius spiritui tuum coniungas et applices, et ita misceas ut unum fieri velis ex duobus, cui te tamquam tibi alteri committas, cui nihil occultes, a quo nihil timeas. Primum certe eligendus est qui ad haec aptus putetur, deinde probandus, et sic demum admittendus. Stabilis enim debet esse amicitia, et quamdam aeternitatis speciem

ought to be loved because of the merit of his virtue flows into another's spirit with the charm of his conduct and the sweetness of his nobler life, and reason is so united with emotion that love is chaste through reason and sweet through affection. Which of these seems to you most suited to friendship?

4. *Walter:* The last one, obviously, which contemplation of virtue forms and charm of conduct adorns. But I desire to know whether all we love in this manner should be admitted into the sweet mystery of friendship.

5. *Aelred:* First we must lay a solid foundation for spiritual love itself, on which its principles should be built, so that one straight line rising to the upper stories may exercise the greatest caution neither to ignore the foundation nor exceed it. That foundation is the love of God, to which everything that either love or affection suggests, everything either prompted secretly by some spirit or openly by a friend, must be referred. The matter calls for close inspection, so that whatever is built suits the foundation. You should not doubt that whatever is perceived as excessive should be trimmed to match the foundation's form and corrected in every respect, in line with the nature of the foundation. 6. Yet not all whom we love should be received into friendship, because not all are found suitable. Since your friend is the partner of your soul—to whose spirit you should join and attach your own and so merge that you create a wish to become one from two, to whom you should entrust yourself as to another self, and from whom you should hide nothing and fear nothing—the one considered suitable for all that is first to be chosen, then tested, and thus finally accepted. Friendship must be stable and, abiding always in affection,

praeferre, semper perseverans in affectu. 7. Et ideo non pue-
rili modo amicos mutare, vaga quadam debemus sententia.
Quoniam enim nemo detestabilior quam qui amicitiam laeserit nihilque magis animum torqueat quam vel deseri ab
amico vel impugnari, cum summo studio eligendus est et
cum maxima cautela probandus. Admissus autem sic tole-
randus, sic tractandus, sic sequendus ut quamdiu a praemisso fundamento irrevocabiliter non recesserit, ille ita
tuus, et tu illius sis, tam in corporalibus quam in spiritalibus,
ut nulla sit animorum, affectionum, voluntatum, senten-
tiarumque divisio. 8. Cernitis ergo quatuor gradus, quibus
ad amicitiae perfectionem conscenditur, quorum primus est
electio, secundus probatio, tertius admissio, quartus *"rerum
divinarum et humanarum cum* quadam *caritate et benevolentia*
summa *consensio."*

9. *Galterus:* Recordor te in prima illa disputatione quam
cum tuo habuisti Ivone, definitionem hanc satis probasse,
sed quia de multis amicitiarum generibus disputasti, utrum
omnes comprehendat, scire desidero.

10. *Aelredus:* Cum vera amicitia nisi inter bonos esse non
possit, qui nihil contra fidem vel bonos mores velle possint
aut facere, profecto non quamlibet, sed ipsam quae vera est
amicitiam definitio ista complectitur.

11. *Gratianus:* Quare non illa quae ante hesternam collationem me plurimum delectabat aeque probanda est, *idem*
scilicet *velle* et *idem nolle?*

12. *Aelredus:* Certe inter eos, quorum fuerint emendati
mores, vita composita, ordinati affectus, nec istam arbitror
repudiandam.

13. *Galterus:* Videat Gratianus ut tam in seipso quam in eo

offer a virtual glimpse of eternity. 7. And so we should not, like children, change friends on some sort of idle whim. Since there is nobody more despicable than one who harms friendship and nothing that torments the mind more than being abandoned or attacked by a friend, they must be chosen with the utmost care and tested with the greatest caution. Once accepted, a friend must be so tolerated, so treated, so supported that as long as he does not withdraw irrevocably from the established foundation, he should be yours and you his in matters both bodily and spiritual in such a way that there should never be any separation of spirit, affection, will, or opinion. 8. You see, then, the four stages of the ascent to the perfection of friendship: the first is choice, the second testing, the third admission, and the fourth "complete *agreement about matters human and divine along with* a certain *love and goodwill.*"

9. *Walter:* I remember that in that first discussion you had with your Ivo, you deemed this definition satisfactory. But because you discussed many kinds of friendship, I would like to know if the definition includes them all.

10. *Aelred:* Since true friendship can only exist among good people, who can never wish or do anything contrary to loyalty or good conduct, obviously that definition includes only true friendship, not just any kind whatsoever.

11. *Gratian:* Why shouldn't the definition that pleased me so much before yesterday's conversation be approved likewise, namely, that it is *to wish* and *not wish the same things?*

12. *Aelred:* I think that definition should not be rejected with regard to those whose conduct has been corrected, life well ordered, and emotions regulated.

13. *Walter:* Gratian should see to it that those traits are in

quem diligit, ista praecedant et sic idem velit et nolit cum ipso, nihil sibi volens concedi, nihil ipse praestare rogatus, quod iniustum, vel inhonestum, vel indecens sit. Sed de quatuor his quae praemisistis, quid sentiendum sit, a te exspectamus doceri.

14. *Aelredus:* Primum igitur de ipsa electione tractemus. Sunt vitia quaedam quibus si quilibet fuerit involutus, non diu amicitiae leges vel iura servabit. Huiusmodi ad amicitiam non facile eligendi sunt, sed si alias eorum vita moresque placuerint, agendum cum eis summopere est, ut sanati ad amicitiam habeantur idonei, videlicet iracundi, instabiles, suspiciosi, verbosi. 15. Difficile quippe est eum quem saepe iracundiae furor exagitat, non aliquando surgere in amicum, sicut in Ecclesiastico scribitur, "*Est amicus, qui odium, et rixam, et convicia denudabit.*" Unde ait scriptura, "*Noli esse amicus homini iracundo, neque ambules cum viro furioso, ne sumas scandalum animae tuae.*" Et Salomon, "*Ira,*" inquit, "*in sinu stulti requiescit.*" At cum stulto diu servare amicitiam quis non credat impossibile?

16. *Galterus:* Et nos te vidimus, si non fallimur, cum iracundissimo homine summa religione colere amicitiam, quem usque ad vitae eius finem numquam a te laesum, quamquam ipse te saepe laesisset, audivimus.

17. *Aelredus:* Sunt quidam ex naturali conspersione iracundi, qui tamen ita hanc comprimere et temperare soliti sunt passionem, ut in quinque quibus, teste scriptura, amicitia dissolvitur atque corrumpitur, numquam prosiliant, quamvis nonnumquam amicum inconsiderato sermone, vel

place in both himself and in the one he loves, and thus may wish and not wish the same things as the other does, desiring to be given nothing unjust, dishonorable, or unseemly, nor to offer it if asked. But we await learning from you what should be thought about the four matters you mentioned before.

14. *Aelred:* Then let us first discuss the choice of a friend. Someone caught up in certain vices will not maintain the laws or rights of friendship for long. Such individuals should not be casually chosen for friendship, but if their lives and conduct are otherwise pleasing, it is necessary to take the greatest pains with them so that once healed, they may be considered suitable for friendship. I refer to the irascible, the unreliable, the suspicious, and the verbose. 15. It indeed is difficult for one frequently roused by the fury of anger not to rise up at times against a friend, as it is written in Ecclesiasticus, *"There are friends who will bare their hatred, quarreling, and taunting."* Hence scripture says, *"Do not be the friend of an irascible man, nor walk with a furious man, or you will take scandal into your soul."* And Solomon says, *"Anger rests in the breast of a fool."* But who would find it hard to believe that it is impossible to maintain friendship for long with a fool?

16. *Walter:* Yet we've seen you, if we're not mistaken, cultivate a deeply devoted friendship with an extremely irascible man, whom we have heard you never hurt to the last day of his life, even though he had often hurt you.

17. *Aelred:* Some people are constitutionally irascible, yet so accustomed to control and moderate passion that they never leap into the five ways in which, according to scripture, friendship is dissolved and destroyed, although at times they offend a friend with thoughtless speech or action

actu, vel zelo minus discreto offendant. Tales si forte in amicitiam receperimus, patienter tolerandi sunt, et cum nobis constet de affectu certitudo, si quis fuerit vel sermonis vel actionis excessus, amico id indulgendum, vel certe sine aliquo dolore iucunde insuper in quo excesserit commonendum.

18. *Gratianus:* Ille tuus quem prae omnibus nobis, ut multis videtur, tibi probas amicum, aliquid quod tibi displicere nullatenus potuit ignorare, ante paucos dies, ut nos putabamus, ira praeventus et dixit, et fecit, cui tamen nihil prioris gratiae imminutum nec credimus, nec videmus. Unde non parum obstupuimus, quod cum tu, ut nos mutuo loquimur, nihil velis vel modicum praeterire, quod velit ipse, ipse modicum quid, tui causa, non potuerit sustinere.

19. *Galterus:* Audacior multo me est iste. Nam et ego ista novi, sed tuum erga eum animum non ignorans, nihil tibi de his loqui praesumpsi.

20. *Aelredus:* Homo certe ille mihi carissimus est, et semel a me receptus in amicitiam, a me numquam poterit non amari. Unde si forte in hac parte fortior illo fui et ubi utriusque voluntas non concurrebat in unum, meam mihi facilius fuit quam illi suam frangere voluntatem. Ubi nulla interveniebat inhonestas, nec fides laedebatur, nec minuebatur virtus, cedendum amico fuit, ut et tolerarem in quo videbatur excessisse, et ubi pax eius periclitabatur, voluntatem eius meae praeferrem.

21. *Galterus:* Sed cum prior ille iam in fata concesserit, alter tibi—licet nos non viderimus—satisfecerit, illa nobis

or ill-advised zeal. If we happen to receive such people as friends, they must be tolerated patiently. Since we may be certain of his affection toward us, we must indulge a friend's excess in word or deed or at least the rebuke for excess must surely be without any resentment and even pleasant.

18. *Gratian:* A few days ago, one whom you esteem, as many see it, more highly as a friend than you do the rest of us, when overcome by anger said and did something, as we understood it, that he could not possibly have been unaware was displeasing to you, yet we neither believe nor see any lessening of your former favor toward him. So as we speak together, we are not a little astounded that although you are unwilling to neglect anything he wishes, however insignificant, in the very way he wishes it, he can't put up with something insignificant for your sake.

19. *Walter:* Gratian has far more nerve than I do. I too am aware of these facts, but knowing your disposition toward him, I didn't presume to speak to you about them.

20. *Aelred:* That man is certainly very dear to me, and once I received him into friendship, I could never not love him. Hence it may be the case that I was stronger on this occasion than he was and where our wills did not coincide, it was easier for me to subdue my will than it was for him to subdue his. Where no dishonor was involved, nor loyalty harmed, nor virtue diminished, I had to yield to a friend so that I could both tolerate the way in which he seemed to have gone too far, and, where his peace of mind was in danger, put his will before mine.

21. *Walter:* Since the first friend of yours we mentioned has died and the other one has made satisfaction to you—although we didn't see it—I'd like you to explain to us in detail

quinque, quibus amicitia sic laeditur ut dissolvatur, velim nobis enuclees, ut eos, qui nullo modo eligendi sunt in amicos, cavere possimus.

22. *Aelredus:* Audite non me, sed scripturam loquentem, *"Qui conviciatur amico, dissolvit amicitiam. Ad amicum,"* inquit, *"etiamsi produxerit gladium non desperes: est enim regressus ad amicum. Si aperuerit os triste, non timeas."* Vide quid dicat. Si forte ira praeventus amicus eduxerit gladium, vel si verbum protulerit triste, si quasi non amans ad tempus tibi sese subtraxerit, si tuo suum aliquando praetulerit consilium, si a te in aliqua sententia vel disputatione dissenserit, non his amicitiam aestimes dissolvendam. 23. *"Est enim,"* ait, *"regressus ad amicum, excepto convicio, et improperio et superbia, et mysterii revelatione, et plaga dolosa. In his omnibus effugiet amicus."* Diligentius proinde haec quinque consideremus, ne nos eis amicitiae vinculis constringamus quos ad haec vitia vel iracundiae furor vel alia quaelibet passio compellere consuevit.

Convicium quippe laedit famam, caritatem extinguit. Tanta est enim hominum malitia utquidquid ira instigante ab amico iaculatum fuerit in amicum quasi a secretorum suorum prolatum conscio, si non credatur, verum tamen esse clametur. 24. Multi enim sicut in propriis laudibus, ita in aliorum vituperationibus delectantur. Quid vero scelestius improperio, quod etiam falsa obiectione innocentis faciem miserando rubore perfundit? At superbia quid minus ferendum, quae solum id quo tactae amicitiae subveniendum foret, humilitatis et confessionis excludit remedium, reddens hominem audacem ad iniuriam, tumidum ad correctionem?

those five things that can so harm friendship that it is dissolved, so that we may be able to be wary of those who should absolutely not be chosen as friends.

22. *Aelred:* Listen not to me but to scripture, where it says, "*He who abuses a friend dissolves friendship. You should not,*" it says, "*despair of a friend even if he has drawn a sword. There can be return to a friend. If he has opened his mouth in harshness, fear not.*" See what it says. If a friend overcome by anger happens to draw a sword, if he has spoken harshly, if he has withdrawn himself temporarily from you as if he does not love you, if he has ever preferred his counsel to yours, if he has disagreed with you in some opinion or discussion, you should not think the friendship must be dissolved on that account. 23. Scripture says, "*There can be return to a friend except in cases of verbal abuse, shaming, pride, the betrayal of secrets, or a treacherous blow. In all those cases, the friend will flee.*" Let us consider this list of five very carefully, then, so we do not bind ourselves tightly in bonds of friendship with those who have become accustomed to be incited to these vices by the fury of anger or some other passion.

Abuse indeed harms reputation and extinguishes love. So great is the malice of men that any charge hurled by a friend in a fit of anger, even if not believed, is yet proclaimed true as if revealed by one with knowledge of his secrets. 24. Many delight in the censure of others just as they do in praise of themselves. But what is more wicked than shaming, which even when the charge is false paints the face of the innocent party with a pitiful blush? And what is more unbearable than pride, which bars the remedy of humility and confession, the only thing that might have healed a stricken friendship, and which makes men daring in wrongdoing and too proud to tolerate criticism?

Sequitur mysteriorum, id est secretorum revelatio, qua nihil est turpius, nihil execrabilius, nihil amoris, nihil gratiae, nihil suavitatis relinquens inter amicos, sed omnia replens amaritudine, et indignationis, et odii atque doloris, felle cuncta conspergens. 25. Hinc scriptum est, "*Qui denudat arcana amici, perdet fidem,*" et paulo post, "*Denudare amici mysteria, desperatio est animae infelicis.*" Quid enim infelicius illo, qui fidem perdit et desperatione languescit? Ultimum illud quo dissolvitur amicitia plaga dolosa est, quae non est aliud quam occulta detractio. Plaga certe dolosa, plaga serpentis et aspidis mortifera. "*Si mordeat serpens in silentio,*" ait Salomon, "*nihil eo minus habet, qui occulte detrahit.*"

26. Quemcumque igitur in his vitiis assiduum inveneris, cavendus tibi est ille, nec donec sanetur, ad amicitiam eligendus. Abiuremus convicia, quorum ultor Deus est. Semei fugientem a facie Absalon sanctum David conviciis impetens, inter haereditaria verba, quae pater filio moriens delegavit, auctoritate Spiritus Sancti decernitur occidendus. Improperium nihilominus caveamus. Infelix Nabal Carmelus, David servitutem et fugam improperans, a Domino percuti meruit et occidi.

Quod si forte contigerit in aliquo nos legem amicitiae praeterire, vitemus superbiam, et amici gratiam humilitatis beneficio repetamus. 27. Rex David amicitiam quam Naas regi filiorum Amon exhibuerat, cum filio eius Hanon misericorditer obtulisset, ille superbus et ingratus amico contumeliam adiecit contemptui. Ob quam causam, tam ipsum

Next comes the betrayal of confidences, that is, secrets, than which nothing is more disgraceful, nothing more despicable, leaving nothing of love, favor, or sweetness between friends, filling everything with bitterness and sprinkling everything with the poison of indignation, hatred, and pain. 25. Hence it is written, "*He who betrays a friend's secrets will lose his loyalty*" and a bit later, "*To betray a friend's confidences is the despair of an unhappy soul.*" What is more unhappy than someone who loses faith and languishes in despair? The last thing that dissolves friendship is a treacherous blow, which is nothing other than hidden disparagement. It is indeed a treacherous blow, the deathly blow of a serpent or asp. As Solomon says, "*If a serpent bites in silence, one who disparages in secret is no better.*"

26. Therefore, you must beware anyone you find unremitting in these vices and he should not be chosen for friendship until he is healed. Let us renounce abuse, because God is its avenger. Shimei assaulted holy David, as he fled from the face of Absalom, with abuse. Among the words that the dying David offered as a legacy to his son, it was decreed by the authority of the Holy Spirit that Shimei should be killed. We should beware shaming no less. The wretched Nabal of Carmel, shaming David's servitude and flight, was rightfully struck and killed by the Lord.

If it happens that we neglect the law of friendship in some way, we should avoid pride and seek to regain our friend's favor through the blessing of humility. 27. When David mercifully offered to Hanun the friendship that he had shown to his father Nahash, king of the Ammonites, Hanun, proud and ungrateful to his friend, added insult to contempt. For that reason, sword and fire together

quam populum eius et urbes, gladius simul et ignis absump-
sit. Super omnia autem amicorum revelare secreta sacrile-
gium arbitremur, quo fides amittitur, et animae captivatae
desperatio importatur. Hinc est quod impiissimus Achi-
tophel parricidae consentiens, cum ei patris consilium prodidisset, cernens suum quod contra illud dederat, non man-
cipatum effectui, dignum proditori finem, laqueo suspensus
promeruit. 28. Postremo detrahere amico venenum amicitiae reputemus, quod Mariae frontem lepra perfudit, et
eiectam extra castra, sex diebus populi communione pri-
vavit.

Nec solum nimium iracundi sed etiam instabiles et suspiciosi in hac electione cavendi sunt. Cum enim magnus amicitiae fructus sit securitas qua te credis et committis amico,
quomodo in eius amore aliqua potest esse securitas, qui
omni circumfertur vento, omni acquiescit consilio? Cuius
affectus molli luto comparatus, diversas et contrarias tota
die, pro arbitrio imprimentis, suscipit et format imagines.
29. Quid praeterea magis competit amicitiae quam pax
quaedam ad invicem et tranquillitas cordis, cuius semper
expers est suspiciosus? Numquam enim requiescit. Suspi-
ciosum quippe semper curiositas comitatur, quae continuos
ei stimulos acuens, inquietudinis et perturbationis ei materias subministrat. Si enim viderit amicum secretius loquentem cum aliquo, proditionem putabit. Si se benevolum praebuerit alteri vel iucundum, ille se minus diligi proclamabit.
Si eum corripuerit, odium interpretabitur. Si laudandum
crediderit, irrisum se calumniabitur. 30. Sed nec verbosum
arbitror eligendum, quia vir linguosus non iustificabitur.

consumed both Hanun and his people and cities. Above all, let us consider it sacrilege to betray a friend's secrets, an act that destroys loyalty and brings despair to the soul that is taken prisoner. Hence the most impious Ahithophel, conspiring with a parricide since he had betrayed to him his father's plans, realized that the counterplot he had devised was not being put into effect and earned the death worthy of a traitor, hung by a noose. 28. Finally, let us consider disparaging a friend as poison to friendship, the act that caused leprosy to cover Miriam's face and deprived her, exiled from the camp, of contact with her people for six days.

In the choice of a friend, we should beware not only of the overly irascible but also the unreliable and the suspicious. Since a great reward of friendship is the security with which you entrust and commit yourself to a friend, how can there be any security in the love of one who is tossed by every wind and assents to all advice? The affection of such a person is like soft clay, taking and forming varied and contrary shapes all day long according to the will of the potter. 29. Furthermore, what corresponds better to friendship than a kind of mutual peace and calmness of heart that the suspicious person always lacks? He is never at rest. For restless anxiety, in fact, is always the companion of the suspicious: it pricks him with endless stinging, supplying him with fodder for restlessness and uneasiness. If he sees his friend speaking privately with anyone, he will think it betrayal. If his friend offers a kindness or favor to another, he will cry out that he is loved less. If his friend corrects him, he will interpret it as hatred. If he believes himself praiseworthy, he will falsely claim that he is being mocked. 30. Nor do I think a verbose man should be chosen, for a talkative

"Vides," inquit sapiens, "hominem promptulum ad loquendum? Magis illo spem habet stultus." Is igitur tibi eligendus est in amicum, quem non iracundiae furor inquietet, non instabilitas dividat, non conterat suspicio, non verbositas a debita gravitate dissolvat. Praecipue utile est, ut eum eligas qui tuis conveniat moribus, tuae consonet qualitati. "*Inter dispares quippe mores,*" ut beatus ait Ambrosius, "*amicitia esse non potest, et ideo convenire debet sibi utriusque gratia.*"

31. *Galterus:* Ubi ergo talis invenietur, qui nec iracundus sit, nec instabilis, nec suspiciosus? Nam verbosus quisquis est profecto latere non potest.

32. [*Aelredus:*] Licet non facile queat reperiri qui non his passionibus saepius moveatur, multi certe sunt qui his omnibus superiores inveniuntur, qui iracundiam patientia comprimant, levitatem servata gravitate cohibeant, suspiciones dilectionis contemplatione propellant. Quos maxime in amicitiam quasi exercitatiores assumendos dixerim, qui vitia virtute vincentes, tanto securius possidentur, quanto fortius, etiam temptantibus vitiis resistere consuerunt.

33. *Gratianus:* Ne quaeso, irascaris, si loquar. Ille tuus, de quo paulo ante fecimus mentionem, quem a te receptum in amicitiam non dubitamus, utrum tibi iracundus videatur, scire desidero.

34. *Aelredus:* Est quidem, at in amicitia minime.

35. *Gratianus:* Quid est, rogo te, in amicitia non esse iracundum?

man will not be justified. As a wise man says, "Do you see a man eager to talk? A fool has more hope than he does." Therefore, that man should be chosen as a friend whom the frenzy of anger does not disturb, nor fickleness tear apart, nor suspicion consume, nor verbosity set free from due seriousness. It is especially beneficial for you to choose one who is suited to your habits and in harmony with your character. Indeed, as Saint Ambrose says, "*There can be no friendship between people of different habits, and therefore the grace of each ought to match that of the other.*"

31. *Walter:* Not irascible, not erratic, not suspicious—where, then, will such a one be found? Obviously, whoever is a great talker can hardly escape notice.

32. *Aelred:* Although it is not easy to find one who is not frequently moved by these passions, certainly there are many who are found to be above them all. They suppress anger with patience, curb levity by remaining serious, ward off suspicion with the contemplation of love. I would say that those especially should be taken into friendship who are better trained for it, so to speak, who, conquering vices with virtue, the more strongly they are accustomed to resist even tempting vices, the more securely they may be kept in friendship.

33. *Gratian:* Please don't be angry if I speak up. I'd like to know whether that friend of yours we mentioned a little while ago, whom we have no doubt you have received into friendship, seems irascible to you.

34. *Aelred:* Oh, he is, but least of all in friendship.

35. *Gratian:* What does it mean, I ask, not to be irascible in friendship?

36. *Aelredus:* Inter nos contractam amicitiam non dubitatis?

Gratianus: Prorsus.

Aelredus: Quando inter nos iras, rixas, dissensiones, aemulationes, vel contentiones ortas audisti?

Gratianus: Numquam. Sed hoc non illius, sed tuae patientiae imputamus.

37. *Aelredus:* Fallimini. Nullo modo enim iram quam non refrenat affectus, cuiusquam patientia refrenabit, cum patientia iracundum magis excitet in furorem, in hoc aliquid sibi vel modicum solatium praestari cupiens, si in iurgiis se illi aliquis parem exhibeat. Ille sane de quo nunc nobis sermo est, ita mihi amicitiae iura conservat, ut commotum aliquando et iamiam prorumpentem in verba, solo nutu cohibeam, et ea quae displicent numquam producat in publicum, sed ad evaporandum suae mentis conceptum, semper expectet secretum. 38. Quod si non ei amicitia, sed natura praescriberet, nec ita virtuosum, nec ita laude dignum iudicarem. Si vero, ut assolet, ab eius aliquando voluntate meus sensus dissentiat, ita alterutro nobis deferimus, ut aliquando ille meam suae, plerumque ego suam meae praeferam voluntatem.

39. *Galterus:* Satis datum est Gratiano. Sed mihi velim enuclees, si forte quis incautius in eorum inciderit amicitias, quos cavendos paulo ante dixisti, vel si qui eorum quos eligendos dixisti, aut in ea ipsa vitia, aut in alia forte deteriora corruerint, qualis eis servanda sit fides, qualis exhibenda gratia.

36. *Aelred:* You do not doubt that friendship has been forged between us?

Gratian: Absolutely not.

Aelred: When have you heard that anger, quarreling, disagreements, rivalries, and disputes have arisen between us?

Gratian: Never. But we attribute that to your patience, not his.

37. *Aelred:* There you are mistaken. For in no way will someone's patience curb anger that affection does not curb, since patience incites an irascible person to fury even more; he desires in that situation to be offered some consolation, however small, if someone else proves his equal at hurling abuse. The man we are now talking about maintains the laws of friendship with me in such a way that when he is upset and already lashing out in words, I restrain him with a mere nod, and he never reveals in public what is bothering him, but always awaits a private conversation to vent about what is on his mind. 38. If nature rather than friendship prescribed him that course of action, I would not judge him so virtuous, nor so praiseworthy. But if, as tends to happen, my sense of things on some occasion differs from his, we defer to each other in such a way that at times he prefers my will to his, but I often prefer his to mine.

39. *Walter:* That's enough of an answer for Gratian. But I would like for you to explain to me what kind of loyalty should be maintained, what kind of favor shown, if someone carelessly happens to fall into friendship with those you said a little while ago are to be guarded against, or if any of those you said should be chosen fall into those very vices or perhaps even worse ones.

40. *Aelredus:* Haec, si fieri potest, in ipsa electione, vel etiam probatione cavenda sunt, ne videlicet nimis cito diligamus maxime indignos. *Digni autem sunt amicitia, quibus in ipsis causa est, cur diligantur.* Attamen in his, qui probati dignique putantur, *erumpunt saepe vitia, tum in ipsos amicos, tum in alienos, quorum tamen ad amicos redundat infamia.* Talibus amicis omnis diligentia adhibenda est, ut sanentur. 41. Quod si impossibile fuerit, non statim amicitiam rumpendam vel discindendam arbitror, sed ut quidam eleganter ait, "Potius paulatim dissuendam, *nisi forte quaedam intolerabilis iniuria exarserit, ut neque rectum, neque honestum sit, ut non statim alienatio* vel disiunctio fiat." Si enim aliquid molitur amicus, aut in patrem, aut in matrem, aut in patriam, quod subita et festinata egeat correctione, non amicitia laedetur si perduellis et inimicus prodatur.

42. Sunt alia vitia pro quibus amicitiam non rumpendam, ut diximus, sed paulatim dissolvendam iudicamus, ita tamen ut non usque ad inimicitias, ex quibus iurgia, maledicta, contumeliaeque gignuntur erumpant. Turpe enim nimis est cum eo huiusmodi bellum gerere, cum quo familiariter vixeris. 43. Nam etsi his omnibus ab eo quem in amicitiam receperas, impetaris, quibusdam quippe moris est ut cum ipsi sic vixerint ut non iam mereantur amari, si forte eis aliquid evenerit adversi, culpam retorqueant in amicum, laesam dicant amicitiam, et omne consilium quod amicus dederit suspectum habeant, et proditi cum eorum in palam culpa

40. *Aelred:* If possible, these situations should be guarded against both in choosing and even testing, obviously so that we do not love too quickly, especially those who are unworthy. *Those are worthy of friendship in whose very selves lies the reason they should be loved.* Yet even in those thought tested and worthy, *vices often erupt, at one time at the expense of friends themselves, at another that of strangers, yet their evil reputation overflows onto their friends.* Every care must be taken for such friends so they may be healed. 41. If that proves impossible, I think friendship should not immediately be broken off or torn asunder, but as someone eloquently put it, "Instead the friendship should be unstitched little by little, *unless an intolerable wrong flares up that makes it neither right nor honorable that desertion* or separation not happen *immediately.*" If a friend undertakes something against his father or his mother or his fatherland that calls for a sudden and accelerated correction, friendship itself will not be harmed if that friend is revealed as a public and private enemy.

42. There are other vices on whose account friendship should not be broken off, as we said, but, we think, dissolved little by little, yet in such a way to avoid an eruption into hostilities from which quarrels, curses, and abuse arise. It is exceedingly shameful to wage war of this sort on someone with whom you have lived on intimate terms. 43. And although you may be attacked in all these ways by the one you had received into friendship, for some it is a habit that when they have lived in such a fashion as to no longer deserve to be loved, should some misfortune befall them, they turn the blame back on a friend, say he has harmed friendship, and consider any advice the friend had given to be suspect. And when they are unmasked and their guilt comes to light in

processerit, non habentes ultra quid faciant, in amicum odia et maledicta congeminent, detrahentes in angulis, in tenebris susurrantes, se mendaciter excusantes, et alios similiter accusantes. 44. Si igitur his omnibus post dimissam amicitiam impetaris quamdiu tolerabilia fuerint, *ferenda sunt et hic honos veteri amicitiae tribuendus, ut in culpa sit qui faciat, non is qui patiatur iniuriam.* Amicitia quippe aeterna est, unde *omni tempore diligit qui amicus est.* Si te laeserit ille quem diligis tu tamen dilige. Si talis fuerit ut ei amicitia subtrahatur, numquam tamen subtrahatur dilectio. Consule quantum potes saluti eius, prospice famae, nec umquam amicitiae eius prodas secreta, quamvis tua ipse prodiderit.

45. *Galterus:* Quae sunt, rogo, illa vitia, pro quibus amicitiam paulatim dicis esse solvendam?

46. *Aelredus:* Quinque illa quae paulo ante descripsimus, maxime autem revelatio secretorum, et occulti morsus detractionum. His sextum addimus: si eos qui tibi aeque diligendi sunt laeserit, eisque quorum tua interest providere saluti, ruinae et scandali materiam etiam correptus praebere non desierit, maxime ubi vitiorum ipsorum te tangit infamia. Non enim amor praeponderare debet religioni, non fidei, non caritati civium, non plebis saluti. 47. Rex Assuerus superbissimum Aman, quem prae caeteris amicum habuerat suspendit in cruce, amicitiae quam ille fraudulentis consiliis laeserat, salutem multitudinis et caritatem praeponens uxoris. Iahel uxor Aber Cinei, licet pax fuerit inter Sisaram et

public, having nothing further to do, they double their hatred and curses against their friend, slandering him in corners, whispering in shadows, lying to excuse themselves and accuse others. 44. If, then, you are attacked in all these ways after a friendship has been abandoned, the abuses *should be endured* as long as they are tolerable, *and this honor paid to a former friendship, that the one who inflicts harm, not the one who suffers it, should take the blame.* Friendship is in fact eternal, hence *he who is a friend loves at all times.* If one you love has harmed you, love him nevertheless. If he becomes the sort from whom friendship is withdrawn, still love should still never be withdrawn. Consider his well-being as much as you can, look out for his reputation, and never betray the secrets of your friendship with him, even if he betrays yours.

45. *Walter:* What are those vices, I ask, for which you say a friendship should be dissolved little by little?

46. *Aelred:* There are the five we described a short while ago, especially the betrayal of secrets and hidden sting of slander. We add a sixth: if a friend harms those who should be equally loved by you, and even when corrected does not stop providing the material for destruction and scandal aimed at those whose well-being you should look out for, especially when the disgrace of those vices touches you. Love should not outweigh religious observance, nor loyalty, nor loving-kindness to fellow citizens, nor the welfare of the people. 47. King Ahasuerus hanged on a cross the supremely arrogant Haman, with whom he had had a friendship beyond all others, preferring the welfare of his people and the love of his wife to the friendship Haman had harmed with deceitful plotting. Jael, Heber the Kenite's wife, despite the peace between Sisera and the house of Heber, still putting

domum Aber, plebis tamen salutem huic amicitiae praeferens, ipsum Sisaram clavo sopivit et malleo. Sanctus propheta David, cum de iure amicitiae cognationi Ionathae
debuerat pepercisse, audiens tamen a Domino, propter Saul
et domum eius et sanguinem, quia occiderat Gabaonitas,
populum fame tribus annis iugiter laborasse, septem viros
de cognatione eius Gabaonitis tradidit puniendos.

48. Hoc autem nolo vos ignorare, inter perfectos quos sa-
pienter electos et caute probatos, vera et spiritalis amicitia
copulavit non posse intervenire discidium. Cum enim amicitia de duobus unum fecerit, sicut id quod unum est non
potest dividi, sic et amicitia a se non poterit separari. Patet
igitur hanc amicitiam quae patitur sectionem, ex ea parte
qua laeditur, numquam fuisse veram, quia *amicitia quae desi-*
nere potest, numquam vera fuit. 49. In hoc tamen amicitia pro-
babilior et magis virtus probatur, quod nec in eo qui laeditur
desinit esse quod fuit, diligens eum a quo non diligitur,
honorans eum a quo spernitur, benedicens eum a quo male-
dicitur, benefaciens ei qui sibi quod perniciosum est machi-
natur.

50. *Galterus:* Quomodo igitur amicitia solvitur, si excluso
talia sunt exhibenda ab eo a quo solvitur?

51. *Aelredus:* Ad amicitiam quatuor specialiter pertinere
videntur: dilectio et affectio, securitas et iucunditas. Ad
dilectionem spectat cum benevolentia beneficiorum exhibitio; ad affectionem interior quaedam procedens delectatio;
ad securitatem sine timore vel suspicione secretorum et consiliorum revelatio; ad iucunditatem de omnibus quae con-
tingunt, sive laeta sint sive tristia, de omnibus quae
cogitantur, sive nociva sint, sive utilia, de omnibus quae

the welfare of her people before friendship, put Sisera to rest with a hammer and nail. Although according to the law of friendship, the holy prophet David should have spared Jonathan's relatives when he heard from the Lord that his people had suffered famine three years in a row because of Saul and his house and the bloodshed of killing the Gibeonites, he handed over seven of Jonathan's relatives to the Gibeonites for punishment.

48. I do not want you to be unaware that between perfect friends wisely chosen and carefully tested, whom a true and spiritual friendship has united, no separation can occur. Since friendship makes one from two, just as what is one cannot be divided, so too friendship cannot be separated from itself. Therefore it is clear that a friendship that suffers division was never true friendship to the degree it is damaged, because *friendship that can end was never true friendship. 49.* Yet friendship is proven more commendable and all the more a virtue because it does not cease to be what it was in the one harmed, who loves one by whom he is not loved, honors one by whom he is scorned, blesses one by whom he is cursed, does good to one who plots evil against him.

50. *Walter:* Then by what means is friendship dissolved, if such generosity to his rejected friend must be shown by the one who did the dissolving?

51. *Aelred:* Four features seem especially characteristic of friendship: love and affection, security and delight. To love belongs the performance of services with goodwill; to affection a certain developing inner pleasure; to security the revelation of secrets and plans without fear or suspicion; to delight the sweet and friendly sharing of everything that happens, whether happy or sad, of everything thought,

docentur vel discuntur, quaedam dulcis et amica collatio.
52. Videsne, in quibus ab his qui merentur solvenda est amicitia? Subtrahitur certe illa interior delectatio quam ex amici
pectore iugiter hauriebat, perit securitas, qua sua illi arcana
revelabat, seponitur iucunditas, quam amica confabulatio
pariebat. Familiaritas proinde illa in qua talia continentur, ei
neganda est, non subtrahenda dilectio, et hoc cum quadam
moderatione et reverentia, ut si non nimius fuerit horror,
semper antiquae amicitiae quaedam videantur remansisse
vestigia.

53. *Gratianus:* Mihi certe perplacent ista quae dicis.

Aelredus: Iam de electione si sufficiunt ista quae diximus,
insinuate.

Galterus: Vellem ut eorum quae dicta sunt, summa sub
brevi nobis epilogo traderetur.

54. *Aelredus:* Geram vobis morem. Amorem amicitiae
diximus esse principium, nec qualemcumque, sed qui de ratione simul et affectu procedit. Qui quidem et castus est ex
ratione, et ex affectu dulcis. Deinde amicitiae ponendum
diximus fundamentum, Dei scilicet dilectionem, ad quam
omnia quae suggeruntur referenda sunt, et utrum ei conveniant, vel ab ea dissideant explorandum. 55. Quatuor sub-
inde gradus in amicitia, quibus ad eius summam pervenitur,
constituendos putavimus, cum amicus primum sit eligendus, deinde probandus, tunc demum admittendus, et sic
postea ut decet tractandus. Et de electione tractantes, ira-
cundos, instabiles, suspiciosos atque verbosos exclusimus—
non omnes tamen, sed eos dumtaxat qui has passiones nec

whether harmful or useful, and of everything taught or learned. 52. Do you see in which of these matters friendship with those who deserved it should be dissolved? Certainly the inner pleasure he used to drink continually from the breast of a friend is removed, the security with which one used to reveal secrets to a friend perishes, and delight produced by friendly conversations is set aside. Accordingly the intimacy in which such things consist must be denied the friend, though love should not be withdrawn and all this should be done with moderation and respect so that if the shock is not too great, some vestiges of the old friendship may always seem to have remained.

53. *Gratian:* What you say really pleases me.

Aelred: Now make it known if what we have said about the choice of a friend is sufficient.

Walter: I'd like us to be given a summary of what has been said as a brief epilogue.

54. *Aelred:* I will humor you. We said that love is the beginning of friendship, not just any kind of love, but one that proceeds from reason and affection together. Surely it is chaste through reason and sweet through affection. Next, we said that the foundation must be laid for friendship, namely the love of God, to which all things prompted should be referred, and we must discover if they conform to or diverge from it. 55. Then we settled that four steps in friendship should be constructed by which its summit is reached, since a friend should first be chosen, then tested, then finally accepted, and thereafter treated as a friend deserves. Considering choice, we excluded the irascible, the unreliable, the suspicious, and the verbose — not all of them, but only those who cannot or will not regulate or moderate

ordinare, nec moderari possunt aut nolunt. Nam multi his perturbationibus sic tanguntur, ut non solum eorum in nullo laedatur perfectio, sed etiam virtus in earum moderatione laudabilius augeatur. 56. Nam qui velut infrenes his passionibus acti semper feruntur in praeceps, in ea vitia inevitabiliter dilabuntur et corruunt, quibus amicitia, teste scriptura, et laeditur et dissolvitur: *convicia* scilicet *et improperium et secretorum revelatio, superbia, et plaga dolosa.*

57. Si tamen haec omnia patiaris ab illo quem semel in amicitiam suscepisti, non statim eam rumpendam dicimus, sed paulatim solvendam, talisque servetur antiquae amicitiae reverentia, ut licet ipsum a secretis tuis amoveas, numquam tamen ei dilectionem subtrahas, auxilium tollas, neges consilium. Quod si etiam ad blasphemias et maledicta eius prorumpat insania, tu tamen defer foederi, defer caritati, ut in culpa sit qui intulit, non ille qui pertulit iniuriam. 58. Porro si patri, si patriae, si civibus, si subditis, si amicis inventus fuerit perniciosus, statim familiaritatis rumpendum est vinculum, nec unius amor perditioni multitudinis praeferatur. Haec ne proveniant, in ipsa electione cavendum, ut videlicet is eligatur, quem non ad ista furor impellat, aut levitas trahat, aut verbositas praecipitet, aut abducat suspicio, maxime qui non nimium a tuis dissentiat moribus, nec a qualitate discordet. 59. Quia vero de vera amicitia loquimur quae non potest esse nisi inter bonos, de illis esse de

these passions. Many are affected by these disturbances but in such a way that not only is their pursuit of perfection in no way harmed, but also virtue is even more laudably increased by the moderation of faults. 56. For those who are continuously borne headlong, as though driven along unbridled by passions, inevitably slip and fall into those vices which, as scripture testifies, are the harm and dissolution of friendship, that is, *slander, shaming, the betrayal of secrets, pride, or a treacherous blow.*

57. Yet if you should suffer all this from one whom you once received into friendship, we say that the friendship should not be broken off at once, but dissolved little by little, and such respect for the former friendship should be maintained that although you exclude your friend from your confidences, you should never withdraw your love for him, refuse him help, or deny him advice. But even if his madness erupts in blasphemies and curses, you should nonetheless respect the bond, respect charity, so that the one who does harm should be to blame, not the one who suffers it. 58. On the other hand, if he is found to be dangerous to his father, his fatherland, his fellow citizens, his dependents, or his friends, the bond of intimacy must be broken immediately so that the love of one should not be preferred to the ruin of many. So that these things do not happen, you must be wary in the choosing itself, namely that the friend chosen is not driven by rage, carried away by frivolity, thrown headlong by verbosity, or led astray by suspicion and in particular, the one chosen should not differ too much from you in character, nor be out of harmony with your nature. 59. But because we are discussing true friendship, which cannot exist except among good people, we have made no mention of those

quibus, quod non sint eligendi, nulla potest esse cunctatio, ut turpes, avari, ambitiosi, criminosi, nullam fecimus mentionem. Si vobis de electione satis datum est, ad probationem deinceps transeamus.

Galterus: Opportunum hoc, nam mihi semper ad ostium oculus est, ne forte quis irrumpat, qui vel nostris deliciis finem ponat, vel quid amaritudinis misceat, vel aliquid superducat inane.

60. *Gratianus:* Cellararius adest, cui si concedatur ingressus, non erit tibi facultas ulterius procedendi. Sed ecce ego observo ianuam; tu, pater, perge quo coeperas.

61. *Aelredus:* Quatuor quaedam probanda sunt in amico: fides, intentio, discretio, patientia. Fides, ut ei te tuaque omnia secure committas. Intentio, ut nihil ex amicitia nisi Deum et naturale eius bonum expectet. Discretio, ut quid praestandum amico, quid ab amico petendum, in quibus contristandum pro amico, in quibus amico congratulandum, et quem amicum nonnumquam corripiendum credimus, pro quibus his id causis fieri debeat, modum etiam ipsum, tempus quoque et locum non ignoret. Patientia vero, ne correptus doleat, ne corripientem contemnat vel odiat, ut eum pro amico quaelibet adversa sustinere non pigeat.

62. Nihil in amicitia fide praestantius, quae ipsius et nutrix videtur et custos. Ipsa se in omnibus, in adversis et prosperis, in laetis et tristibus, in iucundis et amaris, praebet aequalem, eodem intuens oculo humilem et sublimem, pauperem et divitem, fortem et debilem, sanum et aegrum.

about whom there can be no doubt that they should not be chosen: the dishonorable, the greedy, the ambitious, and the slanderous. If you have had a satisfactory answer about choosing a friend, next let us go on to testing.

Walter: This is opportune, since I've always got my eye on the door in fear that someone may burst in and put an end to our pleasure, or mix in bitterness, or introduce foolishness.

60. *Gratian:* The cellarer is here, and if entry is granted him, there will be no opportunity for you to go any further. See, I'm guarding the door; father, go on from where you had started.

61. *Aelred:* Four qualities in a friend should be tested: loyalty, intention, discretion, and patience. Loyalty, so that you may securely entrust yourself and all that is yours to him. Intention, so that he expects nothing from the friendship but God and its natural good. Discretion, so that he should be aware of what should be offered to a friend, what should be asked of a friend, in what circumstances to grieve with a friend or rejoice with him and, since we believe a friend should sometimes be corrected, for what reasons this should be done, as well as the manner, time, and place for it. Certainly patience, so that he may not grieve when corrected, nor defy or hate the one who corrects him, and that it should not annoy him to endure any suffering for his friend.

62. Nothing is more excellent in friendship than loyalty, which seems to be its nurse and guardian. It offers itself as a companion in all situations, in adversity and prosperity, in joy and sadness, in delight and bitterness, gazing with the same eye on the humble and the lofty, the poor and the rich, the strong and the weak, the healthy and the sick. Indeed, a

Fidelis quippe amicus nihil in amico quod extra animum eius sit intuetur, virtutem in propria sua sede complectens, caetera omnia quasi extra eum posita, nec multum probans si adsint, nec si absint requirens. 63. Ipsa tamen fides in prosperis quidem latet, sed eminet in adversis. "In necessitate enim," ut ait quidam, "probatur amicus." Amici divitis multi. Sed utrum vere amici sint, interveniens paupertas explorat. "*Omni tempore,*" ait Salomon, "*diligit qui amicus est, et frater in angustiis comprobatur.*" Et alias, arguens infidelem, "*Dens putridus,*" inquit, "*et pes lassus, qui sperat super infideli in die angustiae.*"

64. *Gratianus:* Si prospera nostra nulla umquam adversitas interpolet, quomodo amici probabitur fides?

65. *Aelredus:* Multa sunt alia quibus fides probatur amici, quamuis in sinistris maxime. Nam ut superius diximus, nihil est quod amicitia magis laeditur quam consiliorum proditio. Evangelica vero sententia est: "Qui in modico fidelis est, et in multo fidelis erit." Amicis itaque quibus adhuc probationem credimus necessariam, non omnia, nec profunda nostra sunt committenda secreta, sed primo exteriora vel modica, de quibus non magnopere curandum est, an celentur, an nudentur. Cum tanta tamen cautione, ac si plurimum obessent prodita, prodessent autem celata. 66. In quibus si fidelis fuerit inventus, in maioribus experiendum non dubites. Quod si forte sinistrum aliquid de te fama vulgaverit, si cuiusquam malitia famam tuam fuerit persecuta, et ille nullius ad credendum adducatur suggestione, nulla moveatur suspicione, nulla dubitatione turbetur, de eius fide

loyal friend sees nothing in a friend as outside his own spirit, embracing virtue in its proper place, considering everything else as if set apart from his friend, neither much valuing these other things if they are present nor missing them if they are absent. 63. Loyalty itself is hidden in good times, but becomes conspicuous in bad ones. As someone says, "A friend is tested in necessity." A rich man has many friends. But the arrival of poverty tests whether they are truly friends. "*He who is a friend loves at all times, and a brother is tested in adversity*," says Solomon. And elsewhere, he censures disloyalty, saying, "*He who pins his hopes on the disloyal in a time of trouble is a rotten tooth and a weary foot.*"

64. *Gratian:* But if no adversity ever interrupts good times, how will a friend's loyalty be tested?

65. *Aelred:* Although it happens especially in hard times, there are many other ways a friend's loyalty is tested. As we said before, nothing harms friendship more than the betrayal of secrets. Indeed, the Gospel sentence is: "He who is loyal in a small matter will also be loyal in a great one." Thus in the case of friends whose testing we still believe necessary, not all secrets, and no deep ones, should be entrusted to them, but rather the superficial or small ones at first, about which it is not a matter of great concern whether they are concealed or revealed. However, this should be done with great caution, as if their revelation would be a great harm and their concealment a great favor. 66. If someone is found loyal in small matters, you should not hesitate to test with greater ones. If it happens that rumor spreads something harmful about you, if someone's malice threatens your reputation and your friend takes nobody's word for it, is moved by no suspicion, is troubled by no doubt, there is no

ulterius nulla tibi debet esse cunctatio, sed quasi de certa et stabili, non parva exultatio.

67. *Gratianus:* Recordor nunc tui illius amici transmarini de quo nobis fecisti saepius mentionem, quem ob hoc verissimum tibi ac fidelissimum probasti amicum, quod falsa de te referentibus, non solum non adhibuerit fidem, sed nec ulla sit haesitatione pulsatus, quod nec de tuo amicissimo, antiquo scilicet Claraevallis sacrista, praesumendum putasti. Sed quoniam de probatione fidei satis actum est, ad caetera enucleanda procede.

68. *Aelredus:* Diximus et intentionem esse probandam. Pernecessarium hoc. Sunt enim plerique qui in rebus humanis nihil bonum norunt, nisi quod temporaliter fructuosum sit. Hi sic amicos sicut boves suos diligunt, ex quibus aliquid commodi se sperant esse capturos, qui profecto germana et spiritali carent amicitia, propter se, et propter Deum et se expetenda, nec in se ipsis naturale amoris contuentur exemplar, ubi facile deprehenditur vis eius et qualis sit, et quanta sit. 69. Ipse Dominus ac salvator noster verae nobis amicitiae formam praescripsit, *"Diliges,"* inquiens, *"proximum tuum sicut te ipsum."* En speculum: diligis te ipsum. Ita plane, si Deum diligis, si nempe talis es, qualem in amicitiam eligendum descripsimus. Aliquam, rogo, a te ipso, huius tuae dilectionis mercedem iudicas exigendam? Minime profecto, sed quod per se sibi quisque carus est. Nisi igitur et tu hunc ipsum in alium transferas affectum, carus ille tibi aeque ut tu esse non poterit. 70. Tunc enim erit ipse quem diligis tamquam alter tu, si tuam tui in ipsum transfuderis caritatem. *"Non enim,"* ut ait sanctus Ambrosius, *"vectigalis amicitia est,*

need for further hesitation on your part about his loyalty, but rather great rejoicing that it is certain and steadfast.

67. *Gratian:* I now recall that friend of yours from overseas you have mentioned to us quite often, whom you proved a most loyal and true friend in that not only had he no faith in those who were telling lies about you, but was also not troubled or stricken by any doubt whatsoever—conduct you did not think you could take for granted in your dearest friend, the former sacristan of Clairvaux. But since enough has been said about testing loyalty, go on to explaining the other qualities.

68. *Aelred:* We said that intention should also be tested. This is absolutely necessary. There are many who recognize nothing good in human affairs unless it is materially advantageous. They love their friends just as they love their cattle, from which they hope to gain some profit. Indeed, they lack the true and spiritual friendship that ought to be sought on its own account and on God's, nor do they perceive in themselves a natural exemplar of love, where friendship's power, nature, and greatness are easily grasped. 69. Our Lord and Savior traced the form of true friendship for us, saying, "*You will love your neighbor as yourself.*" Here is a mirror: you love yourself. Yes, to be sure, if you love God, if you are no doubt the sort of person we have described as suitable to be chosen for friendship. Tell me, do you think some reward should be sought for loving yourself? Of course not, because everyone is dear to himself by nature. Thus unless you transfer that very affection to another, he will not be able to be as dear to you as you are yourself. 70. If you pour your love of yourself into him, then the one you love will be like another self. "*For,*" as Saint Ambrose says, "*friendship is not a tax, but*

sed plena decoris, plena gratiae. Virtus est enim, non quaestus, quia pecunia non parturitur, sed gratia, nec licitatione pretiorum, sed concertatione benevolentiae." Eius igitur quem eligisti, subtiliter est probanda intentio, ne secundum spem commodi cuiuslibet tibi velit in amicitia copulari, mercenariam eam aestimans, non gratuitam.

Certiores autem plerumque sunt amicitiae inopum quam divitum, cum spem lucri sic tollat paupertas, ut amicitiae non minuat, sed potius augeat caritatem. 71. Divitibus itaque assentatorie gratificatur, erga pauperem nemo simulator est. Verum est quidquid defertur pauperi, cuius amicitia invidia vacat. Haec diximus ut in amicis mores probemus, non aestimemus censum. Sic ergo probatur intentio. Si eum videris tuorum magis cupidum quam tui, aucupari semper aliquid quod tua sibi conferri possit industria, honorem, gloriam, divitias, libertatem, in quibus omnibus si dignior illo praeferatur, vel certe in tua non potestate sit quod appetitur, qua tibi intentione adhaeserit facile pervidebis.

72. Iam nunc de discretione videamus. Quidam perverse satis, ne dicam impudenter, talem amicum habere volunt, quales ipsi esse non possunt. Hi sunt, qui leves quoque amicorum transgressiones impatienter ferunt, austere corripiunt, et carentes discretione, magna neglegunt, contra minima quaeque se erigunt. Confundunt omnia, non locum servantes ubi, non tempus quando, non personas, quibus quaelibet vel publicare conveniat vel celare. Quocirca illius quem eligis est probanda discretio, ne si improvidum

full of beauty, full of grace. It is virtue, not profit, because what is
generated is not money but grace, and not by bidding at auction but
by a competition in goodwill." Therefore, the intention of the
one you have chosen must be subtly tested, so he should not
wish to join with you in friendship in the hopes of some material gain, valuing friendship according to profit rather than
spontaneously.

Furthermore, friendships among the poor are generally
more reliable than those among the rich, since poverty so
removes hope of material gain that it does not diminish the
love of friendship but instead increases it. 71. Therefore the
rich are treated with fawning flattery, but nobody plays the
hypocrite for the poor. Whatever is given to a poor man,
whose friendship is devoid of envy, is genuine. We have said
all this so we may test friends' character, not estimate their
wealth. Thus, then, is intention tested. Perhaps you see that
he is more desirous of your property than of you yourself,
always lying in wait for something—honor, glory, riches,
freedom—that can be conferred on him by your efforts. If
he prefers someone better endowed with any of those, and
certainly if what he seeks is not in your power, you will easily
discern his intention in joining himself to you.

72. Now let us see about discretion. Some people per-
versely enough, not to say shamelessly, want to have a friend
such as they themselves cannot be. These are the ones who
endure even minor faults in their friends impatiently, correct them harshly, and in their lack of discretion, neglect
more important faults and get upset at any little thing. They
confuse everything without regard to place, time, or the
people to whom it is suitable to reveal matters and from
whom it is suitable to conceal them. Therefore the discretion of the one you choose must be tested, so that you avoid

quemquam vel imprudentem tibi in amicitia sociaveris, lites quotidianas et iurgia tibi ipse perquiras. 73. Sane hanc in amicitia necessariam esse virtutem satis facile est pervidere, qua si quis caruerit, instar navis absque gubernaculo pro impetu spiritus instabili et irrationabili semper motu feretur. Sic et multae causae deesse non poterunt, quibus illius quem cupis amicum probetur patientia. Cum necesse sit arguere eum quem diligis, quod aliquando quasi ex industria durius fieri oportet, ut sic eius vel probetur, vel exerceatur tolerantia. 74. Id sane attendendum est, ut licet talia reperiantur in eo quem probas, quae offendant animum, vel alicuius secreti incauta revelatione, vel alicuius temporalis commodi cupiditate, vel minus discreta correptione, vel aliqua debitae lenitatis transgressione, non statim a proposita dilectione vel electione resilias, quamdiu correctionis eius spes ulla relucet. Nec quemquam in amicis eligendis vel probandis taedeat esse sollicitum, cum huius laboris fructus vitae sit medicamentum et immortalitatis solidissimum fundamentum. 75. Cum enim plurimi in thesauris multiplicandis, in bobus, in asinis, in ovibus et capris nutriendis, eligendis, comparandis, satis periti sint, certaque in his omnibus cognoscendis non desint indicia, dementiae res est, eamdem in amicis acquirendis vel probandis non dare operam, et quasdam addiscere notas, quibus hi, quos elegimus in amicos, ad amicitiam probentur idonei. Cavendus sane est quidam impetus amoris qui praecurrit iudicium et probandi adimit potestatem. 76. Est proinde viri prudentis sustinere, hunc refrenare impetum, ponere modum benevolentiae, paulatim procedere

allying yourself in friendship with someone thoughtless or unwise, creating for yourself daily quarrels and disputes. 73. Of course in friendship it is easy enough to see that this virtue is necessary, since if someone lacks it, he is like a rudderless ship, always moved by the wind's shifting force and unpredictable course. Thus there cannot fail to be many opportunities by which the patience of the one you want as a friend may be tested. When it is necessary to rebuke the one you love, this should sometimes be done more severely as if on purpose, so that thereby his endurance may be tested or exercised. 74. You must certainly pay attention that although there may be such traits in the one you are testing that offend your spirit—whether through careless revelation of some secret, desire for some worldly gain, indiscriminate reproach, or some lapse in due gentleness—still you should not draw back from the proposed love or choice immediately, as long as there is any flicker of hope for improvement. Nor should it weary anyone to be anxious about the choice and testing of friends, since the reward of this labor is medicine for life and the most solid foundation for immortality. 75. Since there are many quite skilled at increasing their wealth, in rearing, choosing, and matching oxen and donkeys, sheep and goats, and reliable markers of expertise in all these matters are not lacking, it is foolhardiness not to take pains in the selection and testing of friends nor to learn the signs by which those we have chosen as friends may be proven suitable for friendship. One must by all means guard against an impulse for love that runs ahead of judgment and takes away the power of testing. 76. Accordingly, it is the mark of a prudent man to hold back, to rein in this impulse, to put a limit to goodwill, to go forward in affection gradu-

in affectum, donec iam probato se totum dedat et committat amico.

Galterus: Fateor, adhuc me movet illorum sententia, qui sine huiusmodi amicis vivere tutius arbitrantur.

Aelredus: Mirum hoc, cum sine amicis nulla prorsus vita iucunda sit.

Galterus: Cur, rogo te?

77. *Aelredus:* Ponamus totum genus humanum exemptum mundo, te solum superstitem reliquisse. Et ecce coram te omnes mundi deliciae et divitiae, aurum, argentum, lapides pretiosi, urbes muratae, castra turrita, ampla aedificia, sculpturae, picturae. Sed et reformatum te in antiquum cogita statum, omnia habere subiecta, *oves et boves universas, insuper et pecora campi, volucres caeli et pisces maris, qui perambulant semitas maris.* Dic, rogo nunc, utrum sine socio omnia tibi haec possent esse iucunda?

Galterus: Minime.

78. *Aelredus:* Quid si unum haberes cuius nescires linguam, ignorares mores, cuius te lateret et amor et animus?

Galterus: Si non aliquibus signis efficere possem, ut esset amicus, mallem nullum quam talem habere.

Aelredus: Si autem unus adesset quem aeque ut te ipsum diligeres, a quo te similiter diligi non dubitares, nonne omnia quae prius videbantur amara, dulcia redderentur et sapida?

Galterus: Prorsus ita est.

Aelredus: Nonne quanto plures haberes de talibus, tanto feliciorem te iudicares?

Galterus: Verissime.

ally, until he may give himself wholly and commit to a now proven friend.

Walter: I confess that the opinion of those who think it safer to live without friends of this kind still has a hold on me.

Aelred: That is astonishing, since absolutely no life can be pleasant without friends.

Walter: Why, I ask you?

77. *Aelred:* Let us suppose that the entire human race has been banished from the world, leaving you the sole survivor. Look: before you are all the world's delights and riches: gold, silver, precious stones, walled cities, turreted castles, spacious buildings, sculptures, paintings. But think of yourself also restored to your former state, with everything subject to you, *all the sheep and cattle as well as the beasts of the field, the birds of the air, and the fish of the sea, which pass along the paths of the sea.* Now tell me, could all that be pleasing to you without a companion?

Walter: Not at all.

78. *Aelred:* What if there were someone whose language you did not know, of whose customs you were ignorant, whose love and spirit lay hidden from you?

Walter: If I could not make friends with him through signs, I'd prefer nobody at all to one like that.

Aelred: If, however, there were one you could love as you do yourself and by whom you had no hesitation to be loved likewise, would not everything that had formerly seemed bitter be made sweet and delicious?

Walter: Absolutely.

Aelred: Is it not the case that the more such friends you had, the happier you would consider yourself?

Walter: Very true.

79. *Aelredus:* Haec est illa mira et magna felicitas quam expectamus, Deo ipso operante, et diffundente inter se et creaturam suam quam sustulerit, inter ipsos gradus et ordines quos distinxerit, inter singulos quosque quos elegerit, tantam amicitiam et caritatem, ut sic quisque diligat alium sicut seipsum, ac per hoc sicut unusquisque de propria, sic et de alterius felicitate laetetur, et ita singulorum beatitudo omnium sit, et omnium beatitudinum universitas singulorum. 80. Ibi nulla cogitationum occultatio, nulla affectionum dissimulatio. Haec est vera et aeterna amicitia quae hic inchoatur, ibi perficitur, quae hic paucorum est, ubi pauci boni, ibi omnium, ubi omnes boni. Hic necessaria probatio, ubi est sapientium et stultorum permixtio, ibi probatione non egent, quos beatificat angelica illa et quodammodo divina perfectio. Ad hanc proinde similitudinem comparemus amicos quos non secus quam nos ipsos diligamus, quorum nobis nuda sint omnia, quibus omnia nostra pandamus secreta, qui firmi sint et stabiles et constantes in omnibus. Putasne quemquam mortalium esse qui non velit amari?

Galterus: Non aestimo.

81. *Aelredus:* Si quem videres inter multos vivere, et omnes habere suspectos, quasi insidiatores capitis sui timere omnes, nullum diligere, nec se diligi a quoquam putare, nonne eum miserrimum iudicares?

Galterus: Miserrimum plane.

Aelredus: Ergo et ipsum felicissimum non negabis qui in eorum inter quos vivit visceribus requiescit, amans omnes et amatus ab omnibus, quem ab hac suavissima tranquillitate, nec suspicio dividat, nec timor excutiat.

Galterus: Optime ac verissime.

79. *Aelred:* That is the great and wonderful happiness we long for, with God himself acting to pour forth such great friendship and love—between himself and every creature he sustains, between the ranks and orders that he distinguishes, among all individuals whom he chooses—that in this way each may love another as himself, and thereby each may rejoice in his own happiness just as he does in the other's, and thus the blessedness of each individual would be the blessedness of all, and the sum of all blessedness would be the blessedness of each individual. 80. There no thought is hidden, no affection contrived. This is true and eternal friendship that begins here and is perfected there, which is for the few here, but there where all are good it is for all. Here where there is a mix of the wise and the foolish, testing is necessary, but there people do not need testing whom that angelic and in some sense divine perfection makes happy. Henceforth, let us compare to this model the friends we are to love no differently than ourselves, all of whose secrets are to be laid bare to us, to whom we should reveal all ours, who are to be firm, steadfast, and dependable in all things. Do you think there is any mortal who does not want to be loved?

Walter: I don't think so.

81. *Aelred:* If you were to see someone living among many, holding all suspect as if in fear that everyone was plotting his death, loving no one nor thinking himself loved by any one, would you not consider him most miserable?

Walter: Most miserable, certainly.

Aelred: Then you will not deny that he is happiest who rests in the inner heart of those among whom he lives, loving all and loved by all, whom neither suspicion separates nor fear banishes from this sweetest tranquility.

Walter: Perfectly put and perfectly true.

82. *Aelredus:* Quod si forte de omnibus difficile inventu sit in praesenti, cum id nobis in futurum servetur, quanto plures nobis abundant huiusmodi, tanto nobis feliciores aestimabimus? Nudiustertius cum claustra monasterii circuirem, consedente fratrum amantissima corona, et quasi inter paradisiacas amoenitates singularum arborum folia, flores fructusque mirarer. Nullum inveniens in illa multitudine quem non diligerem, et a quo me diligi non confiderem, tanto gaudio perfusus sum ut omnes mundi huius delicias superaret. Sentiebam quippe meum spiritum transfusum in omnibus, et in me omnium transmigrasse affectum, ut dicerem cum propheta, *"Ecce quam bonum et quam iucundum habitare fratres in unum."*

Gratianus: Num omnes illos quos sic diligis et a quibus sic diligeris te in amicitiam assumpsisse putabimus?

83. *Aelredus:* Plerosque omni affectu complectimur, quos tamen ad amicitiae secreta non admittimus, quae maxime in omnium secretorum et consiliorum nostrorum revelatione consistit. Unde Dominus in Evangelio, *"Iam non dicam vos servos,* sed amicos meos," causamque subiungens qua amici nomine digni haberentur, *"Quia omnia,"* inquit, *"quae audivi a patre meo nota feci vobis."* Et alias: *"Vos amici mei estis, si feceritis quae praecipio vobis."* De his verbis, ut sanctus ait Ambrosius, *"Dedit formam amicitiae quam sequamur, ut faciamus amici voluntatem, ut aperiamus secreta nostra amico, quaecumque in pectore habemus, et illius arcana non ignoremus. Ostendamus* nos illi *et ille nobis aperiat sinum. Nihil* enim *occultat amicus. Si verus est, effundit animum suum, sicut effundebat mysteria patris Domi-*

82. *Aelred:* If it is perhaps difficult to find such a state regarding everything in the present life, since it is reserved for us in the future, shall we not think that the more people of that sort there are for us, the more fortunate they are for us? While I was walking around the monastery cloister the day before yesterday, where sat together a most loving circle of brothers, I marveled at the leaves, flowers, and fruits of each single tree, as if in the loveliness of paradise. Finding no one in the crowd I did not love or of whose love for me I was not confident, I was suffused with such joy that it exceeded all the delights of this world. Indeed, I felt my spirit was poured into all and the affection of all had been transferred into me, so that I could say with the prophet, "*See how good and pleasant it is for brothers to live in unity.*"

Gratian: Are we to think that you have taken into friendship all those whom you so love and by whom you are so loved?

83. *Aelred:* We embrace with all affection many whom we nevertheless do not take into the secrets of friendship, which consists especially in revealing all our confidences and plans. Hence the Lord says in the Gospel, "*Now I will call you not servants* but my friends," adding the reason friends should be considered worthy of the name: "*Because everything that I have heard from my father I have made known to you.*" And in another place: "*You are my friends if you do what I command you.*" With these words, as Saint Ambrose says, "*He gave us a model for friendship that we should follow, so that we would do a friend's will, disclose whatever secrets we have in our heart, and not be ignorant of his hidden thoughts. Let us bare our breast* to him *and let him open his to us.* For *a friend hides nothing. If he is a true friend, he pours out his spirit just as the Lord*

nus Iesus." 84. Haec Ambrosius. Quam multos ergo diligimus quibus minus cautum est sic nostrum propalare animum et effundere viscera, quorum vel aetas, vel sensus, sive discretio, ad talia sustinenda non sufficit!

85. *Galterus:* Haec amicitia tam sublimis et perfecta est, ut ad eam aspirare non audeam. Mihi et huic Gratiano illa sufficit, quam tuus Augustinus describit: colloqui scilicet et conridere, et vicissim benevole obsequi, simul legere, simul conferre, simul nugari et simul honestari, dissentire interdum sine odio, tamquam homo sibi, atque ipsa rarissima dissensione, condire consensiones plurimas, docere aliquid invicem aut discere ab invicem, desiderare absentes cum molestia, suscipere advenientes cum laetitia. 86. His atque huiusmodi a corde amantium et redamantium procedentibus signis per os, per linguam, per oculos, et mille motus gratissimos, quasi fomitibus conflare animos, et ex pluribus unum facere. Hoc est quod nos diligendum credimus in amicis, ita ut rea sibi nostra videatur conscientia, si non amaverimus redamantem, aut si amantem non redamaverimus.

87. *Aelredus:* Amicitia haec carnalium est, et maxime adolescentium, quales aliquando fuerant ipse et suus, de quo tunc loquebatur amicus, quae vero exceptis nugis et mendaciis, si nulla intercesserit inhonestas, spe uberioris gratiae toleranda est, quasi quaedam amicitiae sanctioris principia, quibus, crescente religione et spiritalium studiorum parilitate, accedente etiam maturioris aetatis gravitate et

Jesus poured out his father's mysteries." 84. So says Ambrose. How many, therefore, we love and to whom it is yet reckless to reveal our souls and pour out our hearts in this way, for neither their age, feeling, nor discretion is sufficient to sustain such intimacy!

85. *Walter:* This friendship is so sublime and perfect that I would not dare aspire to it. The one your Augustine describes suffices for me and Gratian here, namely to converse and laugh, to submit to one another kindly, to read together and confer together, to laugh together and be serious together, to disagree from time to time without hatred, as a man does with himself, and to season many agreements with that occasional disagreement, to teach each other something and learn something from each other, to long for the absent friend in distress, to welcome the returning friend with joy. 86. Through these and similar signs that emerge from the heart of those who love and are loved in return—from the face, the tongue, the eyes, in a thousand pleasing gestures—spirits flare up as if kindled and make one from many. That is what we believe should be cherished in friends, in such a way that our conscience would appear guilty to itself if we did not love the one who returns our love, or did not love in return one who loves us.

87. *Aelred:* This is carnal friendship, especially common among the young, as Augustine and the friend of whom he spoke once were, but it should be tolerated, with the exception of silliness and lying and as long as there is no dishonor associated with it, in the hopes of richer grace—as the beginnings, so to speak, of a more holy friendship from which, with the growth of devotion and equal spiritual zeal, and with the approach of the seriousness of mature age and the

spiritalium sensuum illuminatione, purgatiori affectu ad altiora, quasi e vicino conscendant, sicut hesterna die ab hominis ad Dei ipsius amicitiam, ob quamdam similitudinem diximus facilius transeundum.

88. Sed iam tempus est, ut quemadmodum amicitia sit colenda deinceps videamus. Firmamentum igitur stabilitatis et constantiae in amicitia fides est. Nihil est enim stabile quod infidum est. Simplices quippe et communes et consentientes et qui iisdem rebus moveantur, esse debent amici ad invicem, quae omnia pertinent ad fidelitatem. Non enim fidum potest esse multiplex ingenium et tortuosum. Neque vero hi qui non eisdem rebus moventur, nec eisdem consentiunt stabiles esse possunt aut fidi. 89. Prae omnibus autem cavenda suspicio est, velut amicitiae venenum, ut numquam male de amico sentiamus, nec mala dicenti credamus vel consentiamus. Accedat huc in sermone iucunditas, hilaritas in vultu, suavitas in moribus, in oculorum etiam nutu serenitas, in quibus haudquaquam mediocre in amicitia condimentum. Tristitia namque et severior facies habet quidem honestam plerumque gravitatem, sed amicitia quasi remissior aliquando debet esse, et liberior et dulcior, ad comitatem facilitatemque sine levitate et dissolutione proclivior.

90. Est praeterea vis amicitiae parem esse inferiori superiorem. Saepe enim quidam inferioris gradus, vel ordinis, vel dignitatis, vel scientiae ab excellentioribus in amicitiam assumuntur, quos oportet omnia quae extra naturam sunt contemnere et aestimare quasi nihilum et inane, et in pulchritudinem amicitiae quae non sericis vel gemmis ornatur, non possessionibus dilatatur, non pinguescit deliciis, nec

illumination of the spiritual senses, they may climb as if from just below to higher ground in purer affection. As we said yesterday, the transition from friendship with man to friendship with God himself should be easier to make because of the similarity between the two.

88. But now it is time that we see in turn how friendship should be cultivated. The foundation of stability and dependability in friendship is loyalty. For nothing is stable that is disloyal. Indeed, those who are straightforward, obliging, sympathetic, and stirred by the same things, which are all aspects of loyalty, should be each other's friends. A changeable and devious character cannot be loyal. Nor can those who are neither stirred by the same things nor in agreement about them be stable or loyal. 89. Above all, suspicion must be guarded against as a poison to friendship, so that we should never think evil of a friend, nor believe or agree with one who speaks evil of him. To these should be added charm in speech, cheerfulness of face, gentleness of manner, even serenity in glance, in which traits there is no small seasoning for friendship. For sadness and a rather severe expression often suggest honorable seriousness, but friendship should at times be more relaxed, so to speak, as well as rather more free, sweet, and inclined to comradeship and ease without frivolity or dissipation.

90. Moreover it is the power of friendship to make the superior equal to the inferior. Often people of inferior rank, order, authority, or knowledge are taken up in friendship by those more eminent. It is suitable both to despise all things outside nature, to consider them as nothing and empty, and always bear in mind that the beauty of friendship is not adorned with silks or gems, nor enlarged by possessions, nor

abundat divitiis, non honoribus extollitur, non dignitatibus inflatur, semper attendere, et sic ad originis recurrentes principium, aequalitatem quam natura dedit, non circumpendentia quae mortalibus cupiditas praestitit, subtili examinatione considerare. 91. Itaque in amicitia quae naturae simul et gratiae optimum donum est sublimis descendat, humilis ascendat, dives egeat, pauper ditescat, et ita unusquisque alteri suam conditionem communicet ut fiat aequalitas, sicut scriptum est: "*Qui multum non abundavit, et qui modicum non minoravit.*" Numquam ergo tuo te praeferas amico, sed si forte in his quae diximus superior inveneris, tunc te magis amico submittere non cuncteris, praestare confidentiam, extollere verecundum, et tanto plus ei conferre honoris quanto minus conferendum conditio vel paupertas praescribit.

92. Praestantissimus iuvenum Ionathas, non regium stemma, nec regni expectationem attendens, foedus iniit cum David et servulum in amicitia adaequans domino, sic fugatum a patre, sic latitantem in heremo, sic adiudicatum morti, neci destinatum sibi praetulit et se humilans et illum exultans, "Tu," inquit, "eris rex, et ego secundus post te." O praeclarissimum verae amicitiae speculum! Mira res! Rex furebat in servum, et quasi in aemulum regni totam patriam excitabat. Sacerdotes arguens proditionis pro sola suspicione trucidat; lustrat nemora, valles exquirit, montes et rupes armata obsidet manu. Omnes se regiae indignationis

fattened by delicacies, nor made abundant with riches, nor exalted by honors, nor puffed up by office holding. Thus returning to the original source of friendship, they should consider in detail the equality nature gives, not the artificial trappings that greed offers mortals. 91. Therefore in friendship, which is the greatest gift of nature and grace together, the lofty should descend and the humble ascend, the rich become poor and the poor become rich, and thus each share his condition with the other to create equality, as it is written: "*He who had much did not have too much, and he who had little did not have too little.*" So you should never prefer yourself to your friend, but if it happens that you are found to be superior in those aforementioned qualities, then you should not hesitate to acquiesce more to your friend, to offer him your confidence, and praise him in his bashfulness, and the less that rank or poverty dictates must be given him, the more you should confer honor on him.

92. Jonathan, the most outstanding youth, paying no mind to his royal pedigree or expectation of the throne, entered into a pact with David that made a humble servant equal to his lord in friendship, so preferring David to himself when David fled Jonathan's father, hid in the desert, was condemned to death, and was destined for slaughter, that he humbled himself and exalted David, saying, "You will be king and I will be second after you." O clearest mirror of true friendship! What a marvel! The king raged against his servant David and roused the whole kingdom against him as if he had designs on the throne. Accusing his priests of betrayal, he executed them based on mere suspicion; he traversed forests, searched valleys, cordoned off mountains and cliffs with an armed escort. All pledged themselves to be

spondent ultores. Solus Ionathas qui solus iustius poterat invidere, patri resistendum putavit, deferendum amico, praebendum in tanta adversitate consilium, et amicitiam regno praeferens: "Tu eris," ait, "rex et ego secundus post te." 93. Et vide, quomodo pater adolescentis contra amicum excitabat invidiam, conviciis urgens, terrens minis, spoliandum regno, honore privandum commemorans. Cum enim in David mortis sententiam protulisset, Ionathas amico non defuit. "Quare," inquit, "morietur David? Quid peccavit? Quid fecit? Ipse posuit animam suam in manu sua, et percussit Philistaeum, et laetatus es. Quare ergo morietur?" Ad hanc vocem versus in insaniam rex, lancea nisus est confodere Ionatham cum pariete, addensque convicia minis. "*Fili,*" inquit, "*mulieris ultro virum rapientis,* scio quia diligis eum *in confusionem tuam, et in confusionem ignominiosae matris tuae.*" 94. Deinde totum virus quo pectus iuvenis aspergeretur evomuit, adiciens verbum ambitionis incitamentum, fomentum invidiae, zeli et amaritudinis incentivum: "Quamdiu vixerit filius Ysai, non stabilietur regnum tuum." Quis non moveretur his verbis, non invideret? Cuius amorem, cuius gratiam, cuius amicitiam non corrumperent, non minuerent, non obliterarent? Ille amantissimus adolescens, amicitiae iura conservans, fortis ad minas, patiens ad convicia, propter amicitiam regni contemptor, immemor gloriae, sed memor gratiae. "Tu eris," inquit, "rex et ego ero secundus post te."

95. Repertos quosdam, dicit Tullius, qui pecuniam praeferre amicitiae sordidum aestimarent, illos autem impossibile reperiri, qui honores, magistratus, imperia, potestates,

avengers of royal wrath. Jonathan alone, who alone could have been more justly envious, thought his father was to be resisted in deference to his friend, offering David advice in such great adversity, and preferring friendship to the throne, he said, "You will be king and I will be second after you." 93. See how the youth's father incited envy against his friend, besetting him with abuse, frightening him with threats, reminding Jonathan that he would be stripped of a kingdom and deprived of honor. Yet when he had decreed a death sentence for David, Jonathan did not fail his friend. "Why is David to die?" he asked. "How has he sinned? What did he do? He took his life into his hands, and killed the Philistine, and you rejoiced. Why, then, is he to die?" At these words the king went mad and tried to pin Jonathan to the wall with his spear, adding abuse to threats. "*Son of a woman who freely ravishes a man,*" he said, "I know that you love David, *to your disgrace and the disgrace of your shameless mother.*" 94. Then he spewed all his venom to stain Jonathan's heart, adding a remark to serve as a spur to ambition, a spark of envy, and an incitement to jealousy and bitterness: "As long as the son of Jesse lives, your kingdom will not be established." Who would not be stirred by these words, who not made envious? Whose love, grace, or friendship would they not corrupt, diminish, and destroy? But this most loving youth, observing the laws of friendship, steadfast against threats, patient in the face of insults, scorning a kingdom for the sake of friendship, unmindful of glory but mindful of grace, said, "You will be king and I will be second after you."

95. Cicero says that some have been found who think it despicable to prefer money to friendship, but it is impossible to find those who do not put honors, political office,

opes amicitiae non anteponant, ut cum ex altera parte proposita haec sint, ex altera vis amicitiae, non multo illa
malint. Imbecillis est enim natura ad contemnendam poten-
tiam. "Ubi enim," ait, "invenies, qui honorem amici anteponat suo?" Ecce inventus est Ionathas victor naturae, gloriae ac potestatis contemptor, qui honorem amici suo
praeferret, "Tu eris," inquiens, "rex et ego ero secundus post
te." 96. Haec est vera, perfecta, stabilis et aeterna amicitia,
quam invidia non corrumpit, non suspicio minuit, non dissolvit ambitio, quae sic tentata non cessit, sic arietata non
corruit, quae tot conviciis pulsata cernitur inflexibilis, tot
lacessita iniuriis permansit immobilis. *Vade* ergo *et tu fac similiter.* Verum, si tibi praeferre quem diligis durum vel etiam
impossibile iudicas, vel parem eum tibi facere, si vis esse
amicus non neglegas. 97. Non enim amicitia recte colitur, a
quibus aequalitas non servatur. *"Defer amico ut aequali,"* ait
Ambrosius, *"nec te pudeat, ut praevenias amicum officio. Amicitia enim nescit superbiam."* Fidelis quippe amicus medicamentum est vitae, immortalitatis gratia.

Iam in beneficiis, quomodo colenda sit, attendamus, et
hinc aliquid de alienis manibus extorqueamus. *"Haec lex,"* ait
quidam, "in amicitia *sanciatur, ut ab amicis honesta petamus,* et
pro amicis *honesta faciamus, nec expectemus ut rogemur.* Cunctatio semper absit, studium semper assit." 98. Si perdenda est
pecunia propter amicum, multo magis amici utilitatibus vel
necessitatibus conferenda. Sed non omnes omnia possunt.

military command, power, or riches before friendship, so
that when those are put on one side and the might of friendship on the other, they much prefer the former. Nature is
weak when it comes to scorning power. "For where," Cicero
said, "will you find one who puts the honor of his friend
ahead of his own?" Behold, Jonathan was found to be a victor over nature, scorning glory and power, preferring his
friend's honor to his own, saying, "You will be king and I will
be second after you." 96. This is true, perfect, steadfast, and
eternal friendship, which envy does not corrupt, suspicion
does not diminish, and ambition does not dissolve, which so
tested, did not yield, so attacked, did not fall, struck by so
many insults appeared unyielding, wounded by so many in-
juries remained steady. Therefore, *go and do likewise.* But if
you judge it difficult or even impossible to prefer the one
you love to yourself, at least do not fail to make him your
equal if you want to be a friend. 97. For they do not rightly
cultivate friendship who do not maintain equality. "*Defer to
your friend as an equal,*" says Ambrose, "*and do not be ashamed
to anticipate a friend in service. For friendship knows no pride.*" A
loyal friend is medicine for this life and a blessing for the
next.

Now let us turn our attention to how friendship should
be cultivated through kindness. On this matter let us snatch
something from others' hands. "*Let this law,*" someone says,
"*be enacted* concerning friendship: *that we ask of friends and do*
for friends *what is honorable, not waiting to be asked.* There
should never be hesitation and there should always be enthusiasm." 98. If we must lose money for a friend, so much
more should it be spent for a friend's advantage or needs.
But not everybody can do everything. This one has plenty of

Abundat iste pecunia, ille agris et possessionibus; alter in consiliis plus potest, alter magis excellit in honoribus. In his qualem te debeas exhibere amico, prudenter adverte. Et de pecunia satis dedit scriptura: *"Perde,"* inquit, *"pecuniam propter amicum."* Sed quia *oculi sapientis in capite eius,* si nos sumus membra et Christus caput, faciamus quod ait propheta, *"Oculi mei semper ad Dominum,"* ut ab eo accipiamus vivendi formam, de quo scriptum est, *"Si quis indiget sapientia, postulet a Domino, qui dat omnibus affluenter et non improperat."*

99. Sic igitur des amico, ut non improperes, non mercedem expectes, non frontem obducas, non vultum avertas, non deponas oculos, sed serena facie, hilari vultu, sermone iucundo intercide verba petentis; occurre benevolentia, ut non rogatus videaris praestare quod petitur. Ingenuus animus nihil magis erubescendum aestimat quam rogare. Cum igitur tibi esse debeat cum amico *cor unum et anima una,* iniuriosum nimis est, si non sit et pecunia una. Haec igitur lex in hac parte inter amicos teneatur: ut sic se sibi suaque impendant, ut qui dat, servet hilaritatem, qui accipit, non perdat securitatem. 100. Booz cum Ruth Moabitis advertisset inopiam, post messores suos legentem spicas alloquitur, consolatur, invitat ad convivium puerorum, et verecundiae eius ingenue parcens, iubet messoribus etiam de industria spicas relinquere, quas illa colligeret absque pudore. Sic et nos debemus amicorum necessitates subtilius explorare, petiturum beneficiis praevenire, talem in dando modum servare, ut ille gratiam videatur praestare qui accipit, magis quam ille qui dedit.

money, that one lands and possessions; one can do more in giving advice, another excels in worldly honors. Consider wisely how you should treat your friend in these matters. Scripture gave much advice about money, saying, "*Lose money for a friend.*" But since *the eyes of a wise man are in his head,* if we are the members and Christ the head, we should do as the prophet says, "*My eyes are always on the Lord,*" so we may accept our way of living from him, concerning whom it is written, "*If someone lacks wisdom, let him seek it from the Lord, who gives generously to all and does not scold.*"

99. Give to a friend, then, in a way that you do not scold, nor expect a reward, nor furrow your brow, nor turn your face aside, nor avert your eyes, but anticipate his request with a calm expression, a cheerful face, and kind words. Approach him with kindness so you seem to offer what is requested without being asked. A noble spirit thinks nothing more embarrassing than to ask. Therefore, since you should be *one heart and one soul* with a friend, it is very hurtful if there should not also be one sum of money. This law, then, should be kept in this respect between friends: that they spend themselves and their goods on each other in such a way that the giver remains cheerful and the receiver does not lose confidence. 100. When Boaz had noted the poverty of Ruth the Moabite, he spoke to her as she was gathering ears of grain behind the reapers, comforted her, and invited her to his servants' table and nobly sparing her modesty, he even ordered his reapers to leave ears of grain on purpose that she could gather without shame. In this fashion we too ought to investigate subtly our friends' needs, to anticipate when one will ask for favors and to maintain such a manner of giving that the one who receives may seem to grant favor more than that the one who gives.

Galterus: Nobis igitur quibus nihil accipere, nihil dare permittitur, qualis erit in hac parte spiritalis amicitiae gratia?

101. *Aelredus:* "Felicissimam vitam," ait sapiens, "ducerent homines, si *duo haec verba de* medio *tollerentur, 'meum' et 'tuum.'*" Magnam certe praestat spiritali amicitiae firmitatem sancta paupertas, quae ideo sancta est, quia voluntaria. Cum enim peremptorium sit amicitiae cupiditas, tanto certe facilius amicitia parta servatur, quanto animus ab illa peste purgatior invenitur. Sunt tamen alia in spiritali amore beneficia, quibus et adesse sibi, et prodesse possunt amici. Primum ut solliciti sint pro invicem, orent pro invicem, erubescant alter pro altero, gaudeat alter pro altero, alterius lapsum ut suum lugeat, alterius profectum, suum existimet. 102. Quibus modis potest erigat pusillanimem, suscipiat infirmum, consoletur tristem, iratum sustineat. Sic praeterea oculos revereatur amici, ut nihil quod inhonestum sit agere, nihil quod dedeceat loqui praesumat. Cum enim quidquid ipse deliquerit, ita redundet in amicum, ut non solum intra se erubescat et doleat, sed etiam his qui videt vel audit, sibi ac si ipse peccasset, improperet. Profecto licet non sibi, amico tamen credit esse parcendum. Optimus itaque comes amicitiae verecundia est, et ideo *maximum ornamentum tollit amicitiae, qui ab ea tollit verecundiam.* 103. Quam saepe conceptam ab intus iracundiae flammam, et iam in publicum erumpentem, amici mei nutus compescuit vel extinxit; quotiens verbum indecens usque ad fauces progressum, austerior illius aspectus repressit! Quam saepe incautius

Walter: But for those of us who are permitted to give and receive nothing, what will be the favor of spiritual friendship in this matter?

101. *Aelred:* "Men would lead the happiest of lives," says a wise man, "if *the two words 'mine' and 'yours' would be removed from* their midst." Holy poverty, holy because it is voluntary, surely offers great strength to spiritual friendship. Since greed is deadly to friendship, surely the more the spirit is found to be purged of that plague, the more easily a friendship, once born, can be maintained. Yet there are other benefits of spiritual love with which friends can aid and support one other. First they may look out for each other, pray for each other, the one blush for the other, the one rejoice for the other, grieve for the other's failings as for his own, and consider the other's progress his own. 102. In whatever ways possible, he should encourage the fainthearted, support the sick, console the sad, bear with the irate. Moreover, he should so respect the eyes of a friend that he presumes to neither do anything dishonorable nor say anything unseemly. For when he fails in any way, it should so reflect on his friend that the friend not only blushes and grieves inwardly, but also reproaches himself for what he sees or hears as if he himself had sinned. In fact, a friend believes that although he should not be pardoned, nonetheless his friend should. Thus the best companion of friendship is modesty, and therefore *he who deprives friendship of modesty deprives it of its greatest adornment.* 103. How often has my friend's nod repressed or even extinguished a flame of inner anger already bursting forth in public, and how many times has his stern glance repressed unbecoming speech that was already on my lips! How often, when I had carelessly burst into

resolutus in risum, vel in otiosa lapsus, in eius adventum debitam gravitatem recepi! Praeterea quidquid suadendum
est, ab amico facilius recipitur, et securius retinetur, cuius
magna in suadendo esse debet auctoritas, cum nec fides eius
dubia, nec adulatio sit suspecta.

104. Amicus igitur amico quod honestum sit suadeat, secure, manifeste, libere. Nec solum monendi sunt amici, sed
si opus fuerit obiurgandi. Nam cum quibusdam molesta sit
veritas, siquidem ex ea nascitur odium secundum illud, "*Obsequium amicos, veritas odium parit,*" obsequium tamen illud
multo molestius est, quod peccatis indulgens, praecipitem
amicum fieri sinit. Maxime autem culpandus est amicus, et
hinc praecipue obiurgandus, si veritatem aspernatur, et obsequiis atque blanditiis in crimen impellitur. Non quod non
debeamus amicis dulciter obsequi, et plerumque blandiri,
sed in omnibus servanda moderatio est, ut monitio acerbi-
tate, obiurgatio contumelia careat. 105. In obsequiis vero vel
blanditiis, suavis quaedam et honesta affabilitas assit. As-
sentatio vero vitiorum nutrix procul amoveatur, quae non
solum amico, sed nec libero quidem digna est. Cuius autem
aures veritati clausae sunt, ut ab amico verum audire ne-
queant, huius salus desperanda est. 106. Quocirca, sicut ait
Ambrosius, "*Si quid vitii in amico deprehenderis, corripe occulte;
si te non audierit, corripe palam. Sunt enim bonae correctiones, et
plerumque meliores quam tacita amicitia. Etsi laedi se putet amicus, tu tamen corripe. Etsi amaritudo correptionis animum eius
vulneret, tu tamen corripe. Tolerabiliora enim sunt amici vulnera
quam adulantium oscula. Errantem igitur amicum corripe.*"

laughter or lapsed into idleness, I recovered due seriousness at his approach! Furthermore, whatever has to be achieved through persuasion is more easily accepted and more securely retained when it comes from one whose authority in persuasion must be great, since his loyalty is beyond doubt, liable to no suspicion of flattery.

104. Therefore a friend should securely, openly, and freely persuade a friend of what is honorable. Friends are not only to be cautioned, but reprimanded if need be. For although truth is annoying to some people, since hatred arises from it, as in, *"Flattery breeds friends and truth breeds hatred,"* still much more harmful is flattery that by indulging sins allows a friend to fall headlong. A friend is especially blameworthy, and hence especially warrants reprimand, if he scorns truth and is driven to crime by flattery and indulgence. Not that we should not indulge friends sweetly, and often flatter them, but moderation is to be preserved in all things, so that admonition should be free of sharpness, and reprimand free of insult. 105. In our indulgence or flattery, there should be a certain pleasant and honorable friendliness. But sycophancy, the nurse of vices, must be banished far away, as it is unworthy not only of a friend, but also of any free person. Hope for salvation is to be given up in the case of one whose ears are closed to the truth so that he cannot bear to hear it from a friend. 106. Therefore, as Ambrose says, *"If you perceive some vice in your friend, correct him secretly; if he does not listen, do so openly. For corrections are good, and often better than friendship that keeps silent. Even if a friend thinks he is injured, correct him nonetheless. Even if the bitterness of correction wounds his soul, correct him nonetheless. Wounds from a friend are more tolerable than the kisses of fawners. Therefore, correct an erring friend."*

Super omnia tamen cavenda est in correptione ira et amaritudo mentis, ne non tam videatur amicum velle corrigere,
quam suo stomacho satisfacere. 107. Vidi enim aliquos in
amicis corrigendis, conceptam amaritudinem ebullientem-
que furorem nunc zeli, nunc libertatis nomine palliare, et
secutos impetum, non rationem, sua tali correptione numquam prodesse, immo et obesse perplurimum. At inter amicos nulla vitii huius excusatio est. Debet enim amicus amico
compati, condescendere, vitium eius suum putare, corripere
humiliter, compatienter. Corripiat eum vultus tristior,
sermo deiectior, intercipiant verba lacrimae, ut non solum
videat, sed etiam sentiat correptionem ex amore et non ex
rancore procedere. Si forte primam correptionem respuerit,
recipiet vel secundam. Tu interim ora, tu plora, tristem praeferens vultum, pium servans affectum. 108. Exploranda est
etiam animi illius qualitas, nam sunt quibus blanditiae pro-
sunt, et his libentius acquiescunt, sunt qui pro nihilo eas du-
cunt, et facilius verbo vel verbere corriguntur. Amicus proinde ita se conformet et aptet amico, ut eius congruit
qualitati, et cui in exteriori adversitate debet adesse, his
quae sunt adversa spiritui, multo magis festinet occurrere.
Igitur sicut monere et moneri proprie amicitiae est, et alterum libere facere, non aspere; alterum patienter accipere,
non repugnanter, sic habendum est, nullam in amicitiis
pestem esse maiorem quam adulationem et assentationem,
quae sunt levium hominum, atque fallacium, ad voluntatem
loquentium omnia, nihil ad veritatem. 109. Nulla proinde
sit inter amicos cunctatio, simulatio nulla, quae maxime

Yet above all, in correction anger and bitterness of spirit are to guarded against, or else one may seem not to want to correct a friend so much as to satisfy bad temper. 107. I have seen, in the correction of friends, some who cloak conceived bitterness and boiling rage now in the name of zeal, now in the name of candor. Following impulse rather than reason, they never did any good with such correction, and often did real harm. But there is no excuse for this vice among friends. A friend should feel compassion for a friend, show good will, consider his friend's sin his own, correct him humbly and compassionately. A sad face and rather dejected speech should correct him, tears should interrupt words, so the friend may not only see but also feel that the correction comes from love, not rancor. If he happens to reject the first correction, he may accept a second. Meanwhile, pray and weep, showing a sad face and maintaining a holy affection. 108. Even the nature of his soul should be examined, for there are those for whom coaxing is effective and they respond to it quite readily, others who scorn it and are corrected more easily with a word or a blow. Accordingly, a friend should conform and adapt himself to a friend in the way suited to his nature, and for one whom he should help in material adversity, all the more should he hasten to his aid in spiritual adversities. Therefore, just as it is characteristic of friendship to caution and be cautioned, and to do the former frankly, not harshly, while accepting the latter patiently, not resentfully, so it should be believed that in friendship there is no greater plague than fawning and sycophancy, the traits of frivolous and deceitful men who say everything in accordance with their wishes, not the truth. 109. Among friends, then, there should be no hesitation and no pretense,

repugnat amicitiae. Debet quippe amico *veritatem, sine qua nomen amicitiae valere non potest.* "*Corripiet me,*" ait sanctus David, "*iustus in misericordia, et increpabit me; oleum autem peccatoris non impinguet caput meum.*" Simulator et callidus provocat iram Dei. Inde Dominus per prophetam: "*Popule meus, qui beatum te dicunt, ipsi te decipiunt, et viam gressuum tuorum dissipant.*" "*Simulator* enim *ore,*" ut ait Salomon, "*decipit amicum suum.*" Quocirca sic colenda est amicitia, ut si forte certis ex causis admittenda videatur dissimulatio, sed simulatio numquam.

Galterus: Quomodo, quaeso, dissimulatio necessaria est, quae ut mihi videtur, semper vitium est.

110. *Aelredus:* Falleris, fili. Nam et Deus dissimulare dicitur peccata delinquentium, nolens mortem peccatoris, sed ut convertatur et vivat.

Galterus: Distingue, rogo, inter simulationem et dissimulationem.

111. *Aelredus:* Simulatio, ut mihi videtur, deceptorius quidam consensus est, contra iudicium rationis, quam Terentius in persona Gnatonis satis eleganter expressit: "*Negat quis? Nego. Ait? Aio. Postremo imperavi egomet mihi omnia assentari.*" Et forte haec ethnicus ille de nostris mutuavit thesauris, sensum prophetae nostri suis exprimens verbis. Nam et hoc ipsum ex persona plebis perversae dixisse prophetam, manifestum est: "Videte nobis vana, *loquimini nobis placentia.*" Et alias: "*Prophetae prophetabant mendacium, et sacerdotes applaudebant manu, et populus meus dilexit talia.*" Hoc vitium ubique detestandum est, semper et ubique cavendum.

which is especially repugnant in friendship. Indeed, a friend owes his friend *the truth, without which the name of friendship has no meaning.* "*The just man,*" says holy David, "*will correct me in mercy and rebuke me; may the oil of a sinner not anoint my head.*" A hypocrite or plotter provokes God's wrath. Hence the Lord through the prophet: "*My people, those who say you are blessed deceive you and destroy the path of your steps.*" As Solomon says, "*A hypocrite deceives his friend with his mouth.*" Therefore friendship should be so cultivated that if dissimulation may perhaps seem permissible for certain reasons, hypocrisy is never permissible.

Walter: How, please, is dissimulation necessary, since it seems to me it is always a vice?

110. *Aelred:* You are mistaken, my son. For even God is said to have dissimulated with regard to the faults of sinners, wanting not the death of a sinner but that he be converted and live.

Walter: Please distinguish between lying and dissimulation.

111. *Aelred:* It seems to me that lying is deceptive agreement, counter to the judgment of reason, which Terence expressed quite elegantly in the character of Gnatho: "*Someone says 'No'? I say 'No.' Someone says 'Yes'? I say 'Yes.' Ultimately, I have ordered everything to agree with me.*" Perhaps that pagan borrowed these ideas from our treasures, expressing the meaning of our prophet in his own words. For it is clear that the prophet had said this very thing when personifying a perverse people: "See vain things for us, *tell us things that please us.*" And elsewhere: "*The prophets were prophesying falsehoods, and the priests were clapping their hands, and my people loved such things.*" This vice is detestable everywhere, to be guarded against always and everywhere.

112. Porro dissimulatio dispensatoria quaedam est, vel poenae, vel correptionis dilatio, sine consensu interiori, pro loco, pro tempore, pro persona. Neque enim si quis amicus constitutus in plebe deliquerit, subito et palam obiurgandus est, sed dissimulandum pro loco, immo et quantum salva veritate fieri potest, excusandum quod fecit, et ad debitam correptionem inferendam expectandum familiare secretum. Sic eo tempore quo animus intentus pluribus, minus est ad ea quae dicenda sunt idoneus, vel, aliis supervenientibus causis, paululum commotior sensus ei fuerit, aliquantulum perturbatus, dissimulatione opus est, donec interiori tumultu sedato, corripientem aure pacatiore sustineat. 113. David rex, cum praeventus concupiscentia homicidium adulterio copulasset, correpturus eum propheta Nathan, regiae deferens maiestati, non subito, nec mente turbata tantae personae crimen impegit, sed congrua dissimulatione praemissa, prudenter ipsius regis contra se ipsum sententiam extorsit.

114. *Galterus:* Mihi perplacet ista distinctio. Sed scire velim si amicus potentior fuerit, possitque ad honores vel quaslibet dignitates, quos voluerit promovere, utrum debeat eos quos diligit et a quibus diligitur, caeteris in tali promotione praeferre, et inter ipsos quem amplius diligit eis quos minus diligit anteferre?

115. *Aelredus:* Et in hac parte quomodo colenda sit amicitia, operae pretium est indagare. Sunt enim nonnulli qui se putent non amari, quia non possunt promoveri, seque contemni causentur, si non curis et officiis implicentur. Unde non parvas discordias inter eos, qui putabantur amici,

112. Dissimulation, on the other hand, is a certain dispensing with or delaying of punishment or correction, without inner agreement, with regard to time, place, and person. If someone you have made your friend errs in public, he should not be rebuked suddenly and openly, but there should be dissimulation with regard to place, and indeed, what he did can be excused as much possible saving the truth, awaiting appropriate privacy for the application of due correction. Likewise, in a moment when the mind is intent on many matters and less receptive to what must be said, or when the friend's understanding is rather unsettled and somewhat distracted for other reasons, dissimulation is necessary until, his inner turmoil calmed, he may bear the one correcting him in a more peaceful frame of mind. 113. When King David, overcome with lust, had added homicide to adultery and the prophet Nathan was about to rebuke him, in deference to royal majesty he did not charge so great a person with crime immediately or in agitation, but instead after suitable dissimulation prudently elicited the king's own verdict against himself.

114. *Walter:* That distinction pleases me very much. But I'd like to know this: if the friend is more powerful and can promote whomever he wants to honors and offices, in such promotions should he prefer to others those he loves and by whom he is loved and give priority among them to one he loves more over those he loves less?

115. *Aelred:* In this matter, too, it is worthwhile to explore how friendship should be cultivated. For there are some who think they are not loved because they cannot be promoted and allege that they are despised if they are not involved in responsibilities and offices. We know that in this

ortas novimus, ita ut indignationem divortium sequeretur, divortium maledicta. Itaque in dignitatibus vel officiis, maxime ecclesiasticis, magna cautio adhibenda est: nec attendendum quid tu possis praestare, sed quid ille cui praestas poterit sustinere. 116. Plures quippe sunt diligendi, qui tamen non sunt promovendi, et multos laudabiliter et dulciter amplectimur, quos non sine gravi nostro peccato et illorum summo periculo, curis et negotiis implicaremus. Quocirca semper in his ratio sequenda est, non affectus, nec his imponendus est honos vel onus istud quos habemus amicitiores, sed quos ad ea sustinenda credimus aptiores. Ubi tamen virtutis invenitur aequalitas, non multum improbo, si aliquantisper affectus suas inserit partes.

117. Nec quisquam se idcirco dicat contemptum, quia non promotum, cum Dominus Iesus Petrum Iohanni in hac parte praetulerit, nec ideo subtraxerit Iohanni affectum quia Petro dederat principatum. Petro commendavit ecclesiam suam, Iohanni commisit dulcissimam matrem suam. Petro dedit claves regni sui, Iohanni reservavit arcana pectoris sui. Petrus ergo sublimior, sed Iohannes securior. Petrus licet in potestate constitutus, dicente Iesu, "*Unus ex vobis tradet me,*" cum caeteris timet et trepidat, Iohannes ex sinus sui participatione factus audacior, innuente Petro quisnam ille esset interrogat. Petrus ergo exponitur actioni, Iohannes reservatur affectui, quia "*Sic,*" inquit, "*eum volo manere, donec veniam.*" Exemplum enim dedit nobis, ut et nos ita faciamus. 118. Praestemus amico quidquid amoris est,

regard, no small discord has arisen among those who are considered friends, to the point that alienation follows indignation and curses follow alienation. Great caution therefore must be exercised with regard to authority and offices, especially ecclesiastical ones: the consideration should be not what you can confer, but what he on whom you confer it can bear. 116. Indeed, many should be loved who nevertheless should not be promoted, and we embrace many in a sweet and praiseworthy manner whom we may not involve in responsibilities and business without grave sin on our part and great danger on theirs. So reason, not affection, must always be followed in these situations, nor should a post and its burden be imposed on those with whom we are more friendly, but on those we believe better equipped to bear them. Yet when there is equality of virtue, I do not much disapprove if affection plays its part.

117. Nobody should say he has been despised because he was not promoted, since the Lord Jesus preferred Peter to John in this regard, nor did he thereby withdraw his affection from John because he had given Peter leadership. He commended his church to Peter and entrusted his dearest mother to John. He gave Peter the keys to his kingdom and revealed his heart's secrets to John. Therefore Peter was more exalted, but John more secure. Even though he had been appointed to power, when Jesus said, *"One of you will betray me,"* Peter was fearful and anxious along with the others, but John, made bolder from resting on Jesus's breast, at a nod from Peter asked who it was. Peter, then, was exposed to action, but John reserved for affection because Jesus said, *"I want him to remain so until I come."* He gave us an example so that we too should do likewise. 118. Let us offer a friend

quidquid gratiae, quidquid dulcedinis, quidquid caritatis. Futiles hos honores et onera illis quos praescripserit ratio imponamus, scientes quia numquam vere diligit amicum, cui amicus ipse non sufficit, nisi haec vilia et contemptibilia adiecerit. Cavendum autem magnopere est, ne tenerior affectus utilitates impediat maiores, dum eos quorum ampliori caritate complectimur, ubi magna spes fructus uberioris elucet, nec absentare volumus, nec onerare. Haec est enim amicitia ordinata, ut ratio regat affectum, nec tam quid illorum suavitas, quam quid multorum petat utilitas attendamus.

119. Recordor nunc duorum amicorum meorum, qui licet exempti praesentibus, mihi tamen vivunt semperque vivent. Quorum primum in initiis meae conversionis, quadam mihi morum similitudine et studiorum parilitate comparaveram, cum adhuc essem adolescens; alterum ab ipso fere pueritiae suae tempore a me electum, et multifarie multisque modis probatum, cum iam aetas mihi variaret capillos, in summam amicitiam assumpsi. Et illum quidem nullo adhuc curae pastoralis onere pressus, nulla rerum temporalium sollicitudine distentus, claustralium deliciarum et spiritalium dulcedinum, quibus tunc initiabar, socium consortemque delegeram, nihil exigens, nihil praestans praeter affectum, et ipsius affectus suave quoddam prout caritas dictabat indicium. Istum iam iuvenem in meae sollicitudinis partem ascitum, in his sudoribus meis habui coadiutorem. Inter utramque hanc amicitiam, memoria praeeunte discernens, video priorem

whatever love, graciousness, sweetness, and kindness we can. Let us impose meaningless posts and burdens on those whom reason dictates, in the knowledge that nobody truly loves a friend for whom the friend himself is only sufficient if he adds these cheap and contemptible distinctions. However, we must also be particularly careful that a more tender affection does not hinder the greater good through our unwillingness to send away or impose a burden on those we embrace with great love when hope for a more bountiful harvest is clear. For this is well-ordered friendship, that reason should rule affection and that we consider not so much what our friends' sweetness seeks as what the common good demands.

119. Now I recall two of my friends who, although delivered from the present life, are nevertheless alive for me and will always be alive. At the beginning of my conversion to religious life, when still a youth, I had joined the first of them with me owing to a certain likeness of character and similarity of interests; the other, chosen by me almost from the time of his boyhood and tested repeatedly in various ways, I admitted to full friendship when age was already turning my hair gray. Not yet weighed down by the burden of pastoral care or distracted by worry about temporal matters, I had chosen the former as my companion and partner in the delights of the cloister and the sweetness of spiritual pursuits into which I was then being initiated, asking nothing, offering nothing except affection and a certain gentle sign of affection itself as loving-kindness dictated. The latter, received when still young as a partner in my worries, was a helper in my labors. Distinguishing between these two friendships as memory permits, I see that the former relied

inniti magis affectui, alterum rationi, quamvis nec illi affectus defuerit, nec illum ratio deseruerit.

120. Denique prior in ipsis amicitiae nostrae principiis ereptus mihi eligi potuit, sicut praescripsimus, non probari. Alter, a puero usque ad mediam aetatem dimissus mihi, et a me dilectus, per omnes amicitiae gradus, quousque talium potuit imperfectio, mecum ascendit. Et primum quidem virtutum eius contemplatio illi meum inclinavit affectum, quem ego olim ab australibus partibus in aquilonalem hanc solitudinem duxi; ego regularibus disciplinis primus institui. Ex tunc ipse victor corporis, laboris etiam et inediae patiens, plurimis exemplo fuit, admirationi multis, mihi gloriae et delectationi. Et iam tunc eum in amicitiae principiis nutriendum putavit, utpote quem onerosum nulli, sed omnibus gratum intuebar. 121. Ingrediebatur et egrediebatur pergens ad imperium seniorum, humilis, mansuetus, gravis moribus, sermone rarus, indignationis nescius, murmuris et rancoris et detractionis ignarus; incedebat quasi surdus non audiens, et sicut mutus non aperiens os suum. Ut iumentum factus est, sequens obedientiae frenum, et iugum disciplinae regularis mente et corpore infatigabiliter portans. Ingressus aliquando adhuc puer cellam infirmorum, correptus est a sancto patre et praedecessore meo, quod tam cito puer se quieti inertiaeque dedisset. Sic erubuit, ut mox egressus, tam ferventer corporalibus se subderet exercitiis, ut multis annis nec cum gravi aegritudine urgeretur aliquid sibi de consueto rigore laxaverit.

more on affection, the latter on reason, although affection was not lacking in the second nor reason in the first.

120. In short, the first, snatched away from me at the very beginning of our friendship, could be chosen by me but not, as we have discussed above, tested. The second, having been entrusted to me and loved by me from boyhood to middle age, ascended all the steps of friendship with me as far as the imperfection of such people allowed. Indeed the contemplation of his virtues first inclined me to affection for him, whom I long ago brought from southern regions to this northern solitude. I first instructed him in monastic discipline. From that time, a conqueror over his body, enduring work and hunger, he was an example to very many, a wonder to many, a glory and delight to me. Already then I thought he should be nurtured in the principles of friendship, since I saw he was troublesome to no one but pleasing to all. 121. He came and went, carrying out the commands of his elders, humble, gentle, serious in manner, speaking rarely, not knowing indignation, a stranger to grumbling, rancor, and detraction; he went about as if deaf, not hearing, and as if dumb, not opening his mouth. He became like a beast of burden, heeding the reins of obedience and bearing the yoke of monastic disciple untiringly in mind and body. Having entered the infirmary once when still a boy, he was scolded by the holy father, my predecessor, for so quickly, as a boy, having given himself over to rest and idleness. He was so ashamed that, having left soon after, he subjected himself to bodily labors so fervently that for many years he did not relieve himself at all of his accustomed rigor even when beset by serious illness.

122. Haec eum mihi invisceraverant miris modis et ita in animum induxerant meum, ut mihi eum de inferiori socium, de socio amicum, de amico amicissimum facerem. Videns enim eum in quosdam canos virtutis et gratiae profecisse, fratrum usus consilio, onus ei subprioratus imposui. Quod quidem invitus, sed quia totum obedientiae sese devoverat, modeste suscepit. Egit tamen mecum multis secreto, ut dimitteretur, praetendens aetatem, praetendens inscitiam, praetendens amicitiam qua iam initiabamur, ne forte hac occasione vel minus diligeret, vel diligeretur minus. 123. Sed his omnibus nihil proficiens, coepit libera voce quidquid timebat utrisque, quidquid sibi in me minus placebat, humiliter et modeste proferre in medium—sperans, ut postea confessus est, hac me quasi praesumptione offensum, ad id posse quod petebat, facilius inclinari. Sed haec eius mentis vocisque libertas amicitiae nostrae cumulum addidit, quia volebam eum amicum habere non minimum. Cernens tunc ille me gratum habere quod dixerat, respondisse humiliter ad singula, satis dedisse de omnibus, se non modo nihil offensionis, sed insuper copiosiorem fructum percepisse, coepit me et ipse arctius solito diligere, habenas laxare affectui, et meo se pectori totum infundere. Ita et mihi eius libertas, et mea sibi probata patientia est.

124. Ego quoque vicem rependens amico, accepta occasione durius obiurgandum putavi, nec quibusdam quasi conviciis parcens, eum libertati meae nec impatientem

122. All this had wonderfully implanted him deep within me and so led him into my spirit that I turned him from an inferior into a companion, from a companion into a friend, and from a friend into my dearest friend. Seeing, as his hair turned gray, that he had progressed in virtue and grace, with the advice of the brothers I imposed on him the burden of the subprior's office. He was in fact unwilling, but because he had devoted himself entirely to obedience, he modestly accepted the burden. Yet he pressed me many times in private to be released, offering as excuses his age, inexperience, the friendship which we were already beginning, and that perhaps he would love less or be loved less on this account. 123. But getting nowhere with any of that, humbly and modestly he began to make public candidly what he feared for us both and what displeased him less in me—hoping, as he confessed afterward, that he could more easily bend me to do what he was asking if I were offended by this presumption. But this candor of mind and speech capped our friendship, because I wanted to have him as my friend no less. Then, perceiving that what he had said pleased me, that I had humbly replied about each of his concerns, that I had satisfied him in all matters, that not only had he occasioned no offense but furthermore had collected a more bountiful harvest, he began also to love me more deeply than before, giving free rein to affection and pouring his entire self into my heart. Thus his candor with me and my patience with him were tested.

124. I, too, repaying my friend in turn, thought that when the occasion presented itself I should reprimand him more severely, sparing no reproach, as it were, and discovered that he was neither impatient with my candor nor ungrateful.

reperi, nec ingratum. Coepi deinde consiliorum meorum ei revelare secreta, et fidelis inventus est. Ita inter nos amor crevit, concaluit affectus, caritas roborabatur, donec ad id ventum est, ut esset nobis *cor unum et anima una, idem velle* et *idem nolle,* essetque hic amor timoris vacuus, offensionis nescius, suspicione carens, adulationem exhorrens. 125. Nihil inter nos simulatum, fucatum nihil, nihil inhoneste blandum, nihil indecenter durum; circuitus nullus, nullus angulus, sed omnia nuda et aperta; qui meum pectus quodammodo suum putarem, et eius meum, ipseque similiter. Ita in amicitia recta linea gradientibus, nullius correptio indignationem, nullius consensio culpam pariebat. Unde se amicum in omnibus probans, meae paci, meae quantum poterat prospiciebat quieti. Ipse se periculis obiiciebat, scandalis emergentibus obviabat. 126. Volebam ei aliquando aliquid de his temporalibus, quia iam infirmabatur, praebere solatium, sed ille prohibebat cavendum dicens ne amor noster secundum hanc carnis consolationem metiretur, ne id magis carnali affectui meo quam eius necessitati ascriberetur, et sic mea auctoritas minueretur. Erat igitur quasi manus mea, quasi oculus meus, *baculus senectutis meae.* Ipse spiritus mei reclinatorium, dolorum meorum dulce solatium, cuius amoris sinus excipiebat laboribus fatigatum, cuius consilium recreabat tristitia vel moerore demersum. 127. Ipse commotum pacificabat, ipse leniebat iratum. Quidquid minus laetum emergebat, referebam ad eum, ut quod solus non poteram, iunctis humeris facilius sustinerem.

Quid ergo? Nonne quaedam beatitudinis portio fuit, sic

Next I began to reveal my secret plans to him, and he was found loyal. In this way love grew between us, affection glowed warmly, and kindness was strengthened until it came to the point that we had *one heart and one soul, wishing* and *not wishing the same things,* and this love was devoid of fear, unaware of offense, free from suspicion, and abhorring flattery. 125. Nothing between us was feigned, nothing falsified, nothing dishonorably pleasant, nothing unsuitably harsh; there was no evasion, no concealment, but everything was exposed and open. I thought my heart was somehow his, and his mine, and he thought likewise. As we thus advanced in friendship along a straight path, neither's correction gave rise to indignation, nor harmony to fault. Hence proving himself a friend in every respect, he looked after my peace and quiet as best he could. He exposed himself to dangers and nipped scandals in the bud. 126. Because he was already becoming infirm, at times I wanted to offer some relief from worldly concerns, but he forbade it, saying it was something to be avoided lest our love be measured according to fleshly comfort or such action be ascribed to my carnal affection, rather than to his need, and my authority be thereby diminished. Consequently he was like my hand, like my eye, *the staff of my old age.* He was a cushion for my spirit, a gentle comfort in my griefs, whose bosom of love received me when tired from my labors and whose advice refreshed me when sunk into sadness or mourning. 127. He calmed me when I was disturbed, soothed me when I was angry. Whatever unpleasantness emerged I referred to him, so that what I could not manage on my own I sustained more easily shoulder to shoulder with him.

What more to say, then? Was it not a share of blessedness

amare et sic amari, sic iuvare et sic iuvari, et sic ex fraternae caritatis dulcedine in illum sublimiorem dilectionis divinae splendorem altius evolare, et in scala caritatis nunc ad Christi ipsius amplexum conscendere, nunc ad amorem proximi ibi suaviter repausandum descendere? In hac igitur amicitia nostra quam exempli gratia inseruimus, si quid cernitis imitandum, ad vestrum id retorquete profectum.

128. Sed ut tandem collationem hanc nostram, vel sole ruente claudamus, ab amore profectam amicitiam non dubitatis. Qui vero semetipsum non amat, alium amare qui potest, cum ex similitudine amoris quo ipse sibi carus est, amorem proximi debeat ordinare? Se autem non diligit, qui turpe aliquid vel inhonestum, vel a se exigit, vel sibi impertit. 129. Primum igitur est ut semetipsum quisque castificet, nihil sibimet indulgens quod indecens sit, nihil sibi subtrahens quod utile sit. Sic vero se ipsum diligens, diligat et proximum, eamdem regulam sequens. Sed quia hic amor multos colligit, ex ipsis eligat quos ad amicitiae secreta lege familiari admittat, in quem suum copiose infundat affectum, denudans pectus suum usque ad inspectionem viscerum et medullarum, cogitationum et intentionum cordis.

130. Eligatur autem non secundum affectionis lasciviam, sed secundum rationis perspicaciam; similitudine morum et contemplatione virtutum. Deinde sic se impendat amico, ut levitas omnis absit, iucunditas assit, nec ordinata desint benevolentiae et caritatis officia vel obsequia. Iam exinde

so to love and be loved, so to help and be helped, and thus to soar higher, from the sweetness of fraternal charity to that more sublime splendor of divine love, and on the ladder of charity at one time ascend to the embrace of Christ himself, at another descend to the love of neighbor to rest sweetly there? Therefore, if you see anything to imitate in this friendship of ours that we have included by way of example, turn it to the advantage of your own spiritual progress.

128. But so we may at last, even as the sun is setting, bring our discussion to a close, you have no doubt that friendship proceeds from love. But can one who does not love himself love another, since he should regulate love of neighbor according to similarity with the love through which he is dear to himself? For one who either asks of himself or gives to himself anything shameful or dishonorable does not love himself. 129. First, then, each person should purify himself, indulging himself in nothing that may be unseemly, turning himself away from nothing that may be useful. Loving himself thus, he should also love his neighbor, following the same rule. But since this love gathers many together, he should choose from among them those he might admit to the mysteries of friendship under the laws of intimacy and into whom he might pour his affection abundantly, baring his breast for inspection of sinews and marrow, of the heart's thoughts and inclinations.

130. A friend should be chosen not according to the wantonness of affection but according to the insight of reason, with regard to likeness of character and contemplation of virtues. Next, he should so devote himself to his friend that all frivolity is absent and delight present and nor should well-ordered duties and services of goodwill and love be

probetur fides eius, probetur honestas, probetur patientia.
Accedat paulatim consiliorum communio, assiduitas pari-
lium studiorum, et quaedam conformatio vultuum. 131. Sic
enim conformari sibi debent amici, ut statim cum alter alterum viderit, etiam similitudo vultus unius in alterum trans-
fundatur; sive fuerit deiectus tristitia, sive iucunditate sere-
nus. Ita electus atque probatus, cum certum tibi fuerit, nihil
eum velle quod dedeceat, vel petere ab amico, vel praestare
rogatus, constiteritque tibi amicitiam eum virtutem, non
quaestum putare, adulationem fugere, detestari assentationem, inventusque fuerit liber cum discretione, patiens in
correptione, firmus et stabilis in dilectione, tunc illa spiritalis sentitur dulcedo, *quam bonum* scilicet *et quam iucundum*
habitare fratres in unum.

132. Quam utile tunc dolere pro invicem, laborare pro invicem, onera sua portare invicem, cum unusquisque pro altero semetipsum neglegere dulce habet, alterius voluntatem
suae praeferre, illius necessitati magis quam suae ipsius occurrere, adversis semet opponere et exponere. Interea quam
dulce habent conferre invicem, sua studia mutuo patefacere,
simul examinare omnia, et de omnibus in unam convenire
sententiam. 133. Accedit et pro invicem oratio, quae in amici
memoria—tanto efficacius, quanto affectuosius—ad Deum
emittitur, profluentibus lacrimis, quas vel timor excutit, vel
affectus elicit, vel dolor educit. Ita pro amico orans Christum, et pro amico volens exaudiri a Christo, ipsum diligenter et desideranter intendit. Cum subito et insensibiliter

lacking. From there, the friend's loyalty should be tested, his honesty tested, and his patience tested. Next, fellowship in plans, enthusiasm for the same pursuits, and a certain compatibility of expression should be added little by little. 131. Friends should be made so like each other so that as soon as one sees the other, even the expression of one is transferred to the other, whether it is downcast with sadness or serene with delight. Once he has thus been chosen and tested—when you are certain that he wants neither to seek anything shameful from you as a friend nor to provide it if asked, and it is clear to you that he thinks friendship virtue, not profit, that he shuns flattery and loathes sycophancy, and that he is found to be discreetly candid, patient under correction, firm and steadfast in love—then you will feel that spiritual sweetness, namely, *how good and pleasant it is for brothers to live in unity.*

132. How beneficial it is, then, to grieve for one another, to work for one another, to carry one another's burdens, while each thinks it sweet to disregard himself for the sake of the other, to prefer the other's will to his own, to attend to the other's needs rather than his own, to oppose and expose himself to adversity. Meanwhile, how sweet friends think it is to confer with one another, to disclose their interests in turn, to explore all matters together, and to reach the same opinion on all matters. 133. Then, too, there is prayer for one another sent forth to God in remembrance of a friend—the more lovingly, the more effectively—in a flood of tears that fear instigates, affection elicits, or grief draws forth. Thus one praying to Christ for a friend and wanting to be heard by Christ for a friend directs his attention to Christ with care and longing. When sometimes one affection sud-

aliquando affectus transiens in affectum, et quasi e vicino ipsius Christi dulcedinem tangens, incipit gustare quam dulcis est et sentire quam suavis est. 134. Ita a sancto illo amore quo amplectitur amicum, ad illum conscendens, quo amplectitur Christum, spiritalem amicitiae fructum pleno laetus ore carpebit, plenitudinem omnium expectans in futurum, quando timore sublato quo nunc pro invicem metuimus et solliciti sumus, omni adversitate depulsa, quam oportet nunc ut pro invicem sustineamus, mortis insuper aculeo cum ipsa morte destructo, cuius nunc punctionibus plerumque fatigati necesse est ut pro invicem doleamus, securitate concepta, de summi illius boni aeternitate gaudebimus, cum haec amicitia ad quam hic paucos admittimus transfundetur in omnes, et ab omnibus refundetur in Deum, cum Deus fuerit omnia in omnibus.

denly and imperceptibly crosses over into another, as if touching the sweetness of Christ himself from close by, the friend begins to taste how sweet and sense how delightful Christ is. 134. So rising from the holy love with which he embraces a friend to that with which he embraces Christ, he will joyfully pluck the spiritual fruit of friendship in his whole mouth, awaiting the abundance of all things in the future. When the dread with which we are now fearful and anxious for one another has been abolished, when all the adversity that we should now bear for one another has been removed, when, furthermore, the sting of death is destroyed along with death itself, by whose pricking pains it is necessary for us often to be tormented now in order to grieve for one another, then, once security is received, we will rejoice in the eternity of supreme goodness as that friendship to which we admit few in this life will be poured out over all and be poured back over God by all since God will be all in all.

A CERTAIN
MARVELOUS MIRACLE

Miracula Domini et manifesta divinae pietatis indicia scire et tegere portio sacrilegii est. Quod enim esse potest praesentibus ad consolationem, ad aedificationem posteris, omnibus ad devotionem, indignum est cunctorum notitiae deperire. Sed plerumque multorum nos terret ineptia, qui vel invidia tabescentes vel infidelitate languentes, de his quae bona sunt, vix de quoquam suis credunt oculis, ad credendum vero de quolibet ea quae mala sunt leni tactu aurium inducuntur. Hinc est quod rem mirabilem et nostris saeculis inauditam tibi potissimum, pater amantissime, credidi revelandam, cuius sancta simplicitas bene sentire de omnibus, de nullo absque certis indiciis sinistrum aliquid suspicari consuevit. Nulla sit de verborum veritate cunctatio, cum ea quae dicenda sunt ex parte propriis oculis viderim, omnia autem mihi tales personae retulerint quas nec aetatis maturitas nec spectata sanctitas ulla sinerent ratione mentiri.

1. Inter monasteria virginum quae vir venerabilis ac Deo dilectus, pater et presbyter Gillebertus, per diversas Angliae provincias miro fervore construxit, unum in provincia Eboracensi situm est, in loco qui aquis et paludibus saeptus ex re nomen accepit. Dicitur enim Wattun id est "umida villa." Qui quondam, ut refert in historia Anglorum venerabilis presbyter Beda, magno sanctarum mulierum pollebat examine, ubi et beatus pontifex Iohannes puellam ob incautam

To know and yet conceal the Lord's miracles and manifest signs of divine love is to commit a kind of sacrilege. It is shameful to keep secret from everyone what can be a consolation to the living, edification for posterity, and an inspiration to devotion for all. But usually we are frightened off by the folly of the many, those who, either wasting away in envy or languishing in lack of faith, scarcely believe anything good seen by their own eyes, yet are persuaded to believe evil about anything by a soft whisper in their ears. For this reason, most beloved father, I believed that a marvelous event totally unheard of in our times ought to be revealed to you above all, who, in your holy simplicity, are accustomed to think well of everyone and to suspect nothing sinister of anyone without certain proof. There should be no hesitation about the truth of my words, since I saw in part with my own eyes what must be recounted and furthermore, persons whose mature age and proven holiness do not allow them to lie reported it all to me.

1. Among the monasteries of virgins that the man venerable and beloved by God, the father and priest Gilbert, built with wondrous fervor in different provinces of England, one was located in the province of York. Surrounded by water and swamps, it took its name from its actual site, for it is called Watton, that is, "wet town." It once thronged with a great crowd of holy women, as the venerable priest Bede reported in his history of the English; there, too, the holy bishop John, with his health-giving touch and prayers cured

sanguinis diminutionem fere desperatam, salubri tactu et
oratione sanavit.

2   Quoniam igitur in eodem loco praedicti patris industria
renovatur antiqua religio, antiqua nihilominus miracula
renovantur. Ita quippe ibi Christi ancillae, inter cotidiana
manuum opera consuetudinemque psallendi, spiritalibus
mancipantur officiis ac caelestibus intersunt theoriis, ut
pleraeque, quasi valedicentes mundo et omnibus quae
mundi sunt, saepe in quosdam indicibiles rapiantur excessus
et angelicis videantur interesse choris. Crebra eis cum bonis
spiritibus confabulatio, a quibus nunc corripiuntur, nunc
erudiuntur, nunc de certis necessariisque praemuniuntur.
Tanta inter eas videtur dilectio, tanta pro invicem sollicitudo, ut cum una obierit, ceterae numquam cessent a precibus donec vel de poena eius vel de gloria certum eis aliquid
eluxerit. Inde est quod, non solum, ut fieri solet, in somnis,
sed et visibiliter carneis oculis, mortuae vivis appareant, et
nunc poenam, nunc gloriam quam singulae meruerunt exponant.

3   Contigit aliquando unam optimae apud omnes opinionis,
relicto corpore, ad caelestia commigrasse. Diligebatur ab
omnibus, sed ab una specialius colebatur. Instat precibus illa
ut ei virginis meritum divina pietas non celaret. Revoluto
anni circulo, dies depositionis eius anniversarius vertebatur.
Solitas orationes puella multiplicat. Accenditur desiderio,
ubertim lacrimis irroratur. Interim pro defunctae excessibus

a girl whose life was nearly despaired of owing to careless bloodletting.

Therefore, as the labor of the abovementioned Father 2 Gilbert is renewing ancient religious practice in that place, ancient miracles are likewise renewed. Here indeed the handmaids of Christ, amid their manual labor and customary psalm singing, are delivered up to spiritual offices and busy with heavenly contemplation to the point that many of them, as if saying farewell to the world and all things of the world, are often seized by certain indescribable raptures and seem to be among the choirs of angels. Among these nuns there are frequent conversations with good spirits, by whom they are in turn rebuked, instructed, and strengthened concerning what is certain and necessary. There is such affection among them, such care for one another, that when one dies, the others never cease from praying until some sure sign shines forth to them concerning either her punishment or her glory. That is why the dead sisters appear to the living—not only, as usually happens, in dreams, but also in a fashion visible to the eyes of the flesh—and lay out in turn the punishment or glory each of them has earned.

Once it happened that one of the best regarded among all 3 the nuns, after leaving her body, had journeyed to the heavenly realms. She was loved by all, but treasured especially by one of them. This nun devoted herself to prayer that divine love would not conceal the reward of the beloved virgin from her. After a year had passed, the anniversary of her death came around. The girl multiplied her customary prayers. She was enflamed by desire, abundantly drenched in tears. Meanwhile, the saving Host was made ready as an

immolanda salutaris hostia parabatur. Sacerdotes debitum officium prosequuntur. Conversa ad altare Christi, virgo desiderii sui praestolabatur effectum, cum ecce radius solis de superioribus ad inferiora demissus ante gradum altaris sese locavit. Intuetur diligentius illa, et mox virginem quam dilexerat nimio splendore coruscam ipsi radio conspicit insidere. Obstupuit et obriguit et, loquente spiritu, carnea lingua tacebat. Quia vero sopitis quodammodo sensibus corpus stabat immobile, accessum virginis, ut evidentius cerneretur, solo desiderio flagitabat. Mox radius solis, a loco quo substiterat elevatus, accessit propius et, ante faciem virginis stans, vultum quem concupierat amanti praebuit comminus contemplandum. Ita ineffabili perfusa gaudio, finem caelestis praestolabatur officii. Cum vero missa voce diaconi clauderetur, illa ad se, radius ad superiora revertitur. His extra propositum praemissis, ad ea quae praeposuimus enarranda transeamus.

2. Pontificante in ecclesia Eboracensi sanctae ac piae recordationis Henrico, puella quaedam quatuor ut putabatur annorum eiusdem sancti precibus patris in eodem monasterio suscipitur nutrienda. Quae mox ut infantilem excessit aetatem, cum puellaribus annis puellarem induit lasciviam. Nullus ei circa religionem amor, nulla circa ordinem sollicitudo, circa Dei timorem nullus affectus. Petulans illi oculus, sermo indecens, lascivus incessus. Incedebat sacro tecta velamine, sed nihil tali dignum habitu praetendebat in opere. Corripitur verbis sed non corrigitur; urgetur verberibus sed non emendatur. Furabatur magistrarum oculis horas ut vel

offering for the sins of the one who had died. The priests proceeded with the requisite service. Turned to the altar, the virgin of Christ was awaiting the fulfillment of her desire when behold, a ray of the sun sent down from above settled before the altar step. She stared intently at it, and immediately she saw the virgin she had loved shining in great splendor seated within the ray itself. Astonished, she stiffened and, as the spirit spoke, her human tongue fell silent. Because her body stood motionless, her senses somehow overcome by sleep, she was asking in her desire alone to approach the beloved virgin in order to see her more clearly. At once the ray of sun rose from where it had stood and came nearer and stopping before the virgin's face, it offered the one who loved her the face she had desired for contemplation near at hand. Suffused with indescribable joy, she awaited the end of the divine service. But when the Mass was ended by the voice of the deacon, she returned to herself, the ray to the heights. Having made a preface to our intended subject, let us proceed to what we think necessary to narrate.

2. When Henry of holy and pious memory was the archbishop of York, a certain girl thought to be about four years old was received to be raised in the monastery of Watton at the request of that same holy father. As soon as she had grown out of childhood, she put on girlish wantonness along with her adolescence. She had no love for religious life, no concern for order, no inclination to the fear of God. Her glance was insolent, her talk unseemly, her gait lewd. She walked about covered in a holy veil, but made no effort worthy of such garb. Reprimanded, she was not corrected; beaten, she was not reformed. Under the eyes of her teachers

indulgeret otio vel signis inordinatis difflueret aut vacaret fabulis aut inutile aliquid aliis suaderet. Disciplina ordinis premebatur et ad exterioris hominis honestatem utcumque servandam cogebatur invita. Omnia ei ex timore constabant, ex amore nihil. Et iam nubilis facta, interioribus exteriora, otiosa quietis, seriis ludicra praeponebat.

2   Accidit autem ut fratres monasterii quibus exteriorum commissa est cura quippiam operis facturi ingrederentur monasterium feminarum. Quod illa perpendens, accessit propius et curiosius ipsorum opera contemplabatur et vultus. Erat inter eos adulescens caeteris formosior facie et aetate viridior. Iniecit in illum oculos misera, ipse vero intendebat in eam. Aspiciunt se oculo blandiori et mox serpens tortuosus, utriusque pectus ingrediens, letiferum insibilat per cuncta vitalia virus.

3   Res primum nutibus agitur, sed nutus signa sequuntur. Tandem, rupto silentio, conserunt de amoris suavitate sermonem. Accendunt se mutuo, spargunt utrimque seminaria voluptatis, libidinis incentiva. Et ille stuprum meditabatur, illa—ut postea dicebat—de solo cogitabat amore. Interim coalescunt affectus, sed ut sibi liberius colloquerentur vel se fruerentur uberius, de loco vel tempore in unam coiere sententiam. Abicientibus itaque arma lucis, nox placebat obscurior; publicum fugitantibus, locus secretior gratus habetur. Dat signum praedae impiissimus praedo, ut ad sonitum lapidis quem vel in parietem vel tectum aedis in qua

she frittered away the hours—whether to indulge her lazi-
ness, or to let herself go in disorderly gestures, waste time in
stories, or encourage others to do some useless thing. She
was constrained by the discipline of the order and was
forced against her will to preserve the respectability of the
outer person at any cost. With her, everything was a matter
of fear, nothing a matter of love. Already now of nubile age,
she preferred the outer to the inner, idleness to quiet, frivolity to seriousness.

Now it happened that the brothers of the monastery to   2
whom care for exterior matters had been delegated entered
the women's monastery to do some work. Paying close attention, she went closer and considered the men's labor and
their faces with some curiosity. Among the men was a youth,
younger and handsomer than the others. The wretch fixed
her eyes on him, and he looked back at her. They made eyes
at one another and soon the crafty serpent, entering each
one's heart, whispered poisonous venom all through their
vitals.

It began with nods, but sign language followed. At last,   3
silence broken, they exchanged words about the sweetness
of love. They inflamed each other mutually, sowing seeds of
pleasure, lures of lust in both of them. His mind was on fornication, she—as she said afterward—was thinking only of
love. All the while their feelings took root, but so they might
converse more freely and enjoy one another more fully, they
came to an agreement about a place and time. Therefore,
having rejected the weapons of light, darker night pleased
them; fleeing public places, they thought a more secluded
spot attractive. The most impious predator gave a sign to his
prey: at the sound of a stone the wretched man promised he

pausare consuevit, infelix se iactaturum promisit, de eius adventu certissima egrederetur ad eum.

3. Ubi tunc, pater G[illebertus], tuus in custodia disciplinae vigilantissimus sensus? Ubi tot tam exquisita ad excludendam vitiorum materiam machinamenta? Ubi tunc illa tam prudens, tam cauta, tam perspicax cura, et circa singula ostia, fenestras, angulos tam fida custodia ut sinistris etiam spiritibus negari videretur accessus? Elusit totam industriam tuam, pater, una puella, quia *nisi Dominus custodierit civitatem, frustra vigilat qui custodit eam.* Fecistis, vir beate, fecisti quicquid potuit homo quoniam sic expediebat. Sed sicut *nemo potest corrigere quem Deus despexerit,* ita nemo potest servare quem non ille servaverit.

2   Et tu, infelix, quid agis? Quid cogitas? Quid tam intentae aures ad tegulas erigis? Ubi timor, ubi amor, ubi illius sanctae congregationis reverentia, ubi beati pontificis qui te huic monasterio tradidit suavis memoria? Nihil horum a tanto te revocat scelere. Deletis his omnibus, solus in corde turpis vivebat affectus. Surgis, misera, pergis ad ostium, conantem egredi divina vis repellit, temptas iterum sed nihil profecisti. Regressa modicum, beatae Virgini solitas vigilias cum duodecim lectionibus celebrasti. Quid ultra tibi facere debuit Christus et non fecit? O mira cordis excaecatio! Quid denuo moliris egressum? Ecce dimitteris instar Balaam, secundum desiderium cordis tui ut eas in adinventionibus tuis. Oportet te duci in Babilonem: ibi forte curaberis.

184

would throw onto either the wall or roof of the house where she usually stayed, she, completely certain he had arrived, would go out to him.

3. Where, then, Father Gilbert, was your most vigilant sense about safeguarding discipline? Where were your many carefully refined devices designed to prevent the opportunity for sin? Where then was your care, so prudent, cautious, and perspicacious, where was the faithful sentinel around every gate, window, and corner so that even evil spirits might seem to be denied access? One girl, Father, mocked all your efforts, because *unless the Lord guards the city, the watchman stays awake in vain.* You did what a man could do, blessed father, since it was useful to do so. But just as *no one can correct whom God has despised,* so nobody can save one whom he has not saved.

And you, unhappy one, what are you doing? What are you thinking? Why do you prick up your ears so attentively to the roof tiles? Where is fear, where is love, where is reverence for this holy community, where is the sweet memory of the blessed bishop who handed you over to this monastery? None of these restrain you from so great a crime. All that being wiped away, only shameful affection was alive in your heart. You rose, wretched girl, you went to the gate, divine will prevented your attempt to leave, you tried again but failed. Retreating for a little while, you celebrated the customary vigils of the Blessed Virgin with its twelve readings. What more should Christ have done for you that he did not do? Oh extraordinary blindness of the heart! Why did you attempt to leave again? Behold, you are forsaken, like Balaam, following your heart's desire and proceeding in subterfuge. You should be taken to Babylon: perhaps you will be cured there.

4. Quid plura? Heu, egreditur. Claudite aures, virgines Christi, oculos operite. Egreditur Christi virgo, adultera post modicum reditura. Egreditur et *quasi columba seducta non habens cor* mox accipitris excipitur unguibus. Prosternitur, os ne clamaret obstruitur, et prius mente corrupta, carne corrumpitur.

2 Experta voluptas nefas compulit iterare. Cum haec saepius agerentur, sorores, sonitum quem crebro audiebant admirantes, fraudem suspicabantur. Illa maxime patuit suspicioni, cuius mores omnibus solebant esse suspecti. Fuga etiam iuvenis suspicionem adauxit. Cum enim concepisse se adultero prodidisset, timens ne et ipse proderetur, relicto monasterio ad saeculum ire perrexit.

5. Tunc matronae sapientiores puellam conveniunt; illa ulterius celare non valens confitetur excessum. Stupor autem apprehendit omnes quae audiebant verbum. Exarsit mox zelus in ossibus earum et aspicientes se mutuo, complosis manibus irruunt super eam, extractoque ab eius capite velo, aliae tradendam flammis, aliae vivam excoriandam, aliae impositam stipiti suppositis carbonibus assandam putarunt. Fervorem adolescentium compescebant matronae. Attamen spoliatur, extenditur, etiam absque ulla miseratione flagellis atteritur. Praeparato ergastulo, vincitur, intruditur. Singulis pedibus duo anuli cum suis catenulis inducuntur, quibus duae non parvi ponderis catenae insertae, quarum una immani trunco clavis infigitur, altera per

4. What more? Alas, she went out. Close your ears, virgins of Christ, cover your eyes. She went out a virgin of Christ, soon to return an adulteress. She went out and *like a deluded, heartless dove*, she was immediately seized by the hawk's talons. She was thrown to the ground, gagged so she should not cry out and already corrupted in spirit, she was now corrupted in flesh.

The experience of pleasure drove her to repeat the wicked act. Since this was going on fairly often, the sisters, puzzled by the noise they heard repeatedly, suspected wrongdoing. She whose habits were customarily held suspect by all was especially open to suspicion. The young man's disappearance further increased their suspicion. For once she had revealed to the adulterer that she was pregnant, fearful that he too would be exposed, he left the monastery and went out into the world.

5. Then the wiser matrons summoned the girl; unable to conceal it any longer, she confessed her sin. All who heard what she said were stunned. Soon zeal burned in their bones and looking at each other, they attacked her with their fists and then, once the veil had been torn off her head, some thought she should be consigned to the flames, others that she should be skinned alive, and still others that she should be tied to a spit and roasted over hot coals. The matrons curbed the vehemence of the younger ones. Nevertheless, she was stripped, stretched out, and even whipped mercilessly. A prison readied, she was bound and thrust into it. Two shackles connected by short chains were fastened to each foot, and two heavy chains were attached, one nailed to a large log and the other, pulled outside the cell through a

foramen extracta foris sera concluditur. Sustentatur pane et aqua, cotidianis opprobriis saturatur.

2   Interea tumens uterus evolvit vel denudavit conceptum. O quantus tunc erat luctus omnium, quanta praecipue virginum lamenta sanctarum, quae suo timentes pudori unius crimen in omnibus metuunt impingendum, etiam quasi iam expositas se omnium oculis illudendas, quasi omnium traditas dentibus corrodendas sentirent. Flebant omnes, flebant singulae, nimioque dolere succensae iterum irruunt in captivam. Et nisi maturiores conceptui pepercissent, vix aliquando ab eius poena quiescerent. Illa universa haec mala sustinet patienter, maioribus se dignam clamat tormentis— credere se tamen ceteras pro eius infidelitate nihil mali passuras.

3   Deliberant quid de his agendum. Si expelleretur, in omnium hoc redundare infamiam, imminereque non parvum omnium animabus periculum si destituta solatio mater cum sobole mortis discrimen incurreret; si servaretur, partum non posse celari clamabant. Tunc una, "Optimum est," inquit, "ut nequissimo iuveni sua meretrix adulterino foetu gravida commendetur eiusque dimittatur curae cuius consensit nequitiae." Ad haec infelix: "Si hoc vobis poterit esse remedio—licet sciam hoc mihi futurum exitio—ecce adolescens nocte illa, hora illa, in loco nostrae iniquitatis conscio mihi sicut promisit occurret. Vestri tunc erit arbitrii me tradere illi. Sicut fuerit voluntas in caelo, sic fiat." Continuo rapiunt verbum de ore eius, iamiamque spirantes

hole, secured with a bolt. She lived on bread and water but was stuffed with daily scolding.

Meanwhile, her swelling belly disclosed and laid bare her 2 pregnancy. Oh, how great the grief of all, how great in particular the lamentation of the holy virgins who, fearing for their own honor, worried that the crime of one would be imputed to all, even feeling as if they were already exposed to mockery in the eyes of all, as if handed over to be gnawed by the teeth of all. They all wept, each one of them wept, and inflamed with excessive grief they once again attacked the prisoner. Had the older nuns not spared what she had conceived, they would hardly ever have ceased their punishment. She endured every abuse patiently, cried out that she deserved greater torture—although she did not believe the others would suffer any harm for her infidelity.

The nuns mulled over what to do. If she were banished, 3 the stigma would attach itself to all of them and threatened no small danger to their souls if the mother, deprived of comfort, suffered the danger of death along with her child; if she were kept there, they exclaimed, the birth could not be concealed. Then one of them said, "It is best that his whore, pregnant with his bastard, be handed over to that vilest of youths and left to the care of the one to whose wickedness she consented." She said unhappily, "If this could bring relief to you—although I know it would mean my ruin—I know that the young man will go, on a certain night and at a certain hour, to the place that shares knowledge of our sin, as he promised me. Then it will be your choice to surrender me to him. Let it be done according to heavenly will." Without hesitation they snatched the words from her mouth and now panting to take vengeance on the

ultionem in iuvenem, quaerunt ab ea de omnibus veritatem. Confitetur illa, affirmans vera esse quae dixerat.

6. Tunc magister congregationis, ascitis quibusdam e fratribus, rem aperit. Iubetque ut nocte illa, unus, tectus velamine caput, designato loco sederet, alios occulte praesentes adesse ut venientem exciperent attrectatumque fustibus vinctum tenerent. Dixit et factum est ita. Adolescens quid cum sua ageretur ignorans, non solum mente sed etiam habitu saecularis advenit. Et ardens libidine, mox ut velamen aspexit, *sicut equus et mulus quibus non est intellectus,* irruit in virum quem feminam esse putabat. At hi qui aderat, amarum ei cum baculis conficientes antidotum, conceptam febrem extinguunt.

2 Res defertur ad virgines. Mox quaedam, zelum Dei habentes etsi *non secundum scientiam,* ulcisci cupientes virginitatis iniuriam, petunt a fratribus iuvenem sibi per modicum tempus dimitti, quasi secretum aliquid ab eo cogniturae. Susceptus ab eis, prosternitur ac tenetur. Adducitur quasi ad spectaculum illa malorum omnium causa. Datur ei in manibus instrumentum ac propriis manibus virum abscidere invita compellitur. Tunc una de astantibus, arreptis quibus ille fuerat relevatus, sicut erant foeda sanguine, in ora peccatricis proiecit.

7. Vides quo zelo urebantur aemulatrices pudicitiae, insectatrices immunditiae, Christi prae omnibus amatrices. Vides quomodo istum mutilando, illam opprobriis et contumeliis insectando Christi ulciscuntur iniuriam. Ecce gladius

youth, asked her for the whole truth. She confessed, declaring that what she had said was true.

6. Then the master of the order, having called together some of the brothers, told them of the matter. He ordered as follows: that on the evening in question one of them, his head covered with a veil, would sit at the designated place with the others hidden so that they could grab the youth when he arrived, beat him with cudgels, and tie him up. It was done as he said. The youth, unaware of what was being done with her, worldly in both mind and clothing, approached. Burning with lust, as soon as he saw the veil, *like a horse or mule without understanding* he rushed upon the man he thought was a woman. Those who lay in wait, putting together a bitter remedy for him with their sticks, extinguished the fever he had contracted.

The situation was reported to the virgins. Immediately some of them, in zeal for God if *not according to knowledge*, desiring to avenge the insult to virginity, asked the brothers that the youth be released to them for a little while on the pretense that they were going to learn some secret from him. Once received by them, he was thrown down headlong and held fast. She, the cause of all these evils, was led forth as if to a spectacle. A tool was given to her and she was forced, unwillingly, to cut off his manhood with her own hands. Then one of the nuns standing by, seizing those parts of which the youth had been relieved, hurled them, fouled with blood as they were, in the sinner's face.

7. You see with what zeal they burn, these strivers after purity, persecutors of filthiness, lovers of Christ above all. You see how by mutilating him and subjecting her to assault and taunts, they avenge the injury to Christ. Behold the

Levi, aemulatio Simeonis, qui violatae castitatis ultores nec circumcisis putant esse parcendum. Ecce zelus Phinees sacerdotis, qui aeternum sacerdotium fornicantium nece promeruerit. Hic etiam sapientia Salomonis elucet, qui virginem Abisac ad concubitum postulantem in proprium fratrem mortis sententiam promulgavit. Non laudo factum sed zelum; nec probo sanguinis effusionem sed tantam contra turpitudinem sanctarum virginum aemulationem extollo. Quid non paterentur, quid non facerent pro castitate servanda, quae tanta potuerunt pro ulciscenda?

8. Sed ut ad propositum redeamus. Abscisus fratribus redditur, mulier in carcerem confusa retruditur. Hactenus, misera mulier, infelicitatis tuae historiam scripsimus. Deinceps quemadmodum super te Christi stillaverit misericordissima pietas stilo prosequamur, *ubi enim abundavit peccatum, superabundavit et gratia.*

2   Iam exacta ultione, tepescente zelo, ad Christi vestigia sacrae virgines provolvuntur. Plorant et orant ut loco parceret, verecundiae virginali consuleret, occurreret infamiae, periculum propulsaret. Et illae quidem cotidie precibus et lacrimis divinam clementiam provocabant. Peccatrix vero pia illa viscera Iesu doloribus et opprobriis contumeliis quoque quas patiebatur commovebat.

9. O bone Iesu, *qui omnipotentiam tuam parcendo maxime et miserando manifestas,* si te praesente quondam in carne, una misera mulier tanta afficeretur miseria, quid ageret illud pium pectus in quo sicut omnis sapientiae et scientiae, ita omnes thesauri misericordiae quieverunt? Audiant iusti *et exultent in conspectu Dei et delectentur in laetitia.* Audiant

sword of Levi, the eagerness of Simeon, who as avengers of violated chastity did not think the circumcised should be spared. Behold the zeal of the priest Phineas, who earned eternal priesthood through the slaying of fornicators. Here shines even the wisdom of Solomon, who pronounced a death sentence against his own brother for asking that the virgin Abishag be his concubine. I praise not the act but the zeal; I do not approve of the bloodshed but extol the striving of the holy virgins against such shameful behavior. What would they not endure, what would they not do to preserve chastity, these who could do such things to avenge it?

8. But let us return to the subject. The castrated youth was returned to the brothers, the dazed woman thrust back into her prison. Until now, wretched woman, we have written the story of your misfortune. Hereafter, let us follow with our pen how the most merciful love of Christ poured down on you, *for where sin flowed, grace too overflowed.*

Vengeance now exacted and their zeal for retribution cooling, the holy virgins prostrated themselves at Christ's feet. They wept and prayed that he spare the place, have regard for their virginal modesty, engage the infamy directly, ward off danger. And indeed, they called forth divine clemency with their daily prayers and tears. The sinner, too, moved the loving heart of Jesus with her misery and disgrace as well as the abuse she was suffering.

9. O good Jesus, *you who show your omnipotence most of all when you spare and take pity,* if when you were here in the flesh, a wretched woman was afflicted with such grief, what would that loving heart have done, the heart in which not only all treasures of wisdom and knowledge repose, but also those of mercy? Let the just hear *and exult in the sight of God*

peccatores ut numquam de illius bonitate desperent qui sic exercet iudicium ut non deserat misericordiam. Respexisti, bone Iesu, respexisti et tot ancillarum tuarum aemulationem et timorem et unius peccatricis tuae afflictionem.

10. Iam infans in ventre vivebat, lac ex uberibus ubertim fluebant, adeo etiam uterus intumescere videbatur ut putaret geminos paritura. Plumbeus color oculos circumfundit, faciem pallor invadit, et nunc vacuatis humore mamillis, post modicum solito liquore replebantur. Iam eam vix capiebat ergastulum, iam partui necessaria praeparantur. Cavent quantum possunt ne fletus infantis partum prodat.

2 Et ecce intempestae noctis silentio cum se misera sopori dedisset, videt in somnis assistere sibi pontificem per quem, ut praediximus, in eodem monasterio divinis est officiis mancipata, amictum pallio, et monachico habitu subinduto. Cumque severiori oculo aspiceret in eam, "Quid est," inquit, "quod me cotidie maledicis?" Negavit illa nimio timore perterrita. Tunc sanctus, "Verum est," ait, "cur negas?" Videns se deprehensam mulier respondit, "Vere, Domine, quia tu me huic monasterio tradidisti, in quo invenerunt me tanta mala." Ad haec antistes, "Tibi hoc potius imputato, quae peccata tua necdum ut oporteret patri spiritali propalasti. Sed vide ut quam citius poteris confitearis et hoc a me suscipiens in mandatis, ut hos psalmos cotidie Christo decantes." Et mox ei numerum et nomen psalmorum describens

and delight in happiness. Let sinners hear that they should never despair of the mercy of the one who carries out justice so as not to abandon mercy. You took care, good Jesus, you took care both for the zeal and fear of so many of your handmaids and for the suffering of one of your sinners.

10. The infant was already alive in her womb, milk flowed freely from her breasts, her belly too seemed to swell so much that she thought she was going to have twins. A leaden gray color encircled her eyes, paleness came over her face, and now, after her breasts had been emptied of fluid, they were shortly thereafter filled with the usual liquid. Now the prison cell could barely hold her, now the things necessary for birth were being made ready. They took the best care they could that the infant's cries would not give away the birth.

And behold, in the silence of the dead of night, when the wretch had gone to sleep, in a dream she saw standing next to her the bishop through whose efforts, as we said before, she had been given over to divine service in that same monastery. He was covered with the pallium worn over a monastic habit. And fixing her with a very stern look, he said, "Why is it that you curse me daily?" Overcome with utter terror, she denied it. The holy man said, "It is true: why do you deny it?" Seeing she was caught, the woman replied, "Truly, my lord, because you handed me over to this monastery in which such evils have come upon me." The bishop answered, "Blame yourself instead, you who have not yet divulged your sins to a spiritual father, as was necessary. But see that you confess as soon as possible and take it as a command from me to chant these psalms to Christ every day." Telling her the names and numbers of the psalms, he van-

disparuit. Evigilans illa et animaequior facta, visionem et psalmos commendat memoriae.

3   Sequenti vero nocte, cum iam putaretur paritura et amara videretur horae illius exspectatio—plus tamen timeretur ipsa partus editio—iterum venerabilis pontifex in somnis apparuit desperanti, duas secum adducens venusta facie mulieres. Accessit ad miseram praesul, et super genua sua capite eius supinato, pallio quo amiciebatur vultum operuit, increpans eam et dicens: "Si fuisses vera confessione purgata, cerneres manifeste ea quae aguntur. Nunc quidem senties beneficium, sed modum et qualitatem facti scire non poteris." Erecta post modicum videt mulieres infantem, ut sibi videbatur, candido coopertum linteo in ulnis ferentes, discedentem sequi pontificem. Expergefacta nihil ponderis sensit in ventre. Attrectat manu corpus et totum vacuum reperitur.

11. Mane autem facto, adsunt custodes, respicientesque in illam vident detumuisse uterum, vultum puellarem—ne dicam virginalem—induisse decorem, oculos perspicaces, plumbeum deposuisse colorem. Et mox quasi propriis non credentes oculis, "Quid est hoc?" inquiunt. "An tot sceleribus tuis et hoc addidisti ut tuum interficeres infantem?" Statimque angustum ergastulum illud in quo catenata sedebat evertunt. Nihil ibi latere pateretur angustia carceris, supellectilis vilitas, tenuitas stramentorum. "Et quid," inquiunt, "misera, num peperisti?" Ipsa se nescire respondit. "Et ubi est," aiunt, "infans tuus?" Respondit, "Nescio." Referensque

ished at once. Waking up and feeling calmer, she committed the vision and the psalms to memory.

On the following night, when she was thought about to give birth and the anticipation of that time seemed bitter— although the outcome of the birth was feared more—again the venerable bishop appeared in a dream to the despairing one, bringing with him two women with beautiful faces. The bishop approached her in her wretchedness, and with her head resting face up on his knees, he covered her face with the pallium he was wearing, scolding her and saying, "If you had been purified by a true confession, you would see clearly what is going on. Now, to be sure, you will experience the benefit, but you will not be able to know the means and nature of the deed." Standing up after a little while, she saw the women, as it seemed to her, carrying in their arms an infant wrapped in a white linen cloth, following the bishop as he departed. Awakened, she felt no heaviness in her belly. She touched her body with her hands and found it completely empty.

11. In the morning, the guards arrived and looking at her they saw that her womb had shrunk and that her face had taken on a pretty, girlish—not to say virginal—beauty, that her eyes were keen and had lost their leaden color. Now, as if not believing their own eyes, they asked, "What is this? Have you added to your many crimes the murder of your baby?" And immediately they ransacked the small prison cell where she sat in chains. But the cramped cell, cheap furnishings, and thin bedding allowed nothing to be hidden there. "What, you wretch?" they asked. "Did you give birth?" She replied that she did not know. "And where is your baby?" She answered, "I don't know." Recounting the

visionem, nihil amplius se scire professa est. Non credunt
rei novitate perterritae. Palpant uterum et ecce, tumori suc-
cesserat tanta gracilitas ut dorso ventrem adhaerere putares.
Temptant ubera, sed nihil humoris eliciunt ex eis. Nec tamen parcentes, premunt fortius, sed exprimunt nihil. Per
singulos artus currunt digiti, explorant omnia, sed nullum
signum partus, nullum conceptus indicium repererunt. Vo-
cantur aliae, et post illas aliae, et unum inveniunt omnes—
sana omnia, munda omnia, pulchra omnia—nihil tamen de-
cernere, nihil sine patris auctoritate iudicare praesumunt.

2   Adhuc tenetur in vinculis, adhuc circa pedes ferrum
durat, stridunt catenae. Duos divinae ministros clementiae
sibi advenisse conspexit et unus catenam qua artius stringe-
batur arrepta socio comitante discessit. Sorores vero adver-
tentes mane deesse catenam mirantur, causam inquirunt,
audiunt, sed parum credentes scrutatae sunt omnem supel-
lectilem eius sed nihil inveniunt. Paulo post inveniunt de
eius pedibus unum de vinculis cecidisse. Quod invenientes
integrum et in ea firmitate qua fuerat fabrilibus instrumentis pedibus eius innexum, admiratae sunt valde. Sed
quid multis morer? Eodem ordine a ceteris absoluta, pes
tantum unus uno compede tenebatur.

12. Interea sanctus pater adveniens, cum evidentibus signis ac veracissimis testibus omnia didicisset, sicut est mirae
humilitatis homo, meam parvitatem de his omnibus credidit consulendam. Veniens igitur ad nostrum monasterium,

vision, she declared that she knew nothing else. They did not believe because they were utterly terrified by the strange occurrence. They touched her womb and, behold! Such slenderness had replaced the swelling that you would have thought her belly was stuck to her back. They felt her breasts, but drew no liquid of out them. Still not sparing her, they pressed harder, but squeezed nothing out. They ran their fingers over each limb, they explored everything, but they discovered no sign of birth, no indication of pregnancy. Others were summoned, and still more after them, and everyone found one thing—all was healthy, clean, beautiful—yet they presumed to decide nothing, to judge nothing, without the authority of the father.

She was still tied down, still endured the iron around her feet. The chains creaked. She saw two ministers of divine mercy had come to her, one cutting off the chain with which she was tightly bound and departing with his companion. In the morning, the sisters were amazed when they noticed that the chain was gone. They asked why, heard why, but hardly believing it searched all the furnishings and found nothing. A little later, they discovered that one of the shackles had fallen from her feet. Finding it whole, and just as strong as it had been when fastened to her feet with iron-makers' tools, they were most astonished. But why delay in much detail? She was released in the same way from the other restraints, with only one foot still bound in a shackle.

12. Meanwhile, the holy father arrived and once he had learned everything from evident signs and utterly trustworthy witnesses, as the man of wondrous humility he is, he believed that my insignificant self should be consulted about it all. Therefore, coming to our monastery, when Christ's

servus Christi, cum mihi aperuisset secreto miraculum,
rogat ut ancillis Christi meam non negarem praesentiam.
Libens annui. Cum vero tam me quam itineris mei socios
humanissime ac iucundissime suscepisset, imus ad cubiculum illud intra cubiculum ubi illa in suo antro sedebat inclusa. Adsunt plures tam virgines quam viduae aevo iam
graves, sapientia et discretione pollentes, spectabiles sancti-
tate et in regularibus disciplinis multum exercitatae. Quae
cum omnia nobis retulissent, coepi compedem propriis manibus attrectare intellixique quod nec ab aliis nec ab ista
sine Dei virtute posset absolvi. Quaedam autem, necdum
timore deposito, quaesierunt a nobis si alia ei vincula
deberent imponi. Prohibui, importunum hoc asserens et
quoddam infidelitatis indicium. Expectandum potius et
sperandum quod is qui eam liberavit ab aliis ab hoc quoque
quo adhuc tenetur eripiet.

13. Patre praeterea praecipiente, relata sunt nobis multa
aeterna memoria digna, quibus manifeste datur intelligi quia
beneplacitum est Domino super timentes eum etiam in eis qui
sperant super misericordia eius. Itaque commendantes nos
sanctis orationibus earum et eas prout potuimus verbo Domini consolantes, ad nostrum monasterium regressi sumus,
laudantes et glorificantes Dominum in omnibus quae audivimus
et vidimus et sanctae virgines narraverunt nobis.

2   Post paucos dies allatae sunt nobis viri illius venerabilis
litterae quibus significavit nobis illum quo eam invenimus
vinctam compedem cecidisse et quid facto deinceps opus
esset meam indignitatem consuluit. Ego vero inter alia haec

servant had revealed the miracle to me in private, he asked that I not deny my presence to Christ's handmaids. I was glad to agree. When he had received both me and my traveling companions most kindly and pleasantly, we went to the cell within the cell where the prisoner sat confined in her cave. Many were present, both virgins and widows already advanced in age, mighty in wisdom and judgment, remarkable for their holiness and long experienced in monastic discipline. When they had reported everything to us, I began to touch the shackle with my own hands and I understood that it could have been released neither by others nor by her without the power of God. Some of the nuns, however, their fear not yet quelled, asked us if other chains should be placed on her. I forbade this, declaring that it was presumptuous and would indicate a lack of faith. Instead, they should wait and hope that he who freed her from the other irons would also rescue her from the one in which she was still held fast.

13. Meanwhile, at the father's instruction, many things worthy of eternal memory were recounted to us, through which it is clearly possible to understand that *the Lord is pleased with those who fear him and even with those who hope in his mercy.* Therefore, commending ourselves to their holy prayers and comforting them as best we could with the word of the Lord, we returned to our monastery, *praising and glorifying the Lord for everything* we heard and saw and the holy virgins told us.

A few days later, a letter from this venerable man was delivered to us in which he told us that the shackle with which we found her bound had fallen off and he consulted my unworthy self about what should be done next. Among other

2

pauca verba rescripsi: "*Quod Deus mundavit tu ne commune dixeris* et quam ipse absolvit tu ne ligaveris."

3 Haec ideo tibi, carissimo meo longe ab his partibus remoto, maxime scribendum putavi, ut et invidis occasionem tollerem et tamen Christi gloriam non tacerem. Vale.

EXPLICIT QUODDAM MIRACULUM MIRABILE
DESCRIPTUM A VIRO VENERABILI
ÆTHELREDO ABBATE RIEVALLIS DE QUADAM
SANCTIMONIALI FEMINA DE WATTUN.

things, I wrote these few words: "*What God has cleansed you should not call common* and the one whom he has loosed you should not bind."

Therefore, my dearest friend, far away from these parts, I ³ thought that I should write about these things to you especially, to deprive the envious of an opportunity and yet not pass over Christ's glory in silence. Farewell.

HERE ENDS A CERTAIN MARVELOUS MIRACLE
DESCRIBED BY THE VENERABLE MAN
AELRED, ABBOT OF RIEVAULX,
CONCERNING A CERTAIN NUN OF WATTON.

TEACHINGS FOR
RECLUSES

Iam pluribus annis exigis a me, soror, ut secundum modum vivendi quem arripuisti pro Christo certam tibi formulam tradam, ad quam et mores tuos dirigere et necessaria religioni possis exercitia ordinare. Utinam a sapentiore id peteres et impetrares, qui non coniectura qualibet, sed experientia didicisset quod alios doceret! Ego certe qui tibi et carne et spiritu frater sum, quoniam non possum negare quidquid iniungis, faciam quod hortaris, et ex diversis patrum institutis aliqua quae tibi necessaria videntur excerpens ad componendum exterioris hominis statum, certam tibi regulam tradere curabo, pro loco et tempore quaedam adiciens et spiritualia corporalibus, ubi utile visum fuerit, interserens.

2. Primum igitur oportet te scire qua causa, quave ratione huiusmodi vita ab antiquis vel instituta sit vel usurpata. Sunt quidam quibus inter multos vivere perniciosum est. Sunt et alii quibus etsi non perniciosum, est tamen dispendiosum. Sunt et nonnulli quibus nihil horum timendum est, sed secretius habitare magis aestimant fructuosum. Itaque antiqui—vel ut vitarent periculum, vel ne paterentur dispendium, vel ut liberius ad Christi anhelarent et suspirarent amplexum—singulariter vivere delegerunt. Hinc est quod plures in eremo soli sedebant, vitam manuum suarum opere sustentantes. Illi vero qui nec hoc sibi securum propter

For many years now, sister, you have been asking me to send you a reliable guide to the way of life you have taken up for Christ, according to which you can both direct your moral conduct and arrange the practices necessary to religious life. How I wish that you would seek and obtain advice from one wiser than I, someone who could teach others what he had learned not through mere guesswork but from experience! But seeing that I am indeed your brother in flesh and spirit, I cannot refuse any task you impose and I will do what you urge. I will undertake to send you a reliable rule, selecting from various teachings of the fathers some things that seem necessary for you to mold the outer person, adding details suited to place and time, and interspersing spiritual matters with corporeal where it seems useful.

2. First, you ought to know the cause or the reason this sort of life was established and adopted by the ancients. There are some for whom it is deadly to live among many. There are others for whom, although not deadly, it is still harmful. And there are still others who have neither of these to fear, but who consider it more advantageous to live in greater seclusion. So the ancients—either to avoid danger, or so as not to suffer harm, or to pant and sigh for Christ's embrace more freely—chose to live by themselves. Consequently, many settled in the wilderness alone, surviving by the labor of their own hands. But those who thought this

solitudinis libertatem et vagandi potestatem arbitrabantur includi potius et infra cellulam obstruso exitu contineri tutius aestimabant. Quod et tibi visum fuit, cum te huic institutioni voveres.

2 Sed multi, rationem huius ordinis vel ignorantes vel non curantes, membra tantum intra parietes cohibere satis esse putant, cum mens non solum pervagatione dissolvatur, curis et sollicitudinibus dissipetur, immundis etiam et illicitis desideriis agitetur, sed etiam lingua tota die per vicos et civitates, per fora et nundinas, per vitas et mores et opera hominum, non solum inutilia, sed etiam turpia curiose discurrat.

3 Vix aliquam inclusarum huius temporis solam invenies ante cuius fenestram non anus garrula vel rumigerula mulier sedeat, quae eam fabulis occupet, rumoribus aut detractionibus pascat, illius vel illius monachi, vel clerici, vel alterius cuiuslibet ordinis viri formam, vultum moresque describat. Illecebrosa quaeque interserat et puellarum lasciviam, viduarum quibus licet quidquid libet libertatem, coniugum in viris fallendis explendisque voluptatibus astutiam depingat. Os interea in risus cachinnosque dissolvitur, et venenum cum suavitate bibitum per viscera membraque diffunditur. Sic cum discedere ab invicem hora compulerit, inclusa voluptatibus, anus cibariis onerata recedit. Reddita quieti misera, eas quas auditus induxerat in corde versat imagines et ignem praemissa confabulatione conceptum vehementius

was not safe for them, because of the freedom of isolation and the opportunity for wandering, considered it much safer to be shut in and confined to a small cell with its exit blocked. So it seemed to you also when you devoted yourself to this way of life.

But many, either ignorant of or disregarding the rationale 2 for this arrangement, consider it enough merely to restrain the body within walls. Meanwhile, not only is the mind freed up for wandering, distracted in cares and concerns, and disturbed as well by unclean and illicit desires, but in addition the tongue roams inquisitively all day long through villages and towns, through squares and marketplaces, through people's lives and behavior and activities—not only the worthless, but also the disgraceful.

These days, you hardly find a single recluse before whose 3 window there sits no chattering old woman or rumormonger distracting her with idle talk, feeding her with scandal and slander, describing the appearance, face, and conduct of this or that monk or cleric or man of any other sort. She weaves in every sort of enticement, describing the lewdness of girls, the freedom of widows who can do whatever they like, and the cunning of wives who deceive their husbands and satisfy their desires. Meanwhile the recluse's face dissolves in laughter and guffawing, and poison drunk down with sweetness spreads through her entire body. Thus, when the hour demands that they part from each other, the recluse withdraws weighed down with pleasures, the old woman with food. The wretched recluse, returned to quiet, turns over in her heart the mental images provoked by what she has heard, and with her musings stokes more fiercely the fire lit by the conversation that passed between them. As if

sua cogitatione succendit. Quasi in psalmis ebria titubat, in lectione caligat, fluctuat in oratione.

4   Refusa mundo luce, citantur mulierculae et addentes nova veteribus, non cessant donec captivam libidinis daemonibus illudendam exponant. Nam manifestior sermo, non iam de accendenda sed potius de satianda voluptate procedens, ubi et quando et per quem possit explere quae cogitat in commune disponunt. Cella vertitur in prostibulum et, dilatato qualibet arte foramine, aut illa egreditur aut adulter ingreditur. Infelicitas haec, ut saepe probatum est, pluribus tam viris quam feminis in hoc nostro saeculo communis est.

3. Sunt aliae quae, licet turpia quaeque declinent, loquaces tamen loquacibus associantur, animum curiositati, linguam et aures tota die otio rumoribusque dedentes. Aliae non multum ista curantes, quod fere vitium per omnes huius temporis serpit inclusas, pecuniae congregandae vel multiplicandis pecoribus inhiant, tantaque cura ac sollicitudine in his extenduntur, ut eas matres vel dominas familiarum aestimes, non anachoritas. Quaerunt animalibus pascua, pastores qui custodiant procurant, annui fructus vel pretium, vel pondus, vel numerum a custodibus expetunt. Sequitur emptio et venditio, ut nummus appositus nummo cumulum erigat et avaritiae sitim accendat. Fallit enim tales spiritus nequam pro impertiendis eleemosynis vel orphanis alendis, pro advenientium parentum vel amicorum caritate et religiosarum feminarum susceptione hoc utile esse ac necessarium suadens.

drunk, she staggers through psalms, is hazy in reading, stumbles in prayer.

When light pours back at dawn, gossips are summoned, 4 and adding new material to the old, they do not cease until they have left the recluse a captive of lust exposed to the deceptions of demons. As franker talk proceeds, now meant not to enflame desire but rather to satisfy it, they plot together where, how, and through whom the recluse can carry out what she has in mind. The cell becomes a brothel, and with its opening expanded by some artifice or other, either she goes out or a lover comes in. This disgrace, as has been frequently demonstrated, is common in our times to many recluses, men and women alike.

3. There are other recluses who, although they shun all wicked deeds, are nonetheless chatterboxes who associate constantly with other chatterboxes, surrendering their minds to prying, their tongues and ears to idleness and gossip all day long. Others, paying little attention to such matters (this vice slithers into nearly all recluses these days), are avid to accumulate money and increase their flocks, and devote themselves to these matters with such care and concern that you would reckon them mothers or mistresses of a household, not anchorites. They seek pastures for their flocks, procure shepherds to watch over them, inquire of their stewards about price, weight, and the amount of annual profit. Next come buying and selling, with the result that coin piled on coin builds up a heap and intensifies the thirst of greed. An evil spirit deludes such women, persuading them that this is useful and necessary for giving alms and feeding orphans, helping out when relatives or friends arrive, and receiving religious women.

2   Non est hoc tuum, ad quam magis pertinet ut pauper cum pauperibus stipem accipias quam, relictis omnibus tuis pro Christo, aliena quaerere ut eroges. Magnae infidelitatis signum est si inclusa de crastino sollicita sit, cum Dominus dicat: *"Primum quaerite regnum Dei, et omnia adicientur vobis."*

4. Quapropter providendum est ut mens omnium rerum temporalium cura exuatur et exoneretur sollicitudine. Quod ut fiat, provideat inclusa ut (si fieri potest) de labore manuum suarum vivat: hoc enim perfectius. Si vero aut infirmitas aut teneritudo non permittit, antequam includatur certas personas quaerat, a quibus singulis diebus quod uni diei sufficiat humiliter recipiat, nec causa pauperum vel hospitum quidquam adiciat. Non circa cellulam eius pauperes clament, non orphani plorent, non vidua lamentetur.

2   "Sed quis hoc," inquis, "poterit prohibere?"

3   Tu sede! Tu tace! Tu sustine! Mox ut scierent te nihil habere, se nihil recepturos, vel fatigati discedent.

4   "Inhumanum hoc!" clamas.

5   Certe si praeter necessarium victum et vestitum aliquid habes, monacha non es. Quid ergo erogabis? Praecipitur tamen inclusae, ut quidquid de labore manuum suarum victui superfuerit, mittat cuilibet fideli, qui pauperibus eroget. Nolo ut insidiatrix pudicitiae, vetula mixta pauperibus accedat propius, deferat ab aliquo monachorum vel clericorum eulogias, non blanda verba in aure susurret, ne pro accepta eleemosyna osculans manum venenum insibilet.

This is not your way. For you it is more suitable to accept 2 a mite as one who is poor among the poor rather than to seek the property of others in order to give alms, since you have renounced all your worldly goods for Christ. It is a sign of great infidelity if a recluse is worried about tomorrow, since the Lord says, "*First seek the kingdom of God, and all things will be given to you.*"

4. Therefore you must take care that the mind is freed from attention to any temporal matters and relieved of worry. To accomplish this, the recluse should if possible see to it that she lives by her own manual labor: this is more perfect. But if illness or youth do not allow it, before she is enclosed she should seek out certain people from whom she may humbly receive every day what suffices for one day, nor should she add anything for the poor or guests. The poor should not cry out around her little cell, nor orphans wail, nor widows lament.

"But who," you ask, "can prevent this?" 2

Sit still! Be silent! Hold firm! As soon as they know that 3 you have nothing, that they will get nothing, even if exhausted, they will depart.

"This is inhuman!" you cry. 4

Surely you are not a nun if you have any more food and 5 clothing than necessary. So what will you give away? All the same, the recluse is instructed that any extra food remaining from her manual labor should be given to some faithful person who will distribute it to the poor. I do not want a way-layer of chastity in the form of an old woman mixed in with the poor to approach the recluse, bringing gifts from some monk or cleric, murmuring flattery into her ear and, while kissing her hand for the alms received, stealthily whispering poison into her ears.

6 Cavendum praeterea est ut nec ob susceptionem religiosarum feminarum quodlibet hospitalitatis onus inclusa suscipiat, nam inter bonas plerumque etiam pessimae veniunt, quae ante inclusae fenestram discumbentes, praemissis valde paucis de religione sermonibus, ad secularia devolvuntur. Inde subtexere amatoria et fere totam noctem insomnem ducere. Cave tu tales, ne cogaris audire quod nolis, videre quod horreas. Forte enim videbuntur amara cum audiuntur vel cernuntur quae postea sentiuntur dulcia cum cogitantur. Si scandalum times eo quod nec pauperibus erogas nec suscipis hospites, cum omnes tuam nuditatem propositumque didicerint, non erit qui reprehendat.

7 Si vero nec pro pauperibus nec pro hospitibus te velim pecuniosam esse, multo utique minus occasione grandioris familiae. Itaque eligatur tibi anus aliqua—non garrula, non litigiosa, non vaga, non rumigerula, sed quae bonos mores excoluerit, et ab omnibus habuerit testimonium sanctitatis. Haec ostium cellae custodiat, et quos debuerit vel admittat vel repellat. Haec quae ad victum necessaria sunt recipiat vel conservet. Habeat sub cura sua fortiorem ad onera sustinenda puellam, quae aquam et ligna comportet, coquat fabas et olera, aut si hoc infirmitas exegerit, praeparet potiora. Haec sub magna disciplina custodiatur ne forte eius lascivia tuum sanctum habitaculum polluatur et ita nomen Domini et tuum propositum blasphemetur.

8 Pueris et puellis nullum ad te concedas accessum. Sunt quaedam inclusae quae docendis puellis occupantur et

Furthermore, the recluse must be wary of taking on any 6
obligation to offer other religious women hospitality, since
often among the good many of the worst appear. Sitting
down in front of the recluse's window, after uttering only a
pious word or two they degenerate into worldly talk. Then
they weave in love stories and pass almost the whole night
without sleep. Be on your guard against such women, so you
are not forced to hear something you do not want to hear,
see something that makes you shudder. It is possible that
what seems bitter when first heard or seen will later, when
mulled over, seem sweet. If you fear scandal because you
neither give alms to the poor nor receive guests, know that
when everyone learns of your nakedness and your chosen
way of life, nobody will criticize.

But if I wish that you not be well supplied with money for 7
the poor or guests, so much less for the sake of a large household. So you should choose some old woman who is not
talkative, quarrelsome, a wanderer, or a gossip, but one who
has cultivated good habits and to whose good character all
testify. Let her keep watch over the door of your cell and either admit or turn away visitors as she ought. It is she who
should receive and keep what is necessary for eating. She
should have under her supervision a girl strong enough to
lift heavy loads, fetch water and wood, cook beans and vegetables, and, if illness necessitates, prepare more nourishing
food. This girl should be kept under strict discipline so that
her lustfulness does not accidentally defile your holy little
dwelling and thereby profane the name of the Lord and your
way of life.

You should allow boys and girls no access to you. There 8
are some recluses who busy themselves teaching girls and

cellam suam vertunt in scholam. Illa sedet ad fenestram, istae in porticu resident. Illa intuetur singulas, et inter puellares motus nunc irascitur, nunc ridet, nunc minatur, nunc blanditur, nunc percutit, nunc osculatur, nunc flentem pro verbere vocat propius, palpat faciem, stringit collum, et in amplexum ruens nunc filiam vocat, nunc amicam. Qualis inter haec memoria Dei, ubi secularia et carnalia, etsi non perficiantur, moventur tamen, et quasi sub oculis depinguntur?

9   Tibi itaque duae illae sufficiant et ad colloquium et ad obsequium.

5. Silentii gravitatem inclusae servandam praecipue suademus. Est enim in ea quies magna et fructus multus. Nam *cultus iustitiae silentium,* et sicut ait Ieremias, *"Bonum est cum silentio exspectare salutare Dei"* et iterum, *"Bonum est viro cum portaverit iugum, ut sedeat solus et taceat."* Unde scriptum est, "Audi, Israel, et tace." Fac ergo quod ait propheta: *"Dixi, custodiam vias meas ut non delinquam in lingua mea; posui ori meo custodiam."* Sic inclusa timens casum linguae, quam secundum apostolum Iacobum *nemo hominum domare potest,* ponat custodiam ori suo, sola sedeat, et taceat ore ut spiritu loquatur et credat se non esse solam quando sola est. Tunc enim cum Christo est, qui non dignatur in turbis esse cum ea.

2   Sedeat ergo sola, taceat, Christum audiens, et cum Christo loquens. Ponat custodiam ori suo, primum ut raro

turn their cells into schools. She sits at the window, they on the porch. She watches each one, and amid their girlish antics at one moment she is angry, at another she smiles, one moment she threatens, at another she wheedles, one moment she slaps, at another she kisses, and at still another she calls closer to her one weeping from a slap, caresses her face, strokes her neck, and rushes to embrace her, calling her first daughter, then friend. What sort of mindfulness of God is there amid all this, where worldliness and carnality, even if they are not acted upon, are still stimulated and sketched, so to speak, before the eyes?

These two women, then, should be sufficient to you for 9 both conversation and service.

5. We particularly urge the recluse to keep strict silence. For to be sure there is great peace and great profit in it. For *silence is the cultivation of justice,* and as Jeremiah says, "*It is good to wait in silence for God's salvation*" and again, "*It is good for a man when he bears the yoke, so that he should sit alone and be silent.*" And so it is written, "Hear, O Israel, and be silent." Therefore, do what the prophet says: "*I have said I will keep watch over my ways so I do not sin with my tongue; I have set a guard at my mouth.*" Likewise, the recluse, fearing the tongue's danger that according to the apostle James *no man can overcome,* should set a guard at her mouth, sit alone, and keep silent with the mouth so that she may speak in her spirit. She should believe she is not alone when she is alone. For then, in fact, she is with Christ, who does not think it fitting to be with her in a crowd.

Therefore, she should sit alone and be silent, listening to 2 Christ and speaking with Christ. She should set a guard on her mouth, and pay attention first to speaking rarely, then to

loquatur, deinde quid loquatur, postremo quibus et quomodo loquatur attendat. "Raro loquatur," id est certis et
constitutis horis de quibus postea dicemus; "quid loquatur,"
id est de necessitate corporis vel animae aedificatione; "quibus loquatur," id est certis personis, et quales ei fuerint de-
signatae; "quomodo loquatur," id est humiliter, moderate,
non alta voce, nec dura, nec blanda, nec mixta risu. Nam si
hoc ad quemlibet virum honestum pertinet, quanto magis
ad feminam, quanto magis ad virginem, quanto magis ad in-
clusam?

3   Sede itaque, soror mea, et tace, et si compelleris loqui,
parum loquere, humiliter, et modeste, sive de corporalium
rerum necessitate, sive de animae salute sermo incubuerit.

6. Iam nunc personas quibus loqui debet designemus. Felix illa quae nec Martinum admisit, nullum virorum nec
videre volens, nec alloqui. Sed quaenam inclusarum hoc sequeretur exemplum? Sufficiunt illis quae modo sunt si hanc
corporalem castitatem conservent, si non onusto ventre ex-
trahantur, si non fletus infantis partum prodiderit. Quibus
quia perpetuum cum viris indicere non possumus silentium,
cum quibus honestius loqui possint videamus.

2   Igitur si fieri potest, provideatur in vicino monasterio vel
ecclesia presbyter aliquis senex, maturis moribus et bonae
opinionis, cui raro de confessione et de animae aedificatione
loquatur, a quo consilium accipiat in dubiis, in tristibus consolationem. Verum quia inclusum membris malum illud
quod timemus plerumque suscitat et emollit emortuam
senectutem, nec ipsi manum suam tangendam praebeat
vel palpandam. Nulla vobis de macie vultus, de exilitate

what she discusses, and finally to whom and how she speaks. "Speaking rarely" means at certain, fixed times that we will discuss later; "what she discusses" includes only bodily needs and the edification of the soul; "to whom she speaks" should be only to certain people of the sort designated for her; "how she speaks" should be humbly, with restraint, not in a loud, strident, or ingratiating voice, nor one mingled with laughter. For if this behavior is appropriate to any honorable man, how much more so is it for a woman, how much more for a virgin, how much more for a recluse?

So, my sister, sit and be silent, and if you are compelled to 3 speak, speak little, humbly, and modestly, whether your words concern bodily needs or salvation of the soul.

6. Now then, let us designate the people to whom the recluse ought to speak. Blessed is she who did not welcome even Saint Martin, wishing neither to see nor to speak to any man. But what recluse would ever follow this example? It suffices women of these times if they preserve their bodily chastity, if they are not dragged out of their cells with wombs laden, if the wailing of an infant does not betray a birth. Since we cannot impose on them a complete prohibition on conversation with men, let us see with whom recluses can speak honorably.

If possible, therefore, let some elderly priest from a 2 nearby monastery or church, of mature conduct and good reputation, be provided. She should speak to him, rarely, for confession and spiritual edification, and take advice from him in doubtful matters, comfort in sorrows. But she should not offer even him her hand to be touched or caressed, for that evil that we fear, enclosed in our limbs, frequently arouses and softens dying old age. There should be no men-

brachiorum, de cutis asperitate sermocinatio sit, ne ubi quaeris remedium incurras periculum.

7. Haec tibi, soror, gratias Deo dicenda non fuerant, sed quia nec solum propter te, sed etiam propter adolescentiores quae similem vitam tuo consilio arripere gestiunt, hanc tibi formulam scribi voluisti, haec interserenda putavi.

2 Si aliqua magni nominis vel bonae aestimationis persona—abbas scilicet aut prior—cum inclusa loqui voluerit, aliquo praesente loquatur. Nullam certe personam te frequentius visitare vellem, nec cum aliqua te crebrius visitante familiare te vellem habere secretum. Periclitatur enim fama virginis crebra certe alicuius personae salutatione, periclitatur et conscientia. Nam quanto saepius eundem videris vultum, vel vocem audieris, tanto expressius eius imago tuae memoriae imprimetur. Et ideo inclusa etiam facie velata loqui debet cum viro, et eius cavere conspectum, cui cum timore solum debet praestare auditum. Nam eandem viri vocem saepe admittere, quibusdam periculosum esse non dubito.

3 Adolescentium et suspectarum personarum devita colloquium, nec unquam tecum nisi in audientia illius qui tibi pro patre est loquatur, et hoc si certa necessitas poposcerit. Cum nullo itaque advenientium—praeter episcopum, aut abbatem, vel magni nominis priorem—sine ipsius presbyteri licentia vel praecepto loquaris, ut ipsa difficultas loquendi tecum maiorem tibi praestet quietem.

4 Numquam inter te et quemlibet virum quasi occasione exhibendae caritatis, vel nutriendi affectus, vel expetendae

tion of drawn face, thin arms, or rough skin, so you do not run into danger where you seek its remedy.

7. Sister, thank God these things did not need to be said to you, but because I wanted this guide to be not only for you, but also for young women who long eagerly to take up a similar way of life following your advice, I thought they should be worked in.

If someone well known and of good reputation—an abbot, say, or a prior—wants to speak with a recluse, he should do so with somebody else present. Of course, I would not want anyone to visit you too frequently, nor for you to have private discussions with any woman who visits you too often. The reputation of a virgin is surely endangered by numerous visits from any person, and her conscience is endangered, too. For the more often you see the same face or hear the same voice, the more distinctly its semblance will be imprinted on your memory. Therefore, a recluse ought to speak to a man with her face veiled too and to be wary of his gaze: she should only listen to him and that in fear. For I have no doubt that often hearing the same man's voice is dangerous for some.

Avoid conversation with young people or those of dubious character. Nobody should ever speak with you except in the earshot of your spiritual father, and that only if undeniable necessity demands it. Therefore, you should speak to nobody who visits—except a bishop, an abbot, or a famous prior—without the permission or instruction of that priest, so that the very difficulty of speaking with you will provide you greater peace of mind.

No messengers should ever run between you and any man on the pretext of showing charity, nourishing affection, or

familiaritatis aut amicitiae spiritualis discurrant nuntii, nec eorum munuscula litterasque suscipias, nec illis tua dirigas, sicut plerisque moris est, quae zonas vel marsupia, diverso stamine vel subtegmine variata, et cetera huiusmodi adolescentioribus monachis vel clericis mittunt. Quod fomentum est amoris illiciti et magni materia mali. Operare proinde ea quae vel necessitas poscit vel praescribit utilitas, et eorum pretium tuis usibus cedat. Quibus si non egueris, aut ecclesiae aut pauperibus, sicut diximus, tribuas.

5   Ornet etiam omnes motus omnesque sermones inclusae verecundia, quae linguam compescat, iram mitiget, iurgia caveat. Nam quam pudere debet honesta loqui, quantae impudentiae est ut inhonesta, aut lacessita iniuriis aut stimulata furore loquatur? Inclusa igitur litiganti non respondeat, detrahenti non improperet, lacessenti non contradicat, sed in omnibus quae in publico vel in occulto aut obiciuntur aut susurrantur, ex conscientiae serenioris arce contemnat, dicens cum Apostolo, "*Mihi autem pro minimo est ut a vobis iudicer.*" Super omnia enim inclusa studere debet ut tranquillitatem spiritus et pacem cordis iugiter retinens, illum sui pectoris aeternum habeat inhabitatorem, de quo scriptum est, "*In pace factus est locus eius.*" Et alias Dominus per prophetam, "Super quem," inquit, "requiescet spiritus meus, nisi super humilem et quietum et trementem sermones meos?"

6   Hunc sacratissimum mentis statum non solum stultiloquia sed etiam multiloquia evertunt, ut advertas, nihil tibi magis esse sectandum quam silentium.

8. Iam nunc tempus loquendi a tacendi tempore distinguamus.

seeking familiar relations or spiritual friendship. Nor should you receive their little gifts or notes, or send yours to them, as is the custom among many who send young monks or clerics belts or pouches decorated with colorful embroidery and other such objects. This is kindling for forbidden love and fuel for great evil. Busy yourself, therefore, with what is either necessary or useful, and let any earnings be for your benefit. If you do not need them, you should give them to the church or the poor, as we have said.

Modesty should adorn every action and word of the recluse, who should hold her tongue, calm her anger, avoid quarrels. Given how she should be bashful about discussing honorable matters, how shameless is it for her to discuss dishonorable ones, even when either provoked by injustice or goaded by rage? Therefore, the recluse should not reply to the quarrelsome, reproach detractors, or contradict those who provoke. Instead, from the stronghold of her serene conscience, she should scorn everything shouted or whispered in private and public, saying with the Apostle, "*For it matters little to me that I should be judged by you.*" Above all, the recluse, always maintaining tranquility of spirit and peace of heart, should strive to hold in her breast that eternal dweller of whom it is written, "*His place was made in peace.*" And at another time the Lord said through the prophet, "On whom will my spirit rest, if not the humble and peaceful man who trembles at my words?"

Not only prattle but also excessive talk will destroy this most holy state of mind, so you should remember that nothing is more important for you to cultivate than silence.

8. Now then, we must distinguish between times for speaking and times for keeping silent.

2   Igitur ab Exaltatione Sanctae Crucis usque ad Quadragesimam post completorium usque ad auroram silentium teneat. Et tunc dicta prima, si aliquid de diurna necessitate voluerit suggerere servienti, paucis hoc faciat verbis, nihil cuiquam postea usque ad tertiam locutura. Inter tertiam vero et nonam, his qui supervenerint personis, si admittendae sunt, competenter respondeat et ministris quod placuerit iniungat. Post nonam sumpto cibo omne colloquium et dissolutionis materiam caveat, ne impingatur ei illud quod scriptum est: "*Sedit populus manducare et bibere, et surrexerunt ludere.*" Porro vespertina laude soluta, cum ministris usque ad tempus collationis de necessariis conferat.

3   Tempore vero Quadragesimae inclusa semper tenere silentium deberet. Sed quia durum hoc impossibileque putatur, cum confessore suo et ministra rarius quam aliis temporibus loquatur—et cum nullo alio, nisi forte aliqua reverenda persona ex aliis provinciis supervenerit.

4   Post Pascha vero usque ad tempus praedictum a completorio usque ad solis ortum silentio custodito, cum horam primam in divinis obsequiis celebraverit, cum ministris suis loquatur, si oportuerit cum supervenientibus inter nonam et vesperam. Finita hora vespertina, disponat cum ministris, si quid opus fuerit, usque ad collationem.

9. His inspectis, operi manuum, lectioni, et orationi certa tempora deputemus.

2   Otiositas quippe inimica est animae, quam prae omnibus cavere debet inclusa. Est enim omnium malorum parens, libidinis artifex, pervagationum altrix, nutrix vitiorum, fomentum acediae, tristitiae incentivum. Ipsa pessimas

Therefore, from the Exaltation of the Holy Cross until 2
Lent the recluse should keep silent from after Compline until dawn. Then after Prime, if she wishes to discuss anything
about the day's needs with her servant, she should do so in
few words, saying nothing to anyone afterward until Terce.
Between Terce and None she should reply as appropriate to
visitors, if they ought to be received, and give orders to her
servants as she pleases. After None, having eaten, she should
avoid any conversation or opportunity for distraction so she
is not accused of what is written: "*The people sat down to eat
and drink, and they got up to play.*" Next, when evening prayer
is completed, she should confer with her servants about necessities until collation.

But during Lent, the recluse should keep silent at all 3
times. But because this is considered harsh and impossible,
let her speak with her confessor and her servant more rarely
than at other times—and with nobody else, unless it happens that some venerable person arrives from another re-
gion.

After Easter until the abovementioned time, having 4
maintained silence from Compline to sunrise, she should
speak with her servants when she has celebrated Prime in
divine worship, with visitors (if appropriate) between None
and Vespers. Once Vespers are finished, let her arrange matters with her servants, if need be, until collation.

9. These matters settled, let us assign fixed times for
handiwork, reading, and prayer.

Idleness is indeed the enemy of the soul, and the recluse 2
should guard against it above all other things. For it is the
mother of all evils, author of lust, nurturer of wandering,
nurse of vices, spark of spiritual weariness, incitement to

cogitationes seminat, affectiones illicitas creat, suscitat desideria. Ipsa quietis fastidium parit, horrorem incutit cellae. Numquam proinde te nequam spiritus inveniat otiosam. Sed quia mens nostra, quae in hac vita subdita est vanitati, numquam in eodem statu permanet, otiositas exercitiorum varietate fuganda est, et quies nostra quadam operum vicissitudine fulcienda.

3   Itaque a Kalendis Novembris usque ad Quadragesimam, secundum aestimationem suam plus media nocte repauset, et sic surgens cum qua potest devotione secundum formam regulae beati Benedicti nocturnas vigilias celebret. Quibus mox succedat oratio secundum quod eam Spiritus Sanctus adiuverit, aut protelare debet aut abbreviare. Caveat autem ne prolixior oratio fastidium pariat. Utilius est enim saepius orare breviter, quam semel nimis prolixe, nisi forte orationem devotio inspirata, ipso nesciente qui orat, prolongaverit.

4   Post orationem, in honore beatae Virginis debitum solvat officium, sanctorum commemorationes adiciens. Cave autem ne de numero psalmorum aliquam tibi legem imponas, sed quamdiu te psalmi delectant, utere illis. Si tibi coeperint esse oneri, transi ad lectionem, quae si fastidium ingerit, surge ad orationem, sic ad opus manuum his fatigata pertransiens, ut salubri alternatione spiritum recrees et pellas acediam.

5   Finitis commemorationibus—quarum numerum non propositi vel voti necessitas extorqueat, sed inspirans devotio dictat—tempus quod restat usque ad auroram, operi

sadness. It sows the worst thoughts, creates forbidden affections, arouses desires. It makes quiet distasteful and the cell frightful. Never, therefore, should the evil spirit find you idle. But because our minds, which are subject to fickleness in this life, never remain in the same state, we must chase away idleness with a variety of occupations and strengthen our peace of mind with some ordered variation of activity.

Therefore, from the Kalends of November to Lent, the 3 recluse should sleep until she guesses it is past midnight, and so arising she should celebrate Vigils with all possible devotion according to the guidance of the Rule of Saint Benedict. Vigils should immediately be followed by prayer that she should prolong or shorten according to how the Holy Spirit helps her. But she should be careful that extended prayer not give rise to tedium. It is better to pray briefly and more often than once and at great length, unless it happens that inspired devotion prolongs the prayer without the knowledge of the one who is praying.

After prayer, she should perform the liturgy owed to the 4 honor of the blessed Virgin, adding commemoration of the saints. But be careful not to impose on yourself any set number of psalms, saying them only as long as they delight you. If they begin to burden you, move along to reading, and if that becomes tedious, rise for prayer. Once you are tired of these, move on to manual labor so in this fashion you may refresh your spirit and ward off spiritual weariness with salutary variety.

Having finished these commemorations—whose number 5 inspired devotion should dictate, rather than intention or vow extracted by torture—she should spend the time remaining until dawn in handiwork accompanied by the

manuum cum psalmorum modulatione deserviat. Albes-
cente aurora matutinas laudes cum horae primae hymnis
persolvat et sic in alternatione lectionum, orationum, psalmorum quoque prout ea devotio variaverit, tertiam exspectet. Qua dicta in opere manuum usque ad horam nonam
occupetur. Cibo autem sumpto et gratiis Deo solutis, ad
praescriptam vicissitudinem redeat spiritalibus exercitiis
opus corporale interserens usque ad vesperam. Facto autem
parvo intervallo aliquam lectionem de vitis patrum vel institutis vel miraculis eorum sibi secretius legat: ut orta ex his
aliqua compunctione, in quodam fervore spiritus completorium dicat et cum pectore pleno devotionis lectulo membra
componat.

6   Illa sane quae litteras non intelligit, operi manuum diligentius insistat, ita ut cum paululum fuerit operata, surgat
et genua flectat, et breviter oret Deum suum, et statim opus,
quod intermiserat, resumat. Et hoc faciat tempore utroque
lectionis scilicet et laboris, dominicam orationem crebrius
inter operandum repetens, et si quos psalmos noverit interserens.

10. A Pascha vero usque ad praedictas Kalendas sic surgat
ad vigilias, ut finitis nocturnis hymnis et orationibus, parvis-
simo intervallo praemisso, matutinas incipiat. Quibus ex-
pletis, usque ad plenum solis ortum orationibus vacet et
psalmis, et tunc, dicta prima, sacrificium diurni operis inco-
het, usque ad horam tertiam. Inde lectione usque ad sextam
spiritum occupet. Post sextam, sumpto cibo, pauset in lectulo suo usque ad nonam, et sic usque ad vesperam manibus
operetur. Post vesperam vero orationibus vacet et psalmis,

chanting of psalms. As dawn lightens the sky, she should perform Lauds with the hymns of Prime, then await Terce by alternating between readings, prayers, and psalms as devotion directs. Once Terce is said, she should busy herself with her hands until None. After a meal and thanksgiving to God, she should return to the prescribed cycle, alternating physical work and spiritual exercises until Vespers. Following a brief pause after Vespers, she should read to herself in private a selection from the lives of the fathers or their teachings or miracles in order that, when they have roused some compunction in her, she should say Compline in fervor of spirit and lay down her limbs on her bed with a heart full of devotion.

Of course, the recluse who cannot read should apply herself more conscientiously to manual labor in this fashion: when she has worked a little while, she should rise and genuflect and pray to her God briefly and immediately resume the work she had interrupted. She should do this in the times designated for both reading and labor, frequently repeating the Lord's Prayer amid her tasks, interposing any psalms she knows.

10. From Easter to the aforementioned Kalends she should arise for Vigils, timing it so that once the nighttime hymns and prayers are finished, she begins Matins after the briefest of pauses. That finished, she should devote herself to prayers and psalms until the sun has risen and then, after Prime, take up the sacrifice of daily work until Terce. Then she should occupy her spirit in reading until Sext. After Sext, having eaten, she should rest in her bed until None, then work with her hands until Vespers. After Vespers, she should devote herself to prayers and psalms, timing colla-

horam collationis ita temperans ut ante solis occasum lectulus membra recipiat. Cavendum enim est omni tempore ne totam diei lucem nox antequam dormitum eat suis obducat tenebris et dormire cogatur cum vigilare debet.

11. De tempore Quadragesimae locuturi, primo excellentiam eius credimus commendandam. Cum multa sunt Christianorum ieiunia, omnibus excellit Quadragesimale ieiunium, quod divina auctoritate non singulis quibusque personis, non illius vel illius ordinis hominibus, sed omnibus indicitur Christianis. Habet autem testimonium excellentiae a Lege, a prophetis, ab Evangelio. Nam Moyses famulus Domini ieiunavit quadraginta diebus et quadraginta noctibus ut legem Domini mereretur accipere. Elias autem propheta cum manducasset de pane subcinericio aquamque bibisset quam ei angelus ministraverat, ieiunavit quadraginta diebus et quadraginta noctibus, et tunc vocem Domini audire promeruit. Dominus et Salvator noster cum ieiunasset quadraginta diebus et quadraginta noctibus superavit tentatorem et accesserunt angeli et ministrabant ei.

2   Est ergo ieiunium contra omnia tentamenta impenetrabile scutum, in omni tribulatione utile refugium, orationibus nostris irrefragabile fulcimentum. Quantae autem virtutis sit ieiunium ipse Christus non tacuit. Qui interrogantibus discipulis cur daemonem qui lunaticum invaserat eicere non potuerant, *"Hoc genus,"* inquit, *"daemoniorum non potest eici, nisi in ieiunio et oratione."*

3   Licet autem religionis comes semper debeat esse ieiunium—sine quo castitas tuta esse non potest—haec tamen Quadragesimalis observatio magnum in se continet sacramentum. Primus locus habitationis nostrae paradisus fuit, secundus mundus iste plenus aerumnis, tertius in caelo cum

tion so that her couch receives her body before sunset. She should be careful that night does not completely cloak the light of day in its shadows before she goes to bed and she be compelled to sleep when she should be awake.

11. Since we are about to discuss the season of Lent, we believe its excellence should be emphasized first. Although there are many Christian fasts, the Lenten fast surpasses them all, because it is decreed by divine authority not for certain individuals nor for one or another order of men, but for all Christians. The Law, the prophets, and the Gospel bear witness to its excellence. Moses, the servant of the Lord, fasted for forty days and forty nights so he would be worthy to accept the Lord's law. The prophet Elijah, once he had eaten the bread baked in ash and drunk the water the angel had provided, fasted for forty days and forty nights, and then merited hearing the voice of the Lord. And when our Lord and Savior had fasted for forty days and forty nights, he overcame the tempter and the angels came and ministered to him.

Fasting, therefore, is an impenetrable shield against all 2 temptation, a sound refuge in every tribulation, an unbreakable support for our prayers. Christ himself did not keep silent about the great power of fasting. When his disciples asked why they had been unable to cast out the demon that had possessed a madman, he said, "*This kind of demon cannot be cast out except by fasting and prayer.*"

Although fasting—without which chastity can never be 3 safe—should always be the companion of religious life, nonetheless this Lenten observance comprises a great sacrament. Our first dwelling place was paradise, the second is this world full of hardships, the third will be in heaven with

angelicis spiritibus. Significant autem isti quadraginta dies totum tempus ex quo pulsus est Adam de paradiso usque ad ultimum diem in quo plene liberabimur ex hoc exilio.

4   Hic autem sumus in timore, in labore, in dolore, proiecti a facie oculorum Dei, exclusi a gaudiis paradisi, ieiuni ab alimento caelesti. Semper autem deberemus hanc miseriam nostram considerare et deplorare, et ostendere in operibus nostris quod sumus advenae et peregrini in mundo. Sed quia hoc facile non potest humana fragilitas, constituit Spiritus Sanctus certum tempus quo id faciamus, et quasdam observationes in Ecclesia fieri ordinavit, quibus ipsius temporis causam animadvertere valeamus. Nam ut ostendat nos pulsos esse et addictos morti propter peccatum, verbum ipsum quod dixit Dominus ad Adam, cum eum expelleret de paradiso cum cinerum aspersione dicitur nobis: "*Pulvis es et in pulverem reverteris.*" Ut sciamus etiam quod in hoc exilio negatur nobis visio Dei, oppanditur velum inter nos et sancta sanctorum. Verum ut reducamus ad memoriam quam longe sumus ab eorum societate de quibus scriptum est, "*Beati qui habitant in domo tua, Domine; in saecula saeculorum laudabunt te,*" usitatum verbum laudis, id est "Alleluia," intermittimus. Quod vero nos tempore hoc arctiori ieiunio constringimur recordari nos facit quod in hac vita caelesti pane non satiamur.

5   In hoc igitur tempore omnis Christianus aliquid addere debet solitis obsequiis et diligentius atque ferventius circa cordis orisque custodiam occupari, sed inclusa maxime quae temporis huius rationem tanto melius intelligit, quanto eam in propria vita sua expressius recognoscit. In his proinde sacris diebus Christo praecipue placere desiderans tota se Deo

the angelic spirits. These forty days signify the entire time from when Adam was banished from paradise to the last day, on which we will be fully freed from this earthly exile.

Here, then, we are in fear, in toil, in suffering, cast away 4 from the face of God, shut out of the joys of paradise, starved of heavenly nourishment. But we should always contemplate and bewail this our misery, and show in our works that we are strangers and pilgrims in this world. But because human frailty cannot manage that easily, the Holy Spirit set a fixed time for us to do it and commanded that certain rituals be observed in the Church, through which we may be able to turn our attention to the purpose of this time. To show us that we are exiled and handed over to death because of sin, the very words the Lord said to Adam when he banished him from paradise are spoken to us with the sprinkling of ashes: "*You are dust, and to dust you will return.*" A veil is spread out between us and the holy of holies so we also know that in this exile, the sight of God is denied us. But so that we recall how far we are from the company of those about whom it is written, "*Blessed are those who live in your house, Lord; they will praise you forever,*" we omit the customary word of praise, that is, "Alleluia." And that we are restricted to a more stringent fast at this time reminds us that in this life, we are not fully satisfied by heavenly bread.

At this time, therefore, every Christian should add some- 5 thing to his usual worship, and occupy himself more conscientiously and ardently to keeping watch over heart and mouth, but this is especially true for the recluse: she will the better understand the purpose of this time the more clearly she recognizes its purpose in her own life. Consequently, desiring especially to please Christ during these holy days, she

voveat atque sanctificet. Omnes delicias respuat, omnes confabulationes abiuret, et quasi dies nuptiarum hoc tempus existimans, ad amplexus Christi omni aviditate suspiret. Frequentius solito incumbat orationi, crebrius se pedibus Iesu prosternat, crebra dulcissimi nominis illius repetitione compunctionem excitet, lacrymas provocet, cor ab omni pervagatione compescat.

6 Finitis itaque sacris vigiliis, intervallum quod a nocturnis laudibus dividit matutinos orationi et meditationi subserviat, dictaque post matutinas prima, usque ad plenam tertiam psalmis et lectionibus vacet. Tertiae vero horae laude completa, operi manuum usque ad horam decimam devota insistat, breves per intervalla orationes interserens. Dicta post haec vespera, corpus reficiat et sic tempus completorii psallens exspectet.

12. Iam de cibi vel potus qualitate vel quantitate ex abundanti quidem est tibi legem imponere, soror, quae ab ipsa infantia usque ad senectutem, quae nunc tua membra debilitat, parcissimo cibo vix corpus sustentas. Pro aliis tamen quibus id utile futurum arbitraris, certam de his praescribere regulam tentabo.

2 Beatus Benedictus libram panis et heminam potus concedit monacho, quod nos inclusis delicatioribus et infirmioribus non negamus. Adolescentulis tamen et corpore robustis, ab omni quod inebriare potest abstinere utillimum est. Panem nitidum et cibos delicatos quasi pudicitiae venenum evitet. Sic necessitati consulat, ut et famem repellat et appetitum non satiet. Itaque quae ad perfectiorem abstinentiam

should vow and sanctify herself utterly to God, refuse all pleasure, renounce all conversation, and thinking of this moment as her wedding day, sigh with every longing for Christ's embrace. She should attend to prayer more often than usual, throw herself at the feet of Jesus more frequently, arouse compunction with repeated repetition of his most sweet name, draw forth tears, restrain her heart from any wandering.

When these holy vigils are finished, she should devote 6 the interval between Lauds and Matins to prayer and meditation, and once Prime has been said after Matins, busy herself with psalms and readings until the end of the third hour. Terce completed, she should devotedly apply herself to manual labor until the tenth hour, at times interrupting it for short prayers. After this, having said Vespers, let her rest, singing psalms while awaiting the time for Compline.

12. Now it is indeed superfluous to regulate the quality and quantity of your food and drink, sister, since from your very infancy to the old age that now weakens your limbs, you have scarcely taken enough nourishment to sustain your body. Nonetheless, I will try to prescribe a definite rule about these matters for the benefit of others for whom you think it will be useful.

Saint Benedict allows a monk a pound of bread and one 2 measure of wine, which we do not deny to more delicate and sickly recluses. However, for the young and strong, it is best to abstain from anything intoxicating. The recluse should shun white bread and delicacies as if poisonous to her chastity. She should consider her needs in such a way that she both stave off hunger and yet not satisfy her appetite. Therefore, those who are unable to progress toward more

progredi non valent, libra panis et hemina lautioris potus contentae sint, sive bis comedant sive semel.

3 Unum habeant de holeribus vel leguminibus pulmentum, vel certe de farinaciis. Cui modicum olei, vel butyri, vel lactis iniciens, hoc condimento fastidium repellat. Et hoc ei si ea die cenatura est sufficiat. Ad cenam vero parum sibi lactis vel piscis modicum, vel aliquid huiusmodi si praesto fuerit, apponat, uno genere cibi contenta cum pomis et herbis crudis, si quas habuerit. Haec ipsa si semel comederit in die praelibato pulmento possunt apponi.

4 In vigiliis tamen sanctorum et Quatuor Temporum ieiuniis, omni etiam feria quarta vel sexta extra Quadragesimam, in cibo Quadragesimali ieiunet. In Quadragesima vero unum ei cottidie sufficiat pulmentum et nisi infirmitas impedierit, sexta feria in pane et aqua ieiunet. Ab Exaltatione sanctae Crucis usque ad Quadragesimam semel in die hora nona reficiat. In Quadragesima vero, dicta vespera, ieiunium solvat. A Pascha usque ad Pentecosten, ad sextam prandeat et ad seram cenet. Quod etiam tota aestate faciat, praeter feriam quartam et sextam, et solemnibus ieiuniis. Diebus autem quibus ieiunat in aestate, liceat ei pro somno meridiano inter matutinos et primam modicum quietis indulgere corpusculo.

13. Porro talia ei vestimenta sufficiant quae frigus repellant. Grossioribus pelliceis utatur et pellibus propter hiemem, propter aestatem autem unam habeat tunicam, utroque vero tempore duas de stupacio camisias vel staminias. Velamen capitis non sit de panno subtili vel pretioso, sed mediocri nigro, ne videatur colore vario affectare decorem.

perfect abstinence should be content with a pound of bread and a measure of wine, whether they eat twice a day or once.

The recluse should have one cooked dish of either vegetables or beans or certainly gruel. Adding a little oil, butter, or milk, she can ward off monotony with this seasoning. But that should suffice for her if she is to have an evening meal that day. Then at supper, she should serve herself a very small portion of milk or fish or something of this sort if it is on hand, content with one type of food plus raw fruit or vegetables if she has any. Those can be served before the main dish if she eats once during the day. 3

However, on the vigils of saints' days, fasts of Ember Days, and on every Wednesday and Friday outside of Lent, she should keep a Lenten fast. During Lent, let one dish daily suffice, and unless illness prevents it, she should keep a bread-and-water fast on Fridays. From the Exaltation of the Holy Cross until Lent, she should eat once a day, after None. But during Lent, she should break her fast only once Vespers have been said. From Easter until Pentecost, she should have dinner after Sext and supper in the evening. She should also do the same all summer except for Wednesdays, Fridays, and solemn fasts. On summer fast days, she may indulge her tired body with a brief rest between Matins and Prime in place of the midday nap. 4

13. Next, let there suffice for her the sort of clothing that keeps off the cold. She should use thicker garments of skin or fur in the winter. In the summer, however, she should have one tunic but, in both seasons, two shirts or shifts of tow cloth. The veil should be made not of refined or expensive cloth, but ordinary black; otherwise, the recluse may seem to aspire to beauty by wearing contrasting colors. She

Calciamenta, pedules, caligas, quantum satis fuerit habeat, et paupertatis suae custos sollicite consideret, ut etiam aliquantulum minus habeat quam indulgere sibi posset iusta necessitas.

2 Haec, soror carissima, de exterioris hominis conversatione non pro antiquitatis fervore, sed pro huius nostri temporis tepore te compellente conscripsi, infirmis temperatum quendam modum vivendi proponens, fortioribus ad perfectiora progrediendi libertatem relinquens.

14. Sed iam nunc audiat et intelligat verba mea quaecumque, abrenuntians mundo, vitam hanc solitariam elegerit, abscondi desiderans, non videri, et quasi mortua saeculo in spelunca Christo consepeliri.

2 Primum cur solitudinem hominum debeas praeferre consortio diligenter attende. "Virgo," inquit Apostolus, "cogitat quae sunt Dei, quomodo placeat Deo, ut sit sancta corpore ac spiritu." Voluntarium hoc sacrificium est, oblatio spontanea, ad quam non lex impellit, non necessitas cogit, non urget praeceptum. Unde Dominus in Evangelio: "*Qui potest capere capiat.*" Quis potest? Ille certe cui Dominus hanc inspiraverit voluntatem et praestiterit facultatem.

3 Primum igitur, O virgo, bonum propositum tuum ipsi qui inspiravit cum summa cordis devotione commenda, intentissima oratione deposcens ut quod tibi impossibile est per naturam facile sentiatur per gratiam. Cogita semper quam pretiosum thesaurum in quam fragili portes vasculo et quam mercedem, quam gloriam, quam coronam virginitas servata ministret. Quam insuper poenam, quam confusionem, quam damnationem importet amissa indesinenter animo revolve.

should have as much as is needed in the way of shoes, leggings, and boots, and as a guardian of her own poverty she should take particular care to have just a little bit less than legitimate necessity could allow her.

Dear sister, at your behest I have written these words 2 concerning the conduct of the outer person, taking into account not the ardor of ancient times but the lukewarm spirit of our own, proposing a certain way of life tempered for the weak and leaving to those who are stronger the freedom to proceed to the more perfect.

14. But now let each one hear and understand my words, who, renouncing the world, has chosen this solitary life, desiring to be hidden away, not to be seen and, as if dead to the world, to be enclosed in the tomb with Christ.

First, pay close attention to why you should prefer soli- 2 tude to human company. "A virgin," says the Apostle, "thinks about what is God's, how she may please God, so she may be holy in body and spirit." This is a voluntary sacrifice, a free offering: law does not require it, nor necessity compel it, nor teaching impel it. And so the Lord in the Gospel: "*Let him who can understand this do so.*" Who can? Surely the one in whom the Lord inspires this wish and provides the means to fulfill it.

Therefore, O virgin, first entrust your good intention to 3 the same one who inspired it with the heart's greatest devotion, asking in most earnest prayer that what is impossible for you by nature may seem easy through grace. Always think about what precious treasure you carry in so fragile a vessel, and what reward, what glory, what a crown the preservation of virginity provides you. Furthermore, ponder unceasingly in your soul what punishment, what shame, what damnation its loss brings with it.

4   Quid hoc pretiosius thesauro, quo caelum emitur, angelus delectatur, cuius Christus ipse cupidus est, quo illicitur
ad amandum et ad praestandum? Quid? Audeo dicere: seipsum et omnia sua. Itaque nardus virginitatis tuae etiam in
caelestibus dans odorem suum facit, ut concupiscat rex decorem tuum et ipse est Dominus Deus tuus. Vide qualem
tibi sponsum elegeris, qualem ad te amicum asciveris. Ipse
est *speciosus forma prae filiis hominum,* speciosior etiam sole et
super omnem stellarum pulchritudinem. *Spiritus eius super
mel dulcis, et hereditas eius super mel et favum. Longitudo dierum
in dextera eius, in sinistra eius divitiae et gloria.*

5   Ipse te iam elegit in sponsam, sed non coronabit nisi pro-
batam—et dicit scriptura qui non est tentatus, non est probatus. Virginitas aurum est, cella fornax, conflator diabolus,
ignis temptatio. Caro virginis vas luteum est in quo aurum
reconditur ut probetur. Quod si igne vehementiori crepue-
rit, aurum effunditur, nec vas ulterius a quolibet artifice re-
paratur.

   15. Haec virgo iugiter cogitans pretiosissimum virginitatis
thesaurum, qui tam utiliter possidetur, tam irrecuperabiliter
amittitur, summa diligentia, summo cum timore custodiat.
Cogitet sine intermissione ad cuius ornatur thalamum, ad
cuius praeparatur amplexum. Proponat sibi Agnum quem
sequi habet quocumque ierit. Contempletur beatissimam
Mariam cum virginitatis tympano choros virginum prae-
cedentem, et praecinentem dulce illud canticum quod
nemo potest canere nisi utriusque sexus virgines, de quibus
scriptum est, "*Hi sunt qui cum mulieribus non sunt coinquinati,*

What is more precious than this treasure through which   4
heaven is gained, which delights the angel, which Christ
himself desires, which entices him to love and to give? What
is it he gives? I dare to say it: himself and all that is his.
Therefore, the nard oil of your virginity, giving forth its
sweet smell even in the heavens, makes the king, your Lord
God himself, long for your beauty. See what kind of spouse
you chose for yourself, what kind of friend you have acquired for yourself. He is *beautiful in form beyond all the sons of
men,* even more beautiful than the sun, and exceeds the stars
in all their loveliness. *His breath is sweeter than honey, and his
inheritance sweeter than honey and the honeycomb. The length of
days is in his right hand, riches and glory are in his left.*

He has already chosen you as his bride, but will not crown   5
you unless you are tested—and scripture says that he who is
not tested is not proven. Virginity is the gold, the cell the
crucible, the devil the bellows pumper, temptation the fire.
A virgin's flesh is a clay vessel in which gold is put to be
tested. If it shatters in the intense heat, the gold is spilled,
and no craftsman can ever repair the vessel.

15. Constantly mindful of these matters, the virgin should
guard her most precious treasure of virginity, possessed so
advantageously and lost so irrecoverably, with the utmost
care and in the utmost fear. She should unceasingly consider
for whose marriage bed she is being adorned, for whose embrace she is being prepared. Let her imagine the Lamb she
must follow wherever he goes. She should contemplate the
most blessed Miriam, preceding choirs of virgins with her
timbrel of virginity, leading that sweet song none but virgins
of either sex can sing, of whom it was written, *"These are the
ones who were not defiled by women, for they are virgins."* You

virgines enim sunt." Nec sic hoc dictum aestimes, quasi non vir sine muliere aut mulier sine viro possit foedari, cum detestandum illud scelus, quo vir in virum, vel femina furit in feminam, omnibus flagitiis damnabilius iudicetur. Sed et absque alienae carnis consortio virginitas plerumque corrumpitur, castitas violatur, si vehementior aestus carnem concutiens voluntatem sibi subdiderit et rapuerit membra.

2   Cogitet semper virgo omnia sua membra sanctificata Deo, incorporata Christo, Spiritui Sancto dedicata. Indignum iudicet quod Christi est tradere Satanae, et virginea eius membra erubescat vel simplici motu maculari. Ita proinde in virginitatis suae custodiam totum animum tendat. Cogitationes expendat, ut virtutis huius perfectionem esuriens, famem delicias putet, divitias paupertatem. In cibo, in potu, in somno, in sermone semper timeat dispendium castitatis, ne si plus debito carni reddiderit, vires praebeat adversario et occultum nutriat hostem.

3   Sedens igitur ad mensam decorem pudicitiae mente revolvat, et ad eius perfectionem suspirans cibos fastidiat, potum exhorreat. Et quod sumendum necessitas iudicaverit aut ratio dictaverit cum dolore aut pudore aliquando cum lacrymis sumat.

4   Si ei sermo fuerit cum aliquo, semper metuat aliquid audire, quod vel modicum serenitatem castitatis obnubilet, deserendam se a gratia non dubitet, si vel unum verbum contra honestatem proferat.

16. Prostrata lectulo pudicitiam tuam commenda Deo et, sic signo crucis armata, revolve animo quomodo die illo vixisti, si verbo, si opere, si affectu Domini tui oculos

should not take this to mean that a man cannot be defiled without a woman or a woman without a man, since that detestable crime in which a man has crazed passion for a man, or a woman for a woman, is judged the most damnable of all sins. But even without union with another's flesh, virginity is often corrupted, chastity violated, if a very heavy tide striking the flesh subjects it to its will and seizes its limbs.

The virgin should always bear in mind that all her members are consecrated to God, joined to the body of Christ, dedicated to the Holy Spirit. She should judge it unworthy to hand over to Satan what is Christ's and blush if her virginal members are stained by even a single stirring. Accordingly, she should direct all her thoughts to safeguarding her virginity so that, starving for the perfection of this virtue, she may think hunger a delicate feast and poverty riches. In food, drink, sleep, and speech she should always fear the loss of chastity, in case by giving the flesh more than its due, she might strengthen her adversary and feed the hidden enemy.

Sitting at table, then, she should ponder the beauty of chastity and, sighing after its perfection, she should shun food, shudder at drink. She should consume only what necessity and reason dictate, with grief and shame, sometimes in tears.

If she speaks with anyone, she should always fear hearing something that could cast even a small cloud over the fair weather of chastity. She should have no doubt that grace will abandon her if she utters even one dishonorable word.

16. Lying on your couch, commend your chastity to God and, armed with the sign of the cross, turn over in your mind how you lived that day, whether you have offended the eyes of your Lord in word, deed, or feeling, whether you have

offendisti, si levior, si otiosior, si negligentior debito fuisti, si plusculo cibo crudior, si potu dissolutior, metas necessitatis excessisti. Si subreptum tibi aliquid horum deprehenderis, suspira, pectus tunde, et hoc sacrificio vespertino tuo reconciliatam sponso, somnus excipiat.

2   Si vigilanti subito, aut ex quiete soporis aut arte temptatoris calor corporis fuerit excitatus, et in somnium callidus hostis invexerit, diversisque cogitationibus quietem pudicitiae infestaverit, proposuerit delicias, vitae durioris horrorem incusserit, veniant tibi in mentem beatae virgines, quae in tenera aetate tam crebro reportarunt de impiissimo hoste triumphum. Cogita Agnetem beatissimam, a qua aurum, argentum, vestes pretiosissimae, lapides pretiosi et tota saecularis gloriae pompa quasi quaedam stercora sunt reputata. Vocata ad tribunal non abfuit. Blandiebatur iudex; contempsit. Minabatur; irrisit, magis metuens ne parceret quam ne puniret. Felix quae lupanar vertit in oratorium, quod cum virgine ingrediens angelus lucem infudit tenebris et insectatorem pudicitiae morte multavit. Si igitur et tu oraveris, et contra libidinis incentorem lacrymarum tuarum arma levaveris, non certe angelus tuo casto deerit cubiculo, qui prostibulo non defuit. Merito beatam Agnetem ignis iste materialis nequivit adurere, cui carnis flamma tepuerat quam ignis succenderat caritatis.

3   Quotienscumque tibi vehementior incubuerit aestus,

been more casual, idle, or negligent than you ought, and whether, suffering from indigestion from a bit too much food or overindulgence in drink, you have exceeded the bounds of necessity. If you recognize that one of these failings has crept up on you, sigh, beat your breast, and then, reconciled to your spouse with this belated sacrifice, let sleep come.

If you awaken suddenly and the heat of your body has been stirred, either by the rest provided by sleep or the cunning of the tempter, if the crafty enemy has invaded your dreams and molested the restfulness of chastity with various thoughts, has proposed delights, or has stricken you with terror concerning your rather austere life, then there should come to your mind the blessed virgins who at a tender age so often triumphed over the most wicked enemy. Think of the most blessed Agnes, who considered gold, silver, overly extravagant clothing, precious stones, and all the pomp of worldly glory as just so much dung. When summoned to the tribunal, she did not fail to appear. The judge wheedled; she scorned him. He threatened; she mocked, afraid that he would spare rather than punish her. Blessed was she who turned a brothel into a chapel because an angel, entering along with the virgin, poured light into the darkness and punished the assaulter of her chastity with death. Therefore, if you, too, pray and raise the weapons of your tears against the inciter of lust, the angel who was not absent from a brothel will certainly be present in your chaste bedchamber. For good reason material fire could not burn the blessed Agnes, in whom the flame of flesh had grown cold, and whom the fire of charity had lit up.

Whenever heat bears violently down on you, every time a 3

quotiens nequam spiritus illicita quaeque suggesserit, illum qui scrutatur corda et renes scito esse praesentem, et sub eius esse oculis quidquid agis vel cogitas. Habe proinde reverentiam angelo quem tibi assistere non dubites, et temptatori responde, "*Angelum Dei habeo amatorem, qui nimio zelo custodit corpus meum.*"

4   Adiuvet conatum tuum in tali necessitate districtior abstinentia, quia ubi multa carnis afflictio, aut nulla aut parva aliqua potest esse delectatio.

17. Nemo se palpet, nemo blandiatur sibi, nemo se fallat: numquam ab adolescentibus sine magna cordis contritione et carnis afflictione castitas conquiritur vel servatur, quae plerumque in aegris vel senibus periclitatur. Nam licet continentia donum Dei sit, et nemo possit esse continens nisi Deus det, nec ullis nostris meritis donum hoc, sed eius gratuitae sit gratiae ascribendum, illos tamen tanto dono indignos iudicat, qui aliquid laboris pro eo subire detrectant, volentes inter delicias casti esse, inter epulas continentes, inter puellas conversari et non temptari, *in commessationibus et ebrietatibus* foedis distendi humoribus et non inquinari, ligare in sinu suo flammas, et non exuri. Difficile hoc utrum aut impossibile, tu videris.

18. Novi ego monachum qui cum in initio suae conversationis tum naturalibus incentivis, tum violentia vitiosae consuetudinis, tum suggestione callidi temptatoris, pudicitiam suam periclitari timeret, erexit se contra se, et adversus carnem suam immanissimum concipiens odium, nihil magis quam quod eam afflictaret appetebat. Itaque inedia macerabat corpus, et quae ei de iure debebantur subtrahens, etiam

wicked spirit suggests something forbidden, know that he who examines hearts and innards is present and that whatever you do or think is in his sight. Have reverence, then, for the angel you should not doubt is with you, and reply to the tempter, "*I have as my lover an angel of God, who guards my body with great zeal.*"

Let a stricter abstinence support your efforts in such difficulties, because where there is great affliction of the flesh there can be little or no pleasure. 4

17. No one should delude himself, no one should flatter himself, no one should deceive himself: the young never seek or maintain chastity without great contrition of heart and affliction of the flesh, and it is often jeopardized among the old and ill. For although continence is a gift of God and no one can be continent unless God grants it, and this gift is not to be ascribed to any merit of ours, but his freely given grace, nonetheless he judges unworthy of such a gift those who decline to undergo some work for it, wishing to be chaste amid pleasures, to be continent amid feasting, to be among girls without being tempted, to be swollen with foul humors *in banquets and drunkenness* without being defiled, to bind flames to their breasts without being burned. Whether this is difficult or impossible, you be the judge.

18. I know a monk who at the beginning of his monastic life feared that his chastity was in danger, sometimes from the goading of nature, at other times from the destructive force of bad habit, and at still other times from suggestions of the cunning tempter. He roused himself against himself and, conceiving a fierce hatred of his flesh, sought nothing more than what would afflict it. Therefore, he weakened his body with starvation and, taking away everything rightfully

motus eius simplices comprimebat. Sed cum iterum nimia debilitas sibi plus indulgere compelleret, ecce caro rursus caput erigens, adquisitam, ut putabatur, infestabat quietem. Plerumque vero se frigidis aquis iniciens, tremens aliquamdiu psallebat et orabat. Saepe etiam illicitos sentiens motus, urticis fricabat corpus, et nudae carni apponens incendium, incendio superabat.

2   Et cum haec omnia non sufficerent et nihilominus eum spiritus fornicationis urgeret, tunc, quod solum superfuit, prostratus ante pedes Iesu orat, plorat, suspirat, rogat, adiurat, obtestatur, ut aut occidat aut sanet. Clamat crebro, "Non abibo, non quiesco, *nec te dimittam nisi benedixeris mihi.*" Praestatur ad horam refrigerium, sed negatur securitas. Quiescentibus enim paululum carnis stimulis, affectiones illicitae pectus invadunt. Deus meus, quas cruces, quae tormenta tunc pertulit miser ille, donec tanta ei infusa est delectatio castitatis, ut omnes quae sentiri possunt vel cogitari carnis vinceret voluptates. Et tunc quoque recessit ab eo, sed usque ad tempus et nunc senectuti morbus accessit, nec sic tamen sibi de securitate blanditur.

19. Unde non parum pudet quorumdam impudentiae qui cum in sordibus senuerint, nec sic suspectarum personarum volunt carere consortio. Cum quibus—quod dictu nefas est—eodem lectulo cubantes, inter amplexus et oscula de sua castitate se dicunt esse securos, quod frigescente corpore ad scelus perficiendum tepescentia membra deficiant.

owed to it, he repressed even its ordinary stirrings. But when great weakness forced him to indulge himself more, his flesh raised its head again, disturbing the peace he thought he had secured. He frequently threw himself into icy water, singing psalms and praying for some time as he shivered. And often, sensing illicit stirrings, he rubbed his body with nettles and conquered the fire of his naked flesh with fire.

And when all these measures did not suffice and the spirit 2 of fornication forced itself on him just the same, then he did the only thing left to do: facedown at Jesus's feet, he prayed, wept, sighed, begged, swore, and entreated that Jesus either kill him or cure him. Repeatedly the monk cried out, "I will not go away, I will not be quiet, *and I will not release you unless you bless me.*" Temporary respite was offered, but freedom from danger denied. For even though the prickings of the flesh quieted down for a while, forbidden feelings assailed his heart. My God, what crosses, what torments that wretch then endured, until such delight in chastity poured into him that it was able to conquer every carnal pleasure that can be felt or imagined. And then too the pleasure of the flesh left him, but only for a time, and even now as the sickness approaches old age, he does not however thus flatter himself that he is safe.

19. There is no small disgrace, then, in the shamelessness of those who, although they have grown old in filthiness, still do not wish to be denied the company of questionable people. Sleeping with them—it is wicked to say—in the same bed, between hugs and kisses they say that they are secure in their chastity, because as their bodies grow cold, lukewarm members are not equipped to carry out sin.

Infelices isti et prae cunctis mortalibus miseri, quibus cum desit sceleris perpetrandi facultas, adhuc manet in ipsa foeditate voluntas. Nec quiescit tempore desiderium, quamvis ei frigiditas neget effectum. Videat tamen utrum verum dicat an mentiatur iniquitas sibi, et dum nititur velare unum, duplex in se prodat flagitium, cum et fere decrepitos nocturnum aliquando phantasma deludat. Emortuam senectutem intestinum hoc malum saepius inquietet.

20. Te, soror, numquam volo esse securam, sed timere semper tuamque fragilitatem habere suspectam et instar pavidae columbae frequentare rivos aquarum et quasi in speculo accipitris cernere supervolantis effigiem et cavere. Rivi aquarum sententiae sunt scripturarum qui de limpidissimo sapientiae fonte profluentes, diabolicarum suggestionum produnt imaginem et sensum quo caveantur elucidant. Nihil enim magis cogitationes excludit inutiles vel compescit lascivas quam meditatio verbi Dei, cui sic animum suum virgo debet assuescere ut aliud volens, non possit aliud meditari. Cogitanti de scripturis somnus obrepat evigilanti primum aliquid de scripturis occurrat, dormientis somnia haerens memoriae aliqua de scripturis sententia condiat.

21. Sed quidam a salutaribus exercitiis quodam retrahuntur timore, ne videlicet propter nimiam abstinentiam vel vigilias immoderatas incidant in languorem, et ita efficiantur aliis oneri, sibi autem dolori.

2   Haec excusatio nostra in peccatis nostris. Quam pauci, quam pauci sunt hodie quos talis fervor ignivit. Omnes

Unhappy and most wretched of mortals are those in whom, although their capacity to commit sin is absent, the will to filthiness persists. Their desire does not calm down with time, even though coldness may deny it an outlet. Let such a person see whether he speaks the truth or whether wickedness lies to him; while he struggles to conceal one sin, he betrays a second one in himself, since nocturnal fantasies may sometimes mock even those who have almost fallen to pieces. This inner evil quite often disturbs the very end of life.

20. Sister, I do not want you to be secure but always afraid. Hold your fragility suspect, spend time by the water streams like a fearful dove and see as if in a mirror the reflection of a hawk flying overhead, and beware. The streams of water are the sentences of the scriptures, flowing from the clearest font of wisdom, that reveal the shape of diabolical suggestions and make clear how to guard against them. Nothing is better at driving out useless thoughts or suppressing lustful ones than meditation on the word of God, with which a virgin must be so familiar that even if she wants to meditate on something else, she cannot. Sleep should steal upon her as she reflects on the scriptures, something from the scriptures should come to her on first awakening, and a sentence from the scriptures, lingering in memory as she sleeps, should give zest to her dreams.

21. But some people are kept from these salutary practices by a certain fear, namely that because of extreme abstinence or excessive vigils they may fall into weakness, thus causing trouble for others as well as grief for themselves.

This is our excuse for our sins. How few there are today, 2 how few, whom such fervor has set afire. We are all wise, all

sapientes sumus, omnes providi, omnes discreti. Procul odoramus bellum et sic morbum corporis antequam sentiatur formidamus, ut languorem animae quem praesentem sentimus territi negligamus—quasi tolerabilius sit flammam libidinis quam ventris tolerare rugitum, aut non multo melius sit continuo languore carnis vitare lasciviam quam sanum et incolumem in eius redigi servitutem! Quid enim interest utrum abstinentia an languore caro superbiens comprimatur, castitas conservetur? "Sed remissio," inquit, "cavenda est, ne forte occasione infirmitatis incurramus illecebras voluptatis." Certe si languet, si aegrotat, si torquentur viscera, si arescit stomachus, quaelibet deliciae oneri magis erunt quam delectationi.

22. Vidi hominem qui cum in pueritia sua, vi consuetudinis oppressus, continere non posset. Tandem in se reversus supra modum erubuit, et mox concaluit cor eius intra eum, et in meditatione eius exarsit ignis. Deinde salubriter irascens sibi, invectione gravissima irruit in seipsum, et bellum indicens corpori, etiam ei quae necessaria videbantur ademit. Successit gravitas levitati, loquacitati silentium. Nemo eum postea vidit iocantem, ridentem nemo conspexit, nemo ex ore eius otiosum sermonem audivit. Temporales consolationes et quidquid carni suave putabat, ita contempsit et exhorruit ut nullam sibi requiem, nullam in cibo vel potu consolationem indulgeri pateretur. Cogitationum suarum ita sollicitus et scrupulosus erat ut in hoc solo nimius videretur. Ita demisso vultu oculisque deiectis stabat, sedebat, et incedebat ut tremens et timens divinis tribunalibus

prudent, all discreet. We scent distant war and we fear bodily disease before it is felt, with the result that in our fright we disregard the weakness of soul we know is already there—as if it were easier to tolerate the flame of lust than the growling of the stomach, or as if it were not much better to escape lust through constant weakening of the flesh than for healthy, strong flesh to be reduced to lust's slavery! What difference does it make whether it is through hunger or weakness that haughty flesh is restrained and chastity preserved? "But," someone says, "we must beware letting up, or it may happen that on the pretext of illness, we meet with the lures of pleasure." Surely if one is weak or ill, if one's bowels are tormented, if one's stomach dries up, any pleasures will be more of a burden than a delight.

22. I saw a man who in his youth, weighed down by force of habit, could not remain continent. Finally, when he came to his senses, he was ashamed beyond measure and quickly his heart warmed within him, and fire lit up his meditation. Next, in healthy anger toward himself, he attacked himself with the most vehement invective and declared war on his body, denying it even what seemed necessary. Seriousness took the place of frivolity and silence that of talkativeness. Afterward, nobody ever saw him joking, nobody caught him laughing, nobody heard idle talk from his mouth. He so despised and feared worldly comforts and whatever he thought pleasing to the flesh that he did not allow himself any indulgence in rest or comfort in food and drink. He was so concerned and careful about his thoughts that in this matter alone he seemed to go too far. He stood, sat, and walked with such a downturned face and downcast eyes that, trembling and fearful, he seemed to be standing before the divine

videretur assistere. Talibus armis gloriosum retulit de tyranno triumphum. Nam gravissimum stomachi incurrens incommodum post diuturnum languorem, cum iam dormitionis eius instaret hora, "Sine," inquit, "ecce Iesus venit."

23. Nec hoc dico ut discretioni, quae omnium virtutum et mater et nutrix est, derogem, sed vitiorum materias, gulam, somnum, requiem corporis, feminarum et effeminatorum familiaritatem atque convictum infra metas necessarias cohibeamus, qui saepe falso nomine discretionis palliamus negotium voluptatis. Vera enim discretio est animam carni praeponere, et ubi periclitatur utraque, nec sine huius incommodo illius potest salus consistere, pro illius utilitate istam negligere.

2   Haec diximus ut quanta tibi debeat in conservanda pudicitia esse sollicitudo adverteres, quae cum omnium virtutum flos sit et ornamentum, sine humilitate tamen arescit atque marcescit.

24. Hoc est certum atque securum virtutum omnium fundamentum, extra quod quidquid aedificas ruinae patet. Initium omnis peccati superbia est, quae angelum de caelo, hominem expulit de paradiso. Huius pessimae radicis cum multi sint rami, omnes tamen in duas species dividuntur, in carnalem scilicet et spiritualem. Carnalis superbia est de carnalibus, spiritualis est de spiritualibus superbire.

2   Carnalis praeterea in duas subdividitur species, iactantiam scilicet et vanitatem. Vanitatis est, si ancilla Christi intus in animo suo glorietur se nobilibus ortam natalibus, si se divitiis paupertatem praetulisse pro Christo delectetur, si se pauperibus et ignobilioribus praeferre conetur, si se

judgment seat. With such weapons he won a glorious triumph over the tyrant. Falling ill with severe stomach trouble, after a long illness, when the hour of his death was at hand, he said, "So be it; behold, Jesus is coming."

23. I do not say this to disparage discretion, the mother and nurse of all virtues, but so that we, who often hide the pursuit of pleasure under the false name of discretion, will confine within strict boundaries the raw material of vices: gluttony, sleep, bodily rest, familiarity and interaction with women and effeminate men. It is true discretion to put the soul before the flesh and, when both are in danger, and the health of the one cannot endure without distress to the other, to neglect the body for the good of the soul.

We have said these things to draw your attention to how   2
much concern you must have to preserve the chastity that, although it is the flower and ornament of all virtues, dries up and withers in the absence of humility.

24. This is the sure and certain foundation of all virtues, without which whatever you build is in danger of collapse. The beginning of all sin is pride, which expelled the angel from heaven and mankind from paradise. Although there are many shoots from this most wicked root, all fall into two categories, namely carnal and spiritual. Carnal pride is being proud about carnal matters, spiritual pride is being proud about spiritual matters.

Carnal pride falls then into two subcategories: boasting   2
and vanity. It is a sign of vanity if a handmaid of Christ boasts inwardly that she was born of noble lineage, if she takes pleasure in having preferred poverty to wealth for Christ's sake, if she tries to put herself before the poor and less noble, if she admires herself for having spurned a mon-

contempsisse divitum nuptias, quasi aliquid magnum admiretur. Est etiam quaedam species vanitatis in affectata aliqua pulchritudine etiam intra cellulam delectari, parietes variis picturis vel caelaturis ornare, oratorium pannorum et imaginum varietate decorare. Haec omnia quasi professioni tuae contraria cave.

3   Qua enim fronte de divitiis vel natalibus gloriaris quae illius vis sponsa videri, qui pauper factus cum esset dives, pauperem matrem, pauperem familiam, domum etiam pauperculam et presaepii vilitatem elegit? Itane gloriandum tibi est quod Dei filium hominum filiis praetulisti, quod foeditatem carnis pro virginitatis decore sprevisti, quod aeternas caeli divitias atque delicias materiis stercorum commutasti?

4   Si gloriaris, in Domino glorieris, serviens ei cum timore. Sed illam te nolim quasi sub specie devotionis sequi gloriam in picturis vel sculpturis, in pannis avium vel bestiarum, aut diversorum florum imaginibus variatis. Sint haec illorum qui nihil intus in quo glorientur habentes, exterius sibi comparant in quo delectantur.

25. Omnis enim *gloria filiae regis ab intus, in fimbriis aureis circumamicta varietatibus.* Si tu iam filia Regis es utpote filii Regis sponsa, patrisque vocem audisti dicentis, *"Audi, filia, et vide, et inclina aurem tuam."*

2   Sit tua omnis gloria ab intus. Vide ut gloria tua sit testimonium conscientiae tuae. Ibi sit pulcherrima virtutum varietas, ibi diversi colores sibi sic conveniant et sic iungantur ut alterius pulchritudinem alter augeat et qui in sui natura minus lucet alterius collatione lucidior appareat. Iungatur

eyed marriage as if that were something great and admirable. It is also a kind of vanity to take delight in any attempt to beautify even the inside of her cell, to adorn the walls with colorful paintings or carvings, to decorate her oratory with an array of hangings and images. Avoid all these things as contrary to your calling.

What impudence do you display if you take pride in 3 wealth or lineage, you who want to be seen as a bride of that one who became poor although he was rich, and chose a poor mother, a poor family, even a hovel and the lowliness of a manger? Should it thus be a matter of pride that you preferred the son of God to the sons of man, rejected the foulness of flesh for the beauty of virginity, exchanged the material of dung for heaven's eternal riches and delights?

If you glory, glory in the Lord, serving him in fear. But I 4 would not have you, on the pretext of devotion, pursue glory in paintings and carvings, in tapestries depicting birds and beasts, or colorful images of different flowers. Let them be for those who, having nothing inward in which to glory, acquire for themselves something outward to enjoy.

25. For *all the glory of the king's daughter, clad in garments fringed with woven gold, is within.* If you are already the King's daughter as the bride of the King's son, you have heard the voice of the father saying, "*Listen, daughter, and see, and incline your ear.*"

All your glory should be within. See to it that your glory 2 bears witness to your conscience. There the most beautiful variety of virtues should be, there different colors should so match one another and so merge so that the one increases the beauty of the other and what shines forth somewhat less by its own nature seems brighter in comparison to some-

castitati humilitas, et nihil erit splendidius. Prudentiae so-
cietur simplicitas, et nihil erit lucidius. Copuletur misericordia iustitiae, et nihil erit suavius. Adde fortitudini mo-
destiam, et nihil erit utilius. In hac varietate tuae mentis
oculos occupa, hanc in anima tua omni studio forma. Cui si
fimbrias aureas addas, vestem polymitam in qua te sponsus
cum summa delectatione conspiciat texuisti. Fimbria ex-
trema pars, quasi finis est vestimenti. *Finis autem praecepti
caritas est, de corde puro et conscientia bona, et fide non ficta.*

26. In his glorieris, in his delecteris—intus non foris, in
veris virtutibus, non in picturis et imaginibus. Panni linei
candidi tuum illud ornent altare, qui castitatem suo candore
commendent et simplicitatem praemonstrent. Cogita quo
labore, quibus tunsionibus terrenum in quo crevit linum
colorem exuerit et ad talem candorem pervenerit ut ex eo
ornetur altare, Christi corpus veletur. Cum terreno colore
omnes nascimur, quoniam *in iniquitatibus conceptus sum et in
peccatis concepit me mater mea.*

2   Primum igitur linum aquis immergitur, nos in aquis baptismatis Christo consepelimur. Ibi deletur iniquitas, sed
necdum sanatur infirmitas. Aliquid candoris recepimus in
peccatorum remissione, sed necdum plene terreno colore
exuimur pro naturali quae restat corruptione. Post aquas
linum siccatur, quia necesse est post aquas baptismatis corpus ut per abstinentiam maceratum illicitis humoribus va-
cuetur. Deinde linum malleis tunditur et caro nostra multis
temptationibus fatigatur. Post haec linum ferreis aculeis

thing else. Let humility be joined to chastity, and nothing will be more brilliant. Let simplicity be combined with wisdom, and nothing will be more dazzling. Let mercy be coupled with justice, and nothing will be sweeter. Add modesty to strength, and nothing will be more useful. Occupy your mind's eye with this variety, make every effort to shape it in your soul. If you add gold fringes to it, you have woven a robe with threads of many colors in which your bridegroom will behold you with the greatest delight. The fringe is the last part, like the end of the garment. *Love from a pure heart and a good conscience and unfeigned faith is indeed the end of law.*

26. In these qualities you should glory, in them you should delight—inwardly, not outwardly, in true virtues, not in paintings and images. Let white linen cloths adorn that altar of yours, to commend chastity and exhibit simplicity in their whiteness. Consider the labor, the poundings through which the flax sheds its earthen color and arrives at such whiteness that it can adorn an altar and cover the body of Christ. We are all born with the color of earth, since *I was conceived in wickedness, and in my sins my mother conceived me.*

First, the flax is plunged in water as we are buried with Christ in the waters of baptism. There wickedness is destroyed, but weakness is not yet healed. We obtain some whiteness through the remission of sins but are not yet fully stripped of our earthy color because of the natural corruption that remains. After soaking the flax is dried, because it is necessary that, after the waters of baptism, our body, weakened by abstinence, be purged of illicit humors. Next, flax is pounded with mallets as our flesh is tormented by many temptations. After that the flax is carded with an iron comb to rid it of superfluous matter and we, scraped by the

discerpitur, ut deponat superflua, et nos disciplinae ungulis rasi, vix necessaria retinemus. Adhibetur post haec lino suaviorum stimulorum levior purgatio et nos victis cum magno labore pessimis passionibus a levioribus et cotidianis peccatis simplici confessione et satisfactione mundamur. Iam tunc a nentibus linum in longum producitur et nos in anteriora perseverantiae longanimitate extendimur. Porro ut ei perfectior accedat pulchritudo, ignis adhibetur et aqua, et nobis transeundum est per ignem tribulationis et aquam compunctionis, ut perveniamus ad refrigerium castitatis.

3   Haec tibi oratorii tui ornamenta repraesentent, non oculos tuos ineptis varietatibus pascant. Sufficiat tibi in altario tuo Salvatoris in cruce pendentis imago, quae passionem suam tibi repraesentet quam imiteris, expansis brachiis ad suos te invitet amplexus in quibus delecteris, nudatis uberibus lac tibi suavitatis infundat quo consoleris. Et si hoc placet, ad commendandam tibi virginitatis excellentiam, virgo mater in sua et virgo discipulus in sua iuxta crucem cernatur imagine, ut cogites quam grata sit Christo utriusque sexus virginitas, quam in matre et prae caeteris sibi dilecto discipulo consecravit. Unde eos pendens in cruce tanto foedere copulavit, ut illam discipulo matrem, illum matri filium delegaret. O beatissimum hoc testamento Iohannem, cui totius humani generis decus, spes mundi, gloria caeli, miserorum refugium, afflictorum solatium, pauperum consolatio, desperatorum erectio, peccatorum reconciliatio,

talons of religious discipline, barely hold onto what is necessary. Then the flax is cleaned more gently with a lighter combing as we, when our worst passions have been defeated through great effort, are cleansed from lesser and everyday sins by simple confession and penance. Now the flax is drawn out in lengths by spinners as we are drawn to what lies ahead through long-lasting perseverance. Finally, the linen is treated with heat and water so it acquires more perfect beauty as we must pass through the fire of tribulation and the water of remorse so that we may come to the cool freshness of chastity.

Let the furnishing of your oratory convey these ideas to 3 you rather than feasting your eyes on foolish variety. An image of the Savior hanging on the cross should suffice for your altar, presenting his passion for you to imitate. Let him invite you, his arms outstretched, into his embrace for your delight; with his breasts bared, let him pour into you the milk of sweetness for your comfort. If you want to commend the excellence of virginity to yourself, an image of the virgin mother may appear on one side of the cross and the virgin disciple on the other, so you may ponder how pleasing the virginity of both sexes is to Christ, virginity that he consecrated in his mother and in the disciple more beloved to him than the others. While hanging on the cross, he joined them in such a close union that he entrusted her to the disciple as a mother and him to his mother as a son. Oh, how very blessed is John in this testament! The beauty of the whole human race, the hope of the world, the glory of heaven, the refuge of the wretched, the solace of the stricken, the consolation of the poor, the lifting up of those in despair, the reconciliation of sinners, and finally the mis-

postremo orbis domina, caeli regina, testamenti auctoritate committitur.

4   Haec tibi incentivum praebeant caritatis, non spectaculum vanitatis. His enim omnibus ad unum necesse est ut conscendas, quoniam unum est necessarium. Illud est unum quod non invenitur nisi in Uno, apud Unum, cum Uno, *apud quem non est transmutatio, nec vicissitudinis obumbratio.* Qui adhaeret ei unus cum eo spiritus efficitur, transiens in illud unum quod semper idem est, et cuius anni non deficiunt. Adhaesio ista caritas, quasi spiritalis ornatus finis et fimbria.

27. Vestis quippe nuptialis ex virtutum varietate contexta oportet ut fimbriis aureis, id est caritatis splendoribus ambiatur, quae omnes virtutes contineat, et constringat in unum, et suam singulis claritatem impertiens, de multis unum faciat, et cum multis uni adhaereat, ut iam omnia non sint multa sed unum.

2   Caritas autem in duo dividitur: in Dei videlicet dilectionem et proximi. Porro dilectio proximi in duo subdividitur, in innocentiam et beneficentiam videlicet, ut nulli noceas, benefacias quibus potueris. Scriptum quippe est, "Quod tibi non vis fieri, alteri ne feceris." Et haec innocentia. Et Dominus in Evangelio, "*Omnia,*" inquit, "*quaecumque vultis ut faciant vobis homines, et vos facite illis.*" Et haec beneficentia.

3   Quantum ad te duo ista pertineant, diligenter adverte. Primum ut nulli noceas: primum illud facile tibi, cum nec id possis, nisi forte lingua percusseris. Secundum illud non erit difficile, si propositum attendas tuum, si professam

tress of the world and the queen of heaven, is given over to him by the authority of this testament.

These images should offer you an incentive to love, not a 4 spectacle of vanity. You must ascend from all these things to one, since only one thing is necessary. That is the oneness found only in the One, beside the One, with the One, *in whom there is no alteration, no shadow of change.* Whoever cleaves to him is made one spirit with him, passing into that oneness that is always the same and whose years never end. This union is love, the fringe and the end, so to speak, of spiritual adornment.

27. Of course it is fitting that the wedding dress, woven from a variety of virtues, should be edged with gold fringes, that is, the sheen of love, which should encompass all virtues and bind them together. Imparting its beauty to each one individually, love should make one out of many and cling to the one along with many virtues, so that in the end all things be not many, but one.

Love is divided into two: love of God and love of neigh- 2 bor. Love of neighbor in turn is subdivided into not harming and doing good, that you should harm no one and that you should do good for whom you are able. Indeed it is written, "What you do not want to be done to you, do not do to another." This is not harming. And the Lord says in the Gospel, "*Everything you want that men do for you, you too do for them.*" And this is doing good.

Pay careful attention to the extent to which those two 3 pertain to you. First, that you should harm no one: this will be easy for you, since you cannot do so, unless perhaps with a tongue-lashing. That second one will not be difficult if you pay attention to your chosen way of life, if you love the

dilexeris nuditatem. Non enim ibi esse poterit erga aliquem malae voluntatis materia, ubi cupiditas nulla, ubi nihil diligitur quod possit auferri, nihil tollitur quod debeat amari.

4 Deinde bene velis omnibus, prosis quibus possis. "In quo," inquis, "cum mihi non liceat vel modicum quod egentibus tribuam possidere?"

28. Agnosce conditionem tuam, carissima. Duae erant sorores Martha et Maria. Laborabat illa, vacabat ista. Illa erogabat, ista petebat. Illa praestabat obsequium, ista nutriebat affectum. Denique non ambulans vel discurrens huc vel illuc, non de suscipiendis hospitibus sollicita, non cura rei familiaris distenta, non pauperum clamoribus intenta sedebat ad pedes Iesu et audiebat verbum illius.

2 Haec pars tua, carissima, quae saeculo mortua atque sepulta, surda debes esse ad omnia quae saeculi sunt audiendum et ad loquendum muta. Nec debes distendi, sed extendi, impleri, non exhauriri. Exsequatur partem suam Martha, quae licet non negetur bona, Mariae tamen melior praedicatur. Numquid invidit Marthae Maria? Illa potius isti. Ita etiam qui optimae videntur vivere in saeculo, tuam vitam aemulentur, non illarum tu.

3 Ad ipsos spectat eleemosynarum largitio, quorum est terrena possessio, vel quibus credita est rerum ecclesiasticarum dispensatio. Quae enim sacrosanctis ecclesiis a fidelibus collata sunt, episcopi, sacerdotes, et clerici dispensanda suscipiunt, non recondenda, non possidenda, sed eroganda. Quidquid habent pauperum est, viduarum, et

nakedness you have vowed. There can be no basis for bad will toward anyone where there is no greed, where there is no love for anything that can be taken away, where nothing that should be loved is taken away.

Then you should wish all well, do good to whom you can. 4 "How," you ask, "since it is not permitted me to possess even a little bit to give to the needy?"

28. Take note of your condition, my dearest one. There were two sisters, Martha and Mary. The one toiled, the other was at leisure. The one paid out, the other asked. The one offered service, the other cultivated affection. In short, not walking or running this way and that like Martha, nor sharing her concern about receiving guests, nor her distraction with household cares, nor her attention to the cries of the poor, Mary sat at the feet of Jesus and listened to his words.

This is your part, dearest: dead and buried to the world, 2 you should be deaf to everything said that concerns the world, unable to speak of it. You should be occupied, not preoccupied, filled, not emptied. Let Martha pursue her part: although there is no denying that it is good, Mary's is proclaimed to be better. Mary certainly did not envy Martha, did she? No, quite the reverse. By the same token, even those who seem to live best in the world should strive after your life, not the other way around.

Distributing alms is for those who have earthly posses- 3 sions, or to whom the management of church property is entrusted. Offerings to the holy churches that bishops, priests, and clerics receive from the faithful are to be distributed, not hoarded, not possessed, but given away. Whatever they have belongs to the poor, widows, and orphans,

orphanorum, et eorum qui altario deserviunt, ut de altario vivant. Sed et ea quae in usus servorum Christi monasteriis conferuntur a certis personis dispensari oportet, ut quod necessitatibus superest fratrum, non includatur marsuppiis, sed hospitibus, peregrinis, atque pauperibus erogetur. Et hoc illorum interest, quibus pars est Marthae commissa, non qui salutari otio vacant cum Maria.

4   Itaque claustralibus nulla debet esse pro pauperibus solli-citudo, nulla pro hospitibus suscipiendis distentio, quippe quibus nulla debet esse de crastino cura, nulla cibi potusve providentia. Nutriantur potius in croceis, spiritalibus pas-cantur deliciis. Hi autem qui contemptibiles sunt constituti ad iudicandum, amplexentur stercora. Ipsi quippe sunt boves, quorum piger stercoribus lapidatur. Sunt enim qui-dam, qui circa spiritalia desides et pigri instar populi pecca-toris, super manna caeleste nauseant, videntesque alios circa temporalia occupatos, invident, detrahunt, murmurant, et pro stercoribus quibus ipsi foedantur, zeli et amaritudinum stimulis feriuntur. De quibus si forte aliquam temporalium dispensationem fuerint adepti, convenienter dici potest, *"Qui nutriti erant in croceis amplexati sunt stercora."*

5   Cum igitur nec illis, qui in coenobiis sunt, quibus cum Martha non parva communio est, circa plurima occupari conceditur, quanto minus tibi, quae totam te saeculo exuisti, cui non solum non possidere, sed nec videre, nec audire licet quae saeculi sunt? Cum enim nihil tibi quisquam det ad ero-gandum, unde habebis quod eroges? Si ex tuo aliquid habes

and to those who serve at the altar so they may live from the altar. But what is offered for the use of Christ's servants in monasteries should also be entrusted to certain people so that anything that exceeds the brothers' needs is not locked up in purses but paid out to guests, pilgrims, and the poor. And this is the concern of those given Martha's part, who are not free for leisure that profits the soul, like Mary.

Therefore, cloistered monks should have no concern for 4 the poor, no preoccupation about receiving guests, since they should have no concern about the morrow, no care about food or drink. Instead, they should be nourished with saffron, fed on spiritual delicacies. Let the despicable ones who have been made judges embrace the dung heap. For they are the oxen with whose dung the slothful man is pelted. For there are some, lazy in spiritual matters and slothful like people of sin, who are nauseated by manna from heaven and, seeing others busy with temporal affairs, envy, disparage, grumble, and are stricken with the torments of jealousy and bitterness on account of the dung with which they themselves are fouled. Of them it can fittingly be said, if they happen to take some responsibility for managing worldly matters, *"Those who were nourished with saffron have embraced dung."*

Therefore, since those in monasteries, who have much in 5 common with Martha, are not allowed to be occupied with too many matters, how much less fitting is it for you, who have totally divested yourself of the world, not only to possess, but also to see and hear the things of the world? For when nobody gives you anything to pay out, how then would you have something you could pay out? If you have something left over from your own labor, give it not with your own hand but through another's. If provisions come to you

labore, da non tua, sed alterius manu. Si aliunde tibi prove-
nit victus, unde tibi aliena distribuere, cum nihil tibi supra
necessarium liceat usurpare?

6   Quid ergo beneficii impendes proximo? "*Nihil ditius bona
voluntate,*" ait quidam sanctus. Hanc praebe. Quid utilius
oratione? Hanc largire. Quid humanius pietate? Hanc impende. Itaque totum mundum uno dilectionis sinu complec-
tere, ibi simul omnes qui boni sunt, considera et congra-
tulare. Ibi malos, intuere et luge. Ibi afflictos conspice et
oppressos, et compatere. Ibi occurrant animo miseria pauperum, orphanorum gemitus, viduarum desolatio, tristium
maestitudo, necessitates peregrinantium, pericula navigan-
tium, vota virginum, tentationes monachorum, praelatorum
sollicitudo, labores militantium. Omnibus pectus tuae dilectionis aperias, his tuas impende lacrymas, pro his tuas
preces effundas.

7   Haec eleemosyna Deo gratior, Christo acceptior, tuae
professioni aptior, his quibus impenditur fructuosior. Huius
munus beneficii tuum propositum adiuvat, non perturbat,
dilectionem proximi auget, non minuit, mentis quietem servat, non impedit.

8   Quid his plura dicam, cum *sancti, ut perfecte possent prox-
imos diligere, studuerunt in hoc* mundo *nihil* habere, *nihil vel
sine appetitu possidere?* Agnoscis verba: beati Gregorii sunt.
Vide quam contra multi sapiunt. Ut enim caritatis impleant
legem, quaerunt ut habeant quod erogent, cum eius perfectionem ipsis adscribat, qui nihil habendum, nihil appeten-
dum, nihil vel sine appetitu possidendum arbitrabantur.

from elsewhere, since it is not permitted for you to acquire anything beyond what is necessary, how can you give away what belongs to someone else?

What good, then, can you do for your neighbor? "*Nothing* 6 *is more precious than goodwill*," says a certain saint. Offer that. What is more useful than prayer? Grant that. What is more humane than piety? Pay that out. So, clasp the whole world in one loving embrace and as you do, consider at the same time all who are good and rejoice with them, look upon the wicked and mourn. In this embrace, fix your eyes on the afflicted and oppressed and take great pity on them. In this embrace, you should call to mind the misery of the poor, orphans' groans, widows' desolation, the sadness of the downcast, pilgrims' needs, sailors' peril, virgins' vows, monks' temptations, prelates' responsibilities, soldiers' labors. Open your loving heart to all, shed tears over them, pour out your prayers for them.

This form of almsgiving is more pleasing to God, more 7 acceptable to Christ, more fitting to your calling, more fruitful for those to whom they are given. This gift of kindness aids rather than disturbs your purpose; it increases rather than diminishes love for your neighbor; it protects rather than hinders your peace of mind.

What more can I say to them, when *holy men, to be able to* 8 *love their neighbors perfectly, strove to have nothing in this* world, to possess *nothing, not even to long for it?* You recognize the words: they are Saint Gregory's. See how many understand the opposite. They seek to have something to give away to satisfy the law of charity, whereas Gregory ascribes the perfection of charity to those precisely who think that nothing should be had, sought, or possessed—even without longing for it.

29. His de proximi dilectione praemissis, de dilectione Dei pauca subiungam. Nam licet utraque soror Deum proximumque dilexerit, specialiter tamen circa obsequium proximorum occupabatur Martha, ex divinae vero dilectionis fonte hauriebat Maria.

2   Ad Dei vero dilectionem duo pertinent: affectus mentis et effectus operis. Et opus hoc in virtutum exercitatione, affectus in spiritalis gustus dulcedine. Exercitatio virtutum in certo vivendi modo, in ieiuniis, in vigiliis, in opere, in lectione, in oratione, in paupertate et caeteris huiusmodi commendatur. Affectus salutari meditatione nutritur. Itaque ut ille dulcis amor Iesu in tuo crescat affectu, triplici meditatione opus habes, de praeteritis scilicet, praesentibus et futuris, id est de praeteritorum recordatione, de experientia praesentium, de consideratione futurorum.

3   Cum igitur mens tua ab omni fuerit cogitationum sorde virtutum exercitatione purgata, iam oculos defaecatos ad posteriora retorque, ac primum cum beata Maria ingressa cubiculum, libros quibus virginis partus et Christi prophetatur adventus evolve. Ibi adventum angeli praestolare ut videas intrantem, audias salutantem, et sic repleta stupore et ecstasi dulcissimam dominam tuam cum angelo salutante salutes, clamans et dicens, "*Ave gratia plena, Dominus tecum: benedicta tu in mulieribus.*" Haec crebrius repetens, quae sit haec gratiae plenitudo, de qua totus mundus gratiam mutuavit, quando *Verbum caro factum est et habitavit in nobis, plenum gratiae et veritatis* contemplare, et admirare Dominum qui terram implet et caelum, intra unius puellae viscera claudi, quam Pater sanctificavit, Filius fecundavit, obumbravit Spiritus Sanctus.

29. After these remarks about the love of one's neighbor, I will add a few words about the love of God. For although each sister loved God and neighbor, nevertheless it was Martha who was especially occupied with service to her neighbor, Mary who drank from the spring of divine love.

In fact, the love of God includes two things: state of mind ₂ and performance of works. The latter is the practice of virtues, the former the sweetness of spiritual savor. The practice of virtues consists of an established way of living, in fasting, vigils, work, reading, prayer, poverty, and other activities of this sort; emotions are nourished in salutary meditation. Therefore, so that the sweet love of Jesus may increase in your affection, you need a threefold meditation, namely on past, present, and future, that is, remembering things past, experiencing things present, and considering things to come.

Therefore, when your mind is purged of all filth through ₃ the practice of virtues, turn your newly purged eyes back to the past. Having first entered the room with the blessed Mary, open the books that prophesy the virgin birth and the coming of Christ. Await the arrival of the angel there so you may see him enter, hear him greeting Mary, and thus filled with wonder and ecstasy, greet your sweetest lady as the angel greets her, crying out and saying, *"Hail, full of grace, the Lord is with you: blessed are you among women."* Repeating these words many times, meditate on what this fullness of grace is, from which the whole world borrowed when *the Word was made flesh and dwelled among us, full of grace and truth.* Marvel that the Lord who fills earth and heaven was enclosed in the womb of one girl whom the Father sanctified, the Son made fertile, the Holy Spirit overshadowed.

4 O dulcis domina, quanta inebriabaris dulcedine, quo
amoris igne succendebaris, cum sentires in mente et in ventre tantae maiestatis praesentiam, cum de tua carne sibi carnem assumeret, et membra in quibus corporaliter omnis
plenitudo divinitatis habitaret, de tuis sibi membris aptaret!

5 Haec omnia propter te, O virgo, ut Virginem quam imi-
tari proposuisti, diligenter attendas, et Virginis filium cui
nupsisti.

6 Iam nunc cum dulcissima domina tua in montana con-
scende, et sterilis et virginis suavem intuere complexum, et
salutationis officium, in quo servulus Dominum, praeco Iudicem, vox Verbum, intus anilia viscera conclusus, in Virginis
utero clausum agnovit, et indicibili gaudio salutavit. Beati
ventres in quibus totius mundi salus exoritur, pulsisque tristitiae tenebris, sempiterna laetitia prophetatur. Quid agis,
O virgo? Accurre, quaeso, accurre et tantis gaudiis admis-
cere, prosternere ad pedes utriusque, et in unius ventre
tuum sponsum amplectere, amicum vero eius in alterius
utero venerare.

7 Hinc matrem euntem in Bethleem cum omni devotione
prosequere, et in hospitium divertens cum illa, assiste et
obsequere parienti, locatoque in praesepi parvulo, erumpe
in vocem exsultationis, clamans cum Isaiah, "*Parvulus natus
est nobis, filius datus est nobis.*" Amplectere dulce illud prae-
sepium, vincat verecundiam amor, timorem depellat affectus, ut sacratissimis pedibus figas labia, et oscula gemines.
Exinde pastorum excubias mente pertracta, angelorum

O sweet lady, with what sweetness you were intoxicated, 4
with what fire of love you were inflamed, when you felt in
your mind and your womb the presence of such majesty,
when he took on flesh from your flesh and put on limbs
from your limbs and all fullness of divinity lived in bodily
form!

All these things were done for you, virgin, so you may at- 5
tentively consider the Virgin whom you have resolved to
imitate and the son of the Virgin whom you have married.

Now then, climb into the mountains with your sweetest 6
lady, behold the sweet embrace of the barren woman and
the Virgin and the kindness of greeting through which the
young servant enclosed in the womb of an old woman recognized his Lord, confined in the Virgin's womb, and hailed
him with inexpressible joy: the herald recognized the Judge,
the voice recognized the Word. Blessed are the wombs from
which the salvation of the whole world arises and from
which, once all shadows of sadness had been dispelled, eternal bliss is prophesied. What are you doing, virgin? Run, I
beseech you, run and join in such joys, throw yourself at the
feet of each of the two women, embrace your bridegroom in
the one's womb, venerate his friend in the other's.

From there, follow the mother in all devotion as she en- 7
ters Bethlehem; stopping at the inn with her, be present and
help her as she gives birth, and when the little one has been
put in the manger, burst out in a voice of exultation, crying
out with Isaiah, "*A child is born to us, a son is given to us.*" Embrace that sweet manger, let love overcome shyness, let affection drive away fear, let your lips press his most sacred
feet and cover them with redoubled kisses. Then direct your
mind to the shepherds' watch, marvel at the host of angels,

exercitum admirare, caelesti melodiae tuas interpone partes, corde simul et ore decantans, *"Gloria in excelsis Deo et in terra pax hominibus bonae voluntatis."*

30. Noli in tua meditatione Magorum munera praeterire, nec fugientem in Aegyptum incomitatum relinquere. Opinare verum esse quod dicitur, eum a latronibus deprehensum in via, et ab adolescentuli cuiusdam beneficio ereptum. Erat is, ut dicunt, principis latronum filius, qui praeda potitus, cum puerulum in matris gremio conspexisset, tanta ei in eius speciosissimo vultu splendoris maiestas apparuit, ut eum supra hominem esse non ambigens, incalescens amore amplexatus est eum et, "O," inquit, "beatissime parvulorum, si aliquando se tempus obtulerit mihi miserendi, tunc memento mei, et huius temporis noli oblivisci." Ferunt hunc fuisse latronem, qui ad Christi dexteram crucifixus, cum alterum blasphemantem corripuisset, dicens, *"Neque tu times Deum, quod in eadem damnatione es, et nos quidem iuste, nam digna factis recipimus? Hic autem nihil mali fecit."* Conversus ad Dominum eum in illa quae in puerulo apparuerat intuens maiestate, pacti sui non immemor, *"Memento,"* inquit, *"mei cum veneris in regnum tuum."* Itaque ad incentivum amoris haud inutile arbitror hac uti opinione, remota omni affirmandi temeritate.

2 Praeterea nihilne tibi suavitatis aestimas accessurum, si eum apud Nazareth puerum inter pueros contempleris, si obsequentem matri, si operanti nutricio assistentem intuearis?

31. Quid si duodennem cum parentibus Ierosolymam ascendentem, et illis redeuntibus et nescientibus in urbe

take part in the heavenly melody, singing from heart and mouth alike, "*Glory to God in the highest, and on earth peace to men of good will.*"

30. Do not pass over the gifts of the Magi in your meditation, nor leave the child unaccompanied on the flight to Egypt. Believe the story that he was seized by thieves along the way and rescued through the kindness of a certain youth. This youth, they say, was the chief bandit's son, who, after he had taken the plunder, when he had caught sight of the little boy in his mother's lap, such splendid majesty appeared to the youth in that most beautiful face that he had no doubt the child was more than human. Glowing with love, he embraced the boy and said, "O most blessed of little children, if ever there is a time when you might have mercy on me, remember me then and do not forget this moment." They say this was the thief crucified on Christ's right, who rebuked the other in his blasphemy, saying, "*Do you not fear God because you are under the same sentence, yet we are condemned justly, we are getting what we deserve for our crimes? But this one? He did nothing wrong.*" Turning back to the Lord, seeing in him that same majesty that was apparent in him as a boy and recalling their agreement, the thief said, "*Remember me when you come into your kingdom.*" And so as an incitement to love I think it worthy to make use of this story, without any heedless affirmation of its truth.

In addition, do you think no sweetness will come to you if you contemplate Jesus as a boy among boys in Nazareth, if you see him obeying his mother and helping his foster father at work?

31. He went up to Jerusalem with his parents at age twelve, and they set out for home, not knowing he had

remanentem per triduum cum matre quaesieris? O quanta copia fluent lacrymae, cum audieris matrem dulci quadam increpatione filium verberantem: *"Fili, quid fecisti nobis sic? Ecce pater tuus et ego dolentes quaerebamus te."*

2   Si autem virginem sequi quocumque ierit delectet, altiora eius et secretiora scrutare, ut in Iordane flumine audias in voce Patrem, in carne Filium, in columba videas Spiritum Sanctum. Ibi tu ad spirituales invitata nuptias, sponsum suscipis datum a Patre, purgationem a Filio, pignus amoris a Spiritu Sancto.

3   Exinde solitudinis tibi secreta ditavit, sanctificavit ieiunium, ibi subeundum docens cum callido hoste conflictum. Haec tibi facta, et pro te facta, et quomodo facta sunt meditare et imitare quae facta sunt.

4   Occurrat iam nunc memoriae mulier illa deprehensa in adulterio et Iesus rogatus sententiam quid egerit quidve dixerit recordare. Cum enim scribens in terra, terrenos eos non caelestes prodidisset, *"Qui sine peccato est,"* inquit, *"vestrum, primum lapidem in illam mittat."* Cum vero omnes sententia terruisset et expulisset e templo, imaginare quam pios oculos in illam levaverit, quam dulci ac suave voce sententiam absolutionis eius protulerit. Puta quod suspiraverit, quod lacrymatus sit, cum diceret, *"Nemo te condemnavit, mulier? Nec ego te condemnabo."* Felix, ut ita dicam, hoc adulterio mulier, quae de praeteritis absolvitur, secura efficitur de futuris. Iesu bone, te dicente "Non condemnabo," quis

stayed in the city. What if you along with his mother look for him for three days? Oh, what a flood of tears will pour forth when you hear his mother giving a tender scolding: "*Son, why did you do this to us? Behold: your father and I have been looking for you in anguish.*"

If it also pleases you to follow your virgin spouse wherever he goes, examine too his secret depths, so that in the Jordan River you may hear the Father in a voice, you see the Son in flesh, and the Holy Spirit in a dove. Invited to a spiritual wedding there, you take the husband given by the Father, purification given by the Son, and a pledge of love given by the Holy Spirit.

Next, he enriched you with hidden places of solitude and sanctified your fasting, teaching you that you must enter into battle there with the crafty enemy. Meditate on these things done for you, and on your account, and about how they were done, and then imitate what was done.

Now you should call to mind the woman caught in adultery and remember what Jesus said and did when asked to pass sentence. Writing on the ground, he had revealed that these men were earthly, not heavenly: "*He among you who is without sin,*" he said, "*should cast the first stone at her.*" But when this sentence had frightened everyone and driven them from the temple, imagine how kind were the eyes he lifted to the woman, with what a sweet and gentle voice he pronounced her absolution. Think how he sighed, how tearful he was when he said, "*Has no one condemned you, woman? I will not condemn you either.*" How fortunate, if I may say so, was the woman in this adultery, who was absolved of past deeds, was made secure for the future. Good Jesus, when you say, "I will not condemn," who will condemn? When it is God who

condemnabit? Deus qui iustificat, quis est qui condemnet? Audiatur tamen de cetero vox tua: *"Vade et iam amplius noli peccare."*

5   Iam nunc domum ingredere Pharisaei et recumbentem ibi Dominum tuum attende. Accede cum illa beatissima peccatrice ad pedes eius, lava lacrymis, terge capillis, demulce osculis, et fove unguentis. Nonne iam sacri illius liquoris odore perfunderis? Si tibi adhuc suos negat pedes, insta, ora, et gravidos lacrymis oculos attolle, imisque suspiriis et inenarrabilibusque gemitibus extorque quod petis. Luctare cum Deo sicut Iacob, ut ipse se gaudeat superari. Videbitur tibi aliquando quod avertat oculos, quod aures claudat, quod desideratos pedes abscondat. Tu nihilominus *insta opportune, importune;* clama, *"Usquequo avertis faciem tuam a me? Usquequo clamabo, et non exaudies? Redde mihi,* Iesu bone, *laetitiam salutaris tui* quia *tibi dixit cor meum,* 'Quaesivi faciem tuam; *faciem tuam, Domine, requiram.'"* Certe non negabit pedes suos virgini, quos osculandos praebuit peccatrici.

6   Sed domum illam non praeteribis ubi per tegulas paralyticus ante pedes eius submittitur, ubi pietas et potestas obviaverunt sibi. *"Fili,"* inquit, *"remittuntur tibi peccata."* O mira clementia, O indicibilis misericordia! Accepit felix remissionem peccatorum, quam non petebat, quam non praecesserat confessio, non meruerat satisfactio, non exigebat contritio. Corporis salutem petebat, non animae; salutem recepit et corporis et animae. Vere, Domine, vita in voluntate tua. Si decreveris salvare me, nemo poterit prohibere. Si aliud decreveris, non est qui audeat dicere, "Cur ita facis?"

justifies, who is there to condemn? Nevertheless, let your words be heard from now on: "*Go, and sin no more.*"

Now enter the Pharisee's house and attend to your Lord 5 reclining at the table. Go to his feet along with that most blessed sinner, wash them with your tears, dry them with your hair, caress them with kisses, cherish them with perfumed oils. Are you not already bathed in the scent of that sacred liquid? If he still denies you his feet, insist, pray, lift eyes brimming with tears, and obtain what you seek in deep sighing and indescribable lamentation. Wrestle with God like Jacob, so he is glad to be beaten. It will seem to you sometimes that he averts his eyes, that he shuts his ears, that he conceals those feet you desire. Nonetheless, *insist fittingly, unfittingly,* and cry, "*How long will you turn your face from me? How long will I cry out without your listening?* Good Jesus, *give me back the joy of your salvation,* because *my heart said to you,* 'I sought your face; *it is your face, Lord, I will seek.*'" Surely, he will not deny a virgin the feet that he offered to a sinful woman for kissing.

But you will not fail to stop at that house where the para- 6 lytic was lowered down to his feet from the roof tiles, where pious love and power met one another. "*My son,*" he said, "*your sins are forgiven.*" O marvelous kindness, O indescribable mercy! The happy man received forgiveness for his sins, which he did not ask; it was neither preceded by confession nor earned through satisfaction and did not require repentance. He was seeking health for his body, not his soul, yet obtained both. Truly, Lord, life is in your hands. If you decide to save me, nobody can stop it. If you decide otherwise, there is no one who will dare say, "Why do you act this way?"

7   Pharisaee, quid murmuras? An oculus tuus nequam est quia ipse bonus est? Certe misereretur cui voluerit. Ploremus et oremus ut velit. Bonis etiam operibus pinguescat oratio, augeatur devotio, dilectio excitetur. Leventur purae manus in oratione, quas non sanguis immunditiae maculavit, tactus illicitus non foedavit, avaritia non coinquinavit. Levetur et cor sine ira et disceptatione, quod tranquillitas sedavit, pax composuit, puritas conscientiae animavit.

8   Sed nihil horum paralyticus iste legitur praemisisse, qui tamen legitur remissionem peccatorum meruisse. Haec est ineffabilis misericordiae eius virtus, cui sicut blasphemum est derogare, ita et hoc sibi praesumere stultissimum. Potest cuicumque vult hoc ipsum efficaciter dicere, quod dixit paralytico: "*Dimittuntur tibi peccata.*" Sed quicumque sine suo labore, vel contritione, vel confessione, vel etiam oratione sibi hoc dicendum exspectat, numquam ei remittentur peccata sua.

9   Sed exeundum est hinc, et ad Bethaniam veniendum, ubi sacratissima foedera amicitiae auctoritate Domini consecrantur. Diligebat enim Iesus Martham et Mariam et Lazarum. Quod ob specialis amicitiae privilegium qua illi familiariori adhaerebant affectu dictum, nemo qui ambigat. Testes sunt lacrymae illae dulces, quibus collacrymatus est lacrymantibus, quas totus populus amoris interpretabatur indicium, "*Vide,*" inquiens, "*quomodo amabat eum.*"

10   Et ecce faciunt ei cenam ibi, et Martha ministrabat. Lazarus autem erat unus ex discumbentibus. Maria autem sumpsit alabastrum unguenti, et *fracto alabastro effudit super*

Pharisee, why are you grumbling? Is your eye evil because 7
he is good? Surely he has mercy on whomever he wants. Let
us weep and pray that he wants it. Through good works, too,
let prayer increase, devotion be enhanced, love be roused.
Let pure hands be lifted in prayer, hands that the blood of
uncleanness has not stained, illicit touch has not fouled,
greed has not contaminated. Let a heart, too, be lifted without the anger and quarreling that tranquility has soothed,
peace has calmed, purity of conscience has animated.

But we do not read that the paralytic had done any of this 8
beforehand, yet we read that he had merited forgiveness of
his sins. This is the inexpressible power of God's mercy,
which it is as blasphemous to scorn as it is foolish to count
on. He can say just as effectively what he said to the paralytic—"*Your sins are forgiven*"—to whomever he wants. But
anyone who expects this to be said to him without his own
work, contrition, confession, or even prayer? His sins will
never be forgiven.

But next you must depart from here to go to Bethany, 9
where the most holy pacts of friendship are being consecrated with the Lord's authority. For Jesus loved Martha,
Mary, and Lazarus. There is no one who doubts that this was
said because of the privilege of special friendship by which
they attached themselves to him in intimate affection. The
witnesses were those sweet tears Jesus wept along with
those weeping, tears everyone interpreted as a sign of love,
saying, "*See how he loved him.*"

And behold, they made dinner for him there, and Martha 10
served. Lazarus was one of those reclining to eat, and Mary
took up an alabaster box of ointment, *and having broken open
the box, she poured the contents upon* Jesus's *head*. Rejoice, I beg

caput Jesu. Gaude, quaeso, huic interesse convivio, singulorum distingue officia: Martha ministrat, discumbit Lazarus,
ungit Maria. Hoc ultimum tuum est. Frange igitur alabastrum cordis tui, et quidquid habes devotionis, quidquid
amoris, quidquid desiderii, quidquid affectionis, totum ef-
funde super sponsi tui caput, adorans in Deo hominem et in
homine Deum.

11   Si fremit, si murmurat, si invidet proditor, si perditionem
vocat devotionem, non sit tibi curae. "*Utquid,*" ait, "*perditio
haec? Posset hoc unguentum venundari multo et dari pauperibus.*"
Pharisaeus murmurat, invidens paenitenti; murmurat Iudas,
invidens unguenti. Sed Iudex accusationem non recipit,
accusatam absolvit. "*Sine,*" inquit, "*illam; bonum enim opus
operata est in me.* Laboret Martha, ministret, paret hospitium
peregrino, esurienti cibum, sitienti potum, vestem algenti.
Ego solus Mariae, et illa mihi, mihi totum praestet quod
habet. A me quidquid optat exspectet."

12   Quid enim? Tune Mariae consulis relinquendos pedes
quos tam dulciter osculabatur, avertendos oculos ab illa spe-
ciosissima facie quam contemplatur, amovendum auditum
ab eius suavi sermone quo reficitur?

13   Sed iam surgentes eamus hinc. Quo, inquis? Certe ut insi-
dentem asello caeli terraeque Dominum comiteris, tantaque
fieri pro te obstupescens, puerorum laudibus tuas inseras,
clamans et dicens, "*Hosanna filio David: benedictus qui venit in
nomine Domini!*"

14   Iam nunc ascende cum eo in cenaculum grande stratum,
et salutaris cenae interesse deliciis gratulare. Vincat verecundiam amor, timorem excludat affectus ut saltem de micis

you, in your presence at this feast. Notice the role each one played: Martha served, Lazarus reclined, Mary anointed. This last part is yours. Therefore, break open the alabaster box of your heart, and whatever devotion, love, desire, and affection you have, pour it all upon the head of your bridegroom, adoring man in God and God in man.

If the betrayer growls, if he grumbles, if he is envious, if 11 he calls your devotion a waste, it should not be a concern to you. He asks, "*Why such waste? This ointment could be sold at a high price and the money be given to the poor.*" The Pharisee grumbled, envious of the penitent; Judas grumbled, envious of the ointment. But the Judge did not entertain the charge and absolved the accused. "*Let her alone,*" he said, "*for she did a good work for me.* Let Martha work, serve, offer welcome to the pilgrim, food to the hungry, drink to the thirsty, clothing to those suffering cold. I alone offer to Mary, and she to me, everything each of us has; let her expect from me whatever she desires."

What, then? Do you counsel Mary to leave the feet she 12 was kissing so sweetly? Are her eyes to be turned away from contemplation of that most beautiful face? Is she to stop listening to his sweet words with which she is refreshed?

But now arising, let us go from here. Where, you ask? 13 Surely so that you may accompany the Lord of heaven and earth as he sat on a donkey and, stunned that such things are being done for you, add your praises to those of the children, crying out and saying, "*Hosanna to the son of David, blessed is he who comes in the name of the Lord!*"

Now then, go up with him into the upper-story room 14 readied for supper and rejoice that you are present for the delights of the banquet of salvation. Let love overcome shyness, affection drive away fear, so that he may at least

mensae illius eleemosynam praebeat mendicanti. Vel a longe sta et quasi pauper intendens in divitem, ut aliquid accipias extende manum, famem lacrymis prode.

15   Cum autem surgens a cena linteo se praecinxerit, posueritque aquam in pelvim, cogita quae maiestas hominum pedes abluit et extergit, quae benignitas proditoris vestigia sacris manibus tangit. Specta et exspecta, et ultima omnium tuos ei pedes praebe abluendos, quia quem ipse non laverit, non habebit partem cum eo.

16   Quid modo festinas exire? Sustine paululum. Videsne? Quisnam ille est, rogo te, qui supra pectus eius recumbit, et in sinu eius caput reclinat? Felix quicumque ille est. O ecce video: *Ioannes est nomen eius.* O Ioannes, quid ibi dulcedinis, quid gratiae et suavitatis, quid luminis et devotionis ab illo haurias fonte edicito. Ibi certe *omnes thesauri sapientiae et scientiae,* ibi fons misericordiae, ibi domicilium pietatis, ibi favus aeternae suavitatis. Unde tibi, O Ioannes, omnia ista? Numquid tu sublimior Petro, Andrea sanctior, et caeteris omnibus apostolis gratior? Speciale hoc virginitatis privilegium, quia virgo es electus a Domino et ideo inter ceteros magis dilectus.

17   Iam nunc exsulta, virgo, accede propius, et aliquam tibi huius dulcedinis portionem vindicare non differas. Si ad potiora non potes, dimitte Ioanni pectus, ubi eum vinum laetitiae in divinitatis cognitione inebriet, tu currens ad ubera humanitatis, lac exprime, quo nutriaris. Inter haec cum sacratissima illa oratione discipulos commendans Patri

offer alms from the crumbs of that table as you beg. Or stand at a distance and, like a poor man looking to a rich one, put out your hand to receive something, reveal your hunger with tears.

When, rising from the table, he has tied a linen cloth 15 around himself and poured water into a basin, ponder what majesty washes and dries the feet of men, what kindness touches the feet of the betrayer with sacred hands. Watch and wait, and as the last of all, offer your feet to him to be washed, because the one he has not himself washed will have no share of him.

Why are you in a hurry to leave now? Stay a little while. 16 Don't you see? Who can that be, I ask you, who rests on his breast and puts his head into his lap? He is happy, whoever he is. Oh, now I see: *his name is John.* O John, tell us what sweetness, what grace and tenderness, what light and devotion you drink from that spring. There, surely, are *all the treasures of wisdom and knowledge,* there the font of mercy, there the dwelling place of love, there the honeycomb of eternal sweetness. From where, O John, did all these things come to you? Are you higher than Peter, holier than Andrew, dearer than all the other apostles? This is the special privilege of virginity, because you were chosen by the Lord as a virgin and therefore you were more loved than the rest.

Now then, rejoice, virgin, go nearer, and do not hesitate 17 to claim some portion of this sweetness for yourself. If you cannot aim higher, leave to John the breast where he may become drunk on the wine of gladness in knowledge of Jesus's divinity; you, running to the breasts of his humanity, squeeze out the milk that nourishes you. Meanwhile, entrusting his disciples to the Father in that most sacred

dixerit, "*Pater, serva eos in nomine tuo.*" Inclina caput, ut et tu
merearis audire, "*Volo ut ubi sum ego, et illi sint mecum.*"

18   Bonum est tibi hic esse, sed exeundum est. Praecedit ipse
ad montem Oliveti. Tu, sequere. Et licet assumpto Petro et
duobus filiis Zebedaei ad secretiora secesserit, vel a longe
intuere, quomodo in se nostram transtulerit necessitatem.
Vide quomodo ille cuius sunt omnia pavere incipit et tae-
dere, "*Tristis est,*" inquiens, "*anima mea usque ad mortem.*"
Unde hoc, Deus meus? Ita compateris mihi te exhibens hominem, ut quodammodo videaris nescire quod Deus es.
Prostratus in faciem oras, et *factus est sudor* tuus, *sicut guttae
sanguinis decurrentis in terram.*

19   Quid stas? Accurre, et suavissimas illas guttas adlambe, et
pulverem pedum illius linge. Noli dormire cum Petro, ne
merearis audire, "*Sic non potuisti una hora vigilare mecum?*"

20   Sed ecce iam proditorem praeeuntem impiorum turba
subsequitur, et osculum praebente Iuda, manus iniciunt in
Dominum tuum. Tenent, ligant, et illas dulces manus vinculis stringunt. Quis ferat? Scio, occupat nunc cor tuum pietas,
omnia viscera tua zelus inflammat. Sine, rogo, patiatur qui
pro te patitur. Quid optas gladium? Quid irasceris? Quid in-
dignaris? Si instar Petri cuiuslibet aurem abscideris, si ferro
brachium tuleris, si pedem truncaveris, ipse restituet omnia,
qui etiam si quem occideris, absque dubio suscitabit.

21   Sequere potius eum ad atrium principis sacerdotum, et
speciosissimam eius faciem, quam illi sputis illiniunt, tu

prayer, he said, "*Father, keep them in your name.*" Bow your head so that you, too, may deserve to hear, "*I want that they, too, may be with me where I am.*"

It is good for you to be here, but one must depart. He 18 himself leads the way to the Mount of Olives. You, follow. And although, having taken up Peter and the two sons of Zebedee, he withdrew to more remote places, observe, if only from afar, how he took our need upon himself. See how he, to whom all belongs, begins to fear and grow weary, saying, "*My soul is sad unto death.*" Where did this come from, my God? Showing yourself in mortal form, you suffer with me so much that somehow you seem not to know that you are God. Lying prostrate, you pray and *your sweat became like drops of blood trickling on the ground.*

Why are you standing still? Run and lap up those sweetest 19 drops and lick the dust from his feet. Do not keep on sleeping like Peter, or you too may deserve to hear, "*Could you not thus stay awake with me for one hour?*"

But now behold a crowd of wicked people following the 20 betrayer as he leads the way, and once Judas has offered the kiss, they lay their hands on your Lord. They grab him, tie him up, and bind those sweet hands in chains. Who could stand it? I know, love now seizes your heart, zealous anger inflames your whole being. Allow him to suffer, I beg, he who suffers for your sake. Why do you want a sword? Why are you angry? Why are you resentful? If like Peter you cut off someone's ear, if you sever an arm with a sword, if you hack off a leg, Jesus will restore them all—and there is no doubt that even if you killed someone, he will revive him.

Instead, follow him to the courtyard of the chief priest, 21 and wash with your tears his beautiful face that they have

lacrymis lava. Intuere quam piis oculis, quam misericorditer, quam efficaciter tertio negantem respexit Petrum, quando ille conversus, et in se reversus, flevit amare. Utinam, bone Iesu, tuus me dulcis respiciat oculus, qui te totiens ad vocem ancillae procacis, carnis scilicet meae, pessimis operibus affectibusque negavi.

22 Sed iam mane facto traditur Pilato. Ibi accusatur, et tacet, quoniam tamquam ovis ad occisionem ducitur, et sicut agnus coram tondente se, non aperuit os suum. Vide, attende quomodo stat ante praesidem, inclinato capite, demissis oculis, vultu placido, sermone raro, paratus ad opprobria et ad verbera promptus. Scio non potes ulterius sustinere, nec dulcissimum dorsum eius flagellis atteri, nec faciem alapis caedi, nec tremendum illud caput spinis coronari, nec dexteram quae caelum fecit et terram arundine dehonestari, tuis oculis aspicere poteris.

23 Ecce educitur flagellatus, portans spineam coronam, et purpureum vestimentum. Et dicit Pilatus, "*Ecce homo.*" Vere homo est. Quis dubitet? Testes sunt plagae virgarum, livor ulcerum, foeditas sputorum. Iam nunc agnosce, zabule, quia est homo. "Vere homo est," inquis. Sed quid est quod in tot iniuriis non irascitur ut homo, non suis indignatur tortoribus ut homo? Ergo plus est quam homo. Sed quis cognoscit illum? Cognoscitur certe homo impiorum iudicia sustinens, sed cognoscetur Deus iudicium faciens.

smeared with spit. See with what loving eyes, how mercifully, with what effect he gazed on Peter, when he denied him the third time, when Peter, turning back and returning to his senses, wept bitterly. Good Jesus, how I wish your sweet eyes would rest on me, who has so many times denied you through the worst deeds and affections at the bidding of that shameless servant, namely my flesh.

But now, in the morning, he is handed over to Pilate. 22 There he is accused and remains silent, for he is led like a sheep to slaughter and, like a lamb before his shearer, does not open his mouth. Look, pay attention to how he stands before the governor, head bowed, eyes cast down, face calm, saying little, prepared for taunts and ready for a beating. I know you cannot endure it any longer, that you will not be able to look with your own eyes at the flesh of his sweetest back being destroyed by whips, nor at his face cut by slapping hands, nor at that awe-inspiring head crowned with thorns, nor at the right hand that made heaven and earth being mocked with a reed.

After he is beaten, he is led out, bearing the crown of 23 thorns and a purple cloak. And Pilate says, "*Behold the man.*" Truly he is a man. Who could doubt it? The whip marks, the bruises, the foulness of spit bear witness. Now, devil, recognize that he is a man. "Truly he is a man," you say. But why is it that amid so much injustice he does not become angry like a man, does not resent his tormenters like a man? Therefore, he is more than a man. But who recognizes him? Doubtless he is known as a man, undergoing the judgments of the wicked, but he will be recognized as God in his judgment.

24   Sero animadvertisti, zabule. Quid tibi per mulierem visum est agere ut dimittatur? Tarde locutus es. Sedet pro tri-
bunali iudex, prolata est sententia, iam propriam portans
crucem ducitur ad mortem. O spectaculum! Videsne? Ecce
principatus super humerum eius. Haec est virga aequitatis, virga
regni eius.

25   Datur ei vinum felle mixtum. Exuitur vestimentis suis,
et inter milites dividuntur. Tunica non scinditur, sed sorte
transit ad unum. Dulces manus eius et pedes clavis perforan-
tur, et extensus in cruce inter latrones suspenditur. Mediator Dei et hominum, inter caelum et terram medius pendens, ima superis unit, et caelestibus terrena coniungit.
Stupet caelum, terra miratur.

26   Quid tu? Non mirum si sole contristante, tu contristaris,
si terra tremiscente, tu contremiscis, si scissis saxis, cor
tuum scinditur, si flentibus iuxta crucem mulieribus, tu col-
lacrymaris.

27   Verum in his omnibus considera illud dulcissimum pectus, quam tranquillitatem servaverit, quam exhibuerit pietatem. Non suam attendit iniuriam, non poenam reputat, non
sentit contumelias, sed illis potius a quibus patitur, ille com-
patitur, a quibus vulneratur, ille medetur, vitam procurat, a
quibus occiditur. Cum qua mentis dulcedine, cum qua spiritus devotione, in qua caritatis plenitudine clamat, "*Pater,
ignosce illis!*"

28   Ecce ego, Domine, tuae maiestatis adorator, non tui corporis interfector, tuae mortis venerator, non tuae passionis
irrisor, tuae misericordiae contemplator, non infirmitatis
contemptor. Interpellet itaque pro me tua dulcis humanitas,

You have understood too late, devil. What did you think 24
you were doing, working through the woman to gain pardon
for him? You spoke too late. The judge is before the judgment seat, the sentence is pronounced, and now, carrying
his own cross, he is led to death. What a sight! Do you see it?
Behold, *princely power is on his shoulder.* This is the scepter of
justice, the scepter of his kingdom.

He is given wine mixed with gall. He is stripped of his 25
clothing and it is divided among the soldiers. His tunic is
not torn up, but falls to one of them by lot. His sweet hands
and feet are pierced with nails and, stretched out on the
cross, he is hung between thieves. The mediator between
God and mankind, hanging midway between heaven and
earth, he unites the depths to the heights and joins earthly
things to heavenly ones. Heaven is stunned, earth marvels.

And you? No wonder if you mourn when the sun is 26
mourning, if you tremble along with the trembling earth, if
your heart is broken when the rocks are broken, if you weep
along with the women weeping by the cross.

But amid all this, consider that sweetest heart, what tran- 27
quility it maintained, what love it showed. He takes no notice of the harm done him, nor thinks about his punishment,
nor feels the insults, but instead suffers along with those
who make him suffer, heals those who wound him, procures
life for those who kill him. With what sweetness of mind,
what devotion of spirit, in what fullness of love he cries out,
"*Father, forgive them!*"

Here I am, Lord, worshiping your majesty, not killing 28
your body, venerating your death, not mocking your suffering, observing your mercy, not scorning your weakness.
Therefore, let your sweet humanity intercede for me, let

commendet me Patri tuo tua ineffabilis pietas. Dic igitur, dulcis Domine, "Pater, ignosce illi."

29 At tu, virgo, cui maior est apud virginis filium confidentia a mulieribus quae longe stant, cum matre virgine et discipulo virgine accede ad crucem, et perfusum pallore vultum comminus intuere. Quid ergo? Tu sine lacrymis, amantissimae dominae tuae lacrymas videbis? Tu siccis manes oculis, et eius animam pertransit gladius doloris? Tu sine singultu audies dicentem matri, "*Mulier, ecce filius tuus,*" et Ioanni, "*Ecce mater tua,*" cum discipulo matrem committeret, latroni paradisum promitteret?

30 Tunc unus ex militibus lancea latus eius aperuit, et exivit sanguis et aqua. Festina, ne tardaveris, comede favum cum melle tuo, bibe vinum tuum cum lacte tuo. Sanguis tibi in vinum vertitur ut inebrieris, in lac aqua mutatur ut nutriaris. Facta sunt tibi in petra flumina, in membris eius vulnera, et in maceria corporis eius caverna, in quibus instar columbae latitans, et deosculans singula ex sanguine eius fiant sicut vitta coccinea labia tua, et eloquium tuum dulce.

31 Sed adhuc exspecta donec nobilis ille decurio veniens, extractis clavis, manus pedesque dissolvat. Vide quomodo felicissimis brachiis dulce illud corpus complectitur ac suo astringit pectori. Tunc dicere potuit vir ille sanctissimus, "*Fasciculus myrrhae dilectus meus mihi, inter ubera mea commorabitur.*" Sequere, tu, pretiosissimum illum caeli terraeque thesaurum, et vel pedes porta, vel manus brachiaque sustenta, vel certe defluentes minutatim pretiosissimi sanguinis stillas curiosius collige, et pedum illius pulverem linge.

your indescribable love commend me to your Father. So, sweet Lord, say, "Father, forgive him."

But you, virgin, more confident before the virgin's son 29 than the women who stand at a distance, approach the cross with the virgin mother and the virgin disciple, and look close up at his face covered by paleness. What, then? Will you be without tears when you see the tears of your most beloved lady? Will you remain dry-eyed as the sword of grief pierces her soul? Will you not sob hearing him saying to his mother, "*Woman, behold your son,*" and to John, "*Behold your mother,*" when he entrusts his mother to the disciple, promises paradise to the thief?

Then one of the soldiers opened his side with a lance, and 30 blood and water came forth. Hurry, do not delay, eat the honeycomb with your honey, drink your wine with your milk. For you the blood is turned into wine to make you drunk, the water is changed into milk to nourish you. The rocks were made into rivers for you, wounds made in his limbs, a hole made in the wall of his body. Hiding in them, like a dove, and kissing them one by one, let your lips become like a scarlet band from the stain of his blood and let your speech become sweet.

But keep waiting until that noble counselor comes and, 31 after pulling out the nails, frees the hands and feet. See how he embraces that sweet body with most blessed arms and clasps it to his chest. Then that most holy man could say, "*My beloved is to me like a bundle of myrrh, he will remain between my breasts.*" You, follow that most precious treasure of heaven and earth and either carry his feet, or lift his hands and arms, or certainly very carefully collect the drops of his most precious blood, falling one by one, and lick the dust on

Cerne praeterea quam dulciter, quam diligenter beatissimus Nicodemus sacratissima eius membra tractavit digitis, fovit unguentis, et cum sancto Ioseph involvit sindone, collocat in sepulcro.

32   Noli praeterea Magdalenae deserere comitatum, sed paratis aromatibus, cum ea Domini tui sepulcrum visitare memento. O si quod illa oculis, tu in spiritu cernere merearis: nunc super lapidem revolutum ab ostio angelum residentem, nunc intra monumentum unum ad caput, alium ad pedes resurrectionis gloriam praedicantes, nunc ipsum Iesum Mariam flentem et tristem tam dulci reficientem oculo, tam suavi voce dicentem, "Maria." Quid hac voce dulcius, quid suavius, quid iucundius? "Maria": rumpantur ad hanc vocem omnes capitis cataractae, ab ipsis medullis eliciantur lacrymae, singultus atque suspiria ab imis trahantur visceribus. "Maria": O beata, quid tibi mentis fuit, quid animi, cum ad hanc vocem te prosterneres, et reddens vicem salutanti inclamares, "Rabbi?" Quo, rogo, affectu, quo desiderio, quo mentis ardore, qua devotione cordis clamasti, "Rabbi?" Nam plura dicere lacrymae prohibent, cum vocem occludat affectus, osque animae corporisque sensus nimius amor absorbeat.

33   Sed, O dulcis Iesu, cur a sacratissimis ac desideratissimis pedibus tuis sic arces amantem? "*Noli,*" inquit, "*me tangere.*" O verbum durum, verbum intolerabile: "*Noli me tangere.*" Ut quid, Domine? Quare non tangam? Desiderata illa vestigia

his feet. See furthermore how sweetly, how carefully the most blessed Nicodemus touches the most sacred limbs with his fingers, soothes them with ointments, and along with holy Joseph wraps them in the shroud and lays them to rest in the tomb.

Do not, furthermore, abandon the companionship of the 32 Magdalene, but remember to visit the tomb of your Lord with her once the spices are prepared. Oh, if you could be worthy to see in spirit what she saw with her eyes: first an angel sitting on the stone rolled away from the entry, then one angel sitting inside at the head of the tomb, another at its feet, proclaiming the glory of the resurrection, and finally Jesus himself restoring the sad and weeping Mary with his ever-so-sweet gaze and saying with his ever-so-gentle voice, "Mary." What is sweeter than this word, what is gentler, what is more pleasing? "Mary": let all your head's floodgates burst at this word, let tears be drawn forth from the very core of your being, let sobbing and sighing be drawn out from deep within your innermost self. "Mary": O blessed one, what was in your mind, what was in your spirit, when you prostrated yourself at that word and, greeting in return the one who greeted you, you called out, "Rabbi?" With what depth of feeling, I ask, with what desire, with what ardor of mind, with what devotion of heart did you cry out, "Rabbi?" Tears make it impossible to say more, since emotion stifles speech and love beyond measure swallows the soul's voice and the body's senses.

But, O sweet Jesus, why do you keep her who loves you 33 from your most sacred and desired feet this way? "*Do not touch me,*" he says. What a harsh, unbearable thing to say, "*Do not touch me.*" But why, Lord? Why should I not touch you?

tua pro me perforata clavis, perfusa sanguine non tangam, non deosculabor? An immitior es solito, quia gloriosior? Ecce, non dimittam te, non recedam a te, non parcam lacrymis, pectus singultibus suspiriisque rumpetur, nisi tangam.

34   Et ille: "Noli timere, non aufertur tibi bonum hoc, sed differtur. Vade tantum et nuntia fratribus meis quia surrexi." Currit cito, cito volens redire. Redit sed cum aliis mulieribus. Quibus ipse Iesus occurrens blanda salutatione, deiectas erigit, tristes consolatur. Adverte. Tunc est datum, quod fuit ante dilatum. Accesserunt enim et tenuerunt pedes eius.

35   Hic quamdiu potes, virgo, morare. Non has delicias tuas somnus interpolet, nullus exterior tumultus impediat.

36   Verum quia in hac misera vita nihil stabile, nihil aeternum est, nec unquam in eodem statu permanet homo, necesse est, ut anima nostra, dum vivimus, quadam varietate pascatur. Unde a praeteritorum recordatione ad experientiam praesentium transeamus, ut ex his quoque quantum a nobis sit diligendus Deus intelligere valeamus.

   32. Non parvum aestimo beneficium quod bene utens malo parentum nostrorum creavit nos de carne illorum, et inspiravit in nobis spiraculum vitae, discernens nos ab illis qui vel abortivi proiecti sunt ab utero, vel qui inter materna viscera suffocati poenae videntur concepti non vitae. Quid etiam quod integra nobis et sana membra creavit, ne essemus nostris dolori, opprobrio alienis?

Will I not touch, will I not kiss those desired limbs, pierced with nails and drenched in blood for me? Are you more severe than usual because you are more glorious? No, I will not let you go, I will not withdraw from you, I will not spare my tears, my breast will burst with sobs and sighs unless I touch you.

He replies, "Do not fear, this happiness is not taken away 34 from you, only postponed. Just go tell my brothers that I have risen." She runs quickly, wanting to return quickly. She returns, but with other women. Jesus, greeting them with kindness, raises up the dejected, comforts the sad. Take note. Now what was postponed was granted, for they approached and clasped his feet.

Linger here as long as you can, virgin. Let no sleep inter- 35 rupt these delights of yours, nor any disturbance from outside interfere with them.

But because nothing is stable in this wretched life, noth- 36 ing is eternal, nor does man ever remain in the same state, it is necessary that our soul feed on a certain variety while we live. For that reason, let us pass from remembering things past to the experience of things present, so that from these, too, we may be able to understand how we must love God.

32. I count it no small blessing that, making good use of our parents' evil, God created us from their flesh and breathed the breath of life into us. He set us apart from those who, either cast out of the maternal womb prematurely or suffocated within it, seem to have been conceived for punishment rather than life. Why is it also the case that he created full and healthy limbs for us, so we would not be a burden to our family, a reproach to strangers?

2   Magnum certum certe et hoc. Sed quomodo illud quantae bonitatis fuerit aestimabimus, quod eo tempore, et inter tales nos nasci voluit, per quos ad fidem suam et sacramenta perveniremus? Videamus innumerabilibus milibus hominum hoc negatum quod nobis gratulamur esse concessum, cum quibus nobiscum una esset eademque conditio. Illi derelicti per iustitiam; nos vocati sumus per gratiam. Procedamus intuentes munus eius fuisse, quod educati a parentibus fuimus, quod nos flamma non laesit, quod non absorbuit aqua, quod non vexati a daemone, quod non percussi a bestiis, quod praecipitio non necati, quod usque ad congruam aetatem in eius fide et bona voluntate nutriti.

3   Hucusque simul cucurrimus, soror, quibus una fuit eademque conditio, quos idem pater genuit, idem venter complexus est, eadem viscera profuderunt. Iam nunc in me, soror, adverte quanta fecerit Deus animae tuae. Divisit enim inter te et me quasi inter lucem et tenebras, te sibi conservans, me mihi relinquens. Deus meus, quo abii, quo fugi, quo evasi? Eiectus quippe a facie tua sicut Cain, habitavi in terra Naid, vagus et profugus, et quicumque invenit me occidit me. Quid enim ageret miserabilis creatura, a suo derelicta creatore? Quo iret vel ubi lateret ovis erronea, suo destituta pastore? O soror, fera pessima devoravit fratrem tuum. In me igitur cerne quantum tibi contulerit, qui te a tali bestia conservavit illaesam.

4   Quam miser ego tunc qui meam pudicitiam perdidi; tam beata tu, cuius virginitatem gratia divina protexit. Quotiens tentata, quotiens impetita, tua tibi est castitas reservata,

This, too, is surely a great thing. But how will we know 2
what great kindness it was that he wanted us to be born at
that time and among those people with whose guidance we
came to his faith and sacraments? Let us see that what we
rejoice was granted to us was denied to untold thousands of
people, although we share one and the same condition with
them. They were forsaken by reason of justice; we were
called by reason of grace. Let us proceed, recognizing that it
was God's gift that we were raised by our parents, that no
fire harmed us, that no water swallowed us, that we were not
tormented by a demon, nor trampled by animals, nor killed
by a fall, that we were raised to a fitting age in God's faith
and goodwill.

We ran along together this far, sister, we whose condition 3
was one and the same, whom the same father sired, the same
womb enclosed and brought forth. Right now, sister, turn
your attention to how much God did for your soul through
me. For he separated you and me like light and darkness,
keeping you for himself, leaving me to myself. My God,
where did I go, where did I flee, where did I escape? Indeed,
driven away from your face like Cain, I lived in the land of
Nod, a wanderer and a fugitive, and whoever met me killed
me. What, then, could he do, a miserable creature abandoned by his creator? Where could the wandering sheep,
deprived of its shepherd, go or hide? O sister, the worst wild
beast devoured your brother. By my example, therefore,
perceive how much he, in keeping you unharmed by such a
beast, conferred on you.

What a wretch I was then, my chastity lost; how blessed 4
are you, whose virginity divine grace protected. Every time
it was tempted, every time it was assailed, your chastity was

cum ego libens in turpia quaeque progrediens, coacervavi mihi materiam ignis quo comburerer, materiam foetoris quo necarer, materiam vermium a quibus corroderer.

5   Recole si placet illas foeditates meas pro quibus me plangebas, et corripiebas saepe puella puerum, femina masculum. Sed non fallit scriptura quae ait, *"Nemo potest corrigere, quem Deus despexerit."* O quantum diligendus est a te qui cum me repelleret, te attraxit, et cum esset aequa utriusque conditio, cum me despiceret, te dilexit!

6   Recole nunc, ut dixi, corruptiones meas, cum exhalaretur nebula libidinis ex limosa concupiscentia carnis et scatebra pubertatis, nec esset qui eriperet et salvum faceret. *Verba* enim *iniquorum praevaluerunt super me,* qui in suavi poculo amoris propinabant mihi venenum luxuriae, convenientesque in unum affectionis suavitas et cupiditatis impuritas rapiebant imbecillem adhuc aetatem meam per abrupta vitiorum atque mersabant gurgite flagitiorum. Invaluerat super me ira et indignatio tua, Deus, et nesciebam. *Ibam longius a te, et sinebas. Iactabar et effundebar,* diffluebam per immunditias meas, *et tacebas.*

7   Eia, soror, diligenter attende omnia ista turpia et nefanda, in quae me meum praecipitavit arbitrium, et scito te in haec omnia corruisse, si non te Christi misericordia conservasset.

8   Nec haec dico quasi nihil mihi contulerit boni, cum exceptis his quae superius diximus utrisque collata, mira patientia meas sustinuit iniquitates, cui debeo quod me terra

preserved for you, while I, willingly advancing in every filthy behavior, piled up combustible matter to burn me, stinking matter to kill me, matter for the worms that would gnaw me.

Consider, if you please, those foul deeds of mine that 5 caused you to mourn for me, often as a girl reproaching me in boyhood, then as a woman reproaching me in manhood. Scripture does not err when it says, "*No one can correct whom God has despised.*" Oh, how much you should love him, who attracted you when he repelled me, and although our condition was the same, he loved you when he spurned me!

Now consider, as I said, my corruptions, when a fog of 6 lust was exhaled from the flesh's slimy longing and youth's gushing torrent and there was nobody to snatch me out of it and save me. For *the words of the wicked prevailed over me,* and they set before me the poison of depravity in a sweet cup of love, dissolving into one drink the sweetness of affection and the impurity of desire, that threw my still-weak youth down the precipices of vice and plunged it into an abyss of degradation. Your anger and displeasure with me grew stronger, God, and I did not know. *I went further from you, and you let me. I was tossed about and cast away* and I was dissolved in my filth, *yet you kept silent.*

Come now, sister, consider carefully all these shameful 7 and wicked deeds into which my will hurled me headlong, and know that you would have fallen into all of them had Christ's mercy not kept you safe.

I do not say these things as if he conferred no good on me 8 when, beyond those favors conferred on both of us that I mentioned before, his wonderful patience endured my wickedness, and I owe it to him that the earth did not

non absorbuit, non fulminavit caelum, non flumina submer-
serunt. Quomodo enim sustineret creatura tantam iniuriam
creatoris, si non impetum eius cohiberet ipse qui condidit,
qui non vult mortem peccatoris, sed ut convertatur et vivat?

9   Ad illud quantae fuit gratiae, quod fugientem prosecutus
est, timenti blanditus quod erexit in spem totiens despera-
tum, quod suis obruit beneficiis ingratum, quod gustu in-
terioris dulcedinis immundis assuetum delectationibus attraxit et illexit, quod indissolubilia malae consuetudinis
vincula solvit, et abstractum saeculo benigne suscepit.

10   Taceo multa et magna misericordiae suae circa me opera,
ne aliquid gloriae quae tota illius est, ad me videatur trans-
ire. Ita enim secundum hominum aestimationem sibi co-
haerent gratia dantis et felicitas recipientis, ut non solum
laudetur, quia solus laudandus esset ille qui dedit, sed etiam
ille qui recipit. Quid enim habet aliquis quod non accepit? Si
autem gratis accepit, quare laudatur velut promeruerit? Tibi
igitur laus, Deus meus, tibi gloria, tibi gratiarum actio, mihi
autem confusio faciei, qui tot mala feci, et tot bona recepi.

11   "Quid igitur," inquis, "me minus accepisti?" O soror,
quam felicior ille est cuius navem plenam mercibus et onus-
tam divitiis flatus mitior integram revexit in portum, quam
qui passus naufragium vix nudus mortem evasit. Tu ergo in
his quas tibi divina gratia servavit, exsultas divitiis; mihi
maximus labor incumbit ut fracta redintegrem, amissa recu-
perem, scissa resarciam. Verumtamen et me nolo aemuleris,

swallow me, lightning strike me, rivers drown me. For how could a creature endure such injury from his creator except that he who made him, wanting not the death of a sinner but that he be converted and live, refrained from attack?

In addition, how great a grace it was that he followed me 9 in my flight, soothing my fearful self, lifted me to hope so many times when I despaired, overwhelmed my ingratitude with his kindnesses, attracted and enticed one accustomed to filthy delights with a taste of interior sweetness, broke the unbreakable shackles of accustomed wickedness, and kindly received me after he rescued me from the world.

I am silent concerning the many and great works of his 10 mercy toward me, so that none of the glory that is wholly his should seem to pass over to me. For according to human judgment the grace of the giver and the good fortune of the receiver are so intertwined that not only is he praised who alone deserves to be praised—he who gave—but also he who receives. What does anyone have that he has not received? If he received the gift freely, why is he praised as if he deserved it? Therefore, my God, to you be the praise, to you the glory, to you the thanksgiving, but to me, the blushing face of one who did so much evil and received so much good.

You ask, "In what, then, did you receive less than me?" O 11 sister, how much happier is he whose ship, filled with goods and weighed down with riches, was carried by a gentle breeze into port unharmed, than he who has suffered shipwreck and, naked, barely escaped death. Rejoice, then, in the riches divine grace has preserved for you, whereas for me there is still immense labor to repair what is broken, recover what is lost, mend what is torn. Nevertheless, I do not

valdeque putes erubescendum, si post tot flagitia in illa vita tibi fuero inventus aequalis, cum saepe virginitatis gloriam intervenientia quaedam vitia minuant, et veteris conservationis opprobrium morum mutatio et succedentes vitiis virtutes obliterent.

12   Sed iam illa in quibus tibi sola conscia es divinae bonitatis inspice munera: quam iucunda facie abrenuntianti saeculo Christus occurrit, quibus esurientem deliciis pavit, quas miserationum suarum divitias ostendit, quos inspiravit affectus, quo te caritatis poculo debriavit. Nam si fugitivum servum suum et rebellem sola sua miseratione vocatum spiritalium consolationum non reliquit expertem, quid dulcedinis crediderim eum virgini contulisse? Si tentabaris, ille sustentabat; si periclitabaris, ille erigebat; si tristabaris, ipse confortabat; si fluctuabas, ille solidabat. Quotiens prae timore arescenti pius consolator astabat, quotiens aestuanti prae amore ipse se tuis visceribus infundebat, quotiens psallantem vel legentem spiritalium sensuum lumine illustrabat, quotiens orantem in quoddam ineffabile desiderium sui rapiebat, quotiens mentem tuam a terrenis subtractam, ad caelestes delicias et paradisiacas amoenitates transportabat!

13   Haec omnia revolve animo, ut in eum totus tuus resolvatur affectus. Vilescat tibi mundus, omnis amor carnalis sordescat. Nescias te esse in hoc mundo, quae ad illos qui in caelis sunt et Deo vivunt, tuum transtulisti propositum. *Ubi est thesaurus tuus, ibi* sit *et cor tuum.* Noli cum argenteis

want you to emulate me, and you should think it something to blush at deeply, if after so many sins, I am found equal to you in the next life, for often the onset of certain vices may threaten the glory of virginity and a changed way of life may obliterate the disgrace of old habits as virtues take the place of vices.

But now consider those gifts of divine goodness of which 12 you alone are aware: with what a cheerful face Christ meets you as you renounce the world, with what delicacies he feeds your hunger, what riches of his mercy he shows you, what affection he inspires in you, with what cup of love he intoxicates you. For if he did not leave bereft of spiritual consolations his fugitive, rebellious slave, summoned by his mercy alone, what sweetness should I believe has he not granted a virgin? If you were tempted, he supported you; if you were in danger, he rescued you; if you were sad, he comforted you; if you wavered, he steadied you. How often did the loving consoler stand by you when you dried up in fear, how often did he pour himself into your innermost being as you burned with love, how often did he illuminate you with the light of spiritual meanings as you sang psalms or read, how often did he seize you with some indescribable desire for him as you prayed, how often did he transport your mind, withdrawn from earthly matters, to heavenly delight and the pleasures of paradise!

Turn all of this over in your mind so that all your feelings 13 are poured out to him. Let the world become worthless to you, all carnal love grow foul. You should not know you are in this world, for you have shifted your purpose in life toward those who are in heaven and live with God. *Where your treasure is, there your heart* should be *too.* Do not imprison

simulacris vili marsupio tuo tuum includere animum qui numquam cum nummorum pondere poterit transvolare ad caelum. Puta te cottidie morituram, et de crastino non cogitabis, non te futuri temporis sterilitas terreat, non futurae famis timor tuam mentem deiciat, sed ex ipso tota fiducia tua pendeat qui aves pascit et lilia vestit. Ipse sit horreum tuum, ipse apotheca, ipse marsupium, ipse divitiae tuae, ipse deliciae tuae. Solus sit tibi omnia in omnibus.

14   Et haec interim de praesentibus satis sint.

33. Qui autem tanta suis praestat in praesenti, quantum illis servat in futuro!

2   Principium futurorum et finis praesentium mors est. Hanc cuius natura non horret, cuius non expavescet affectus? Nam bestiae fuga, latibulis, et aliis mille modis mortem cavent, vitam tuentur. Iam nunc diligenter attende quid tua tibi respondeat conscientia, quid praesumat fides tua, quid spes promittat quid expectet affectus.

3   Si vita tua tibi oneri est, si mundus fastidio, si caro dolori, profecto desiderio tibi mors est, quae vitae huius onus deponit, finem ponit fastidio, corporis dolorem absumit. Hoc unum dico omnibus mundi huius praestare deliciis, honoribus, atque divitiis, si ob conscientiae serenitatem, fidei firmitatem, spei certitudinem, mortem non timeas. Quod ille maxime poterit experiri qui aliquo tempore sub hac servitute suspirans, in liberioris conscientiae auras evasit. Hae sunt futurae beatitudinis tuae primitiae salutares, ut morte

your spirit with silver images in your worthless purse, which will never be able to fly its way to heaven weighed down by coins. Reflect every day that you are going to die, and you will not consider the morrow. Let no future barrenness frighten you, nor fear of future hunger depress you, but let all your trust depend on the one who feeds the birds and clothes the lilies. He himself should be your barn, your storehouse, your purse, your wealth, your delight. He alone should be all things in all for you.

Let this be enough, for the moment, about things pres- 14
ent.

33. But he who offers such wonderful things to his people in the present keeps so much in reserve for them in the future!

The beginning of things to come and the end of things 2
present is death. Whose nature does not tremble before it, whose feelings do not dread it? Animals guard against death and preserve life through flight, concealment, and a thousand other strategies. Now then, pay close attention to what your conscience advises, what your faith trusts, what your hope promises, what your feelings await.

If your life is a burden to you, if the world is disgust, if 3
flesh is pain, then death is truly what you desire, death that casts aside the burden of this life, puts an end to disgust, takes away bodily pain. I mean that the only thing surpassing all the pleasures, honors, and riches of this world is if, in serenity of conscience, firmness of faith, and certainty of hope, you do not fear death. He can best experience this relief who, sighing beneath the burden of his present slavery, has at some time escaped to the fresh air of a freer conscience. These are the salvific first fruits of your future

superveniente, naturalem horrorem fides superet, spes temperet, conscientia secura repellat.

4   Et vide quomodo mors beatitudinis principium est laborum meta, peremptoria vitiorum. Sic enim scriptum est: "*Beati mortui qui in Domino moriuntur. Amodo iam dicit Spiritus, ut requiescant a laboribus suis.*" Unde propheta reproborum ab electorum mortem discernens, "*Omnes,*" inquit, "*reges dormierunt in gloria, vir in domo sua, tu autem proiectus es de sepulchro tuo quasi stirps inutilis, pollutus et obvolutus.*" Dormiunt quippe in gloria quorum mortem bona commendat conscientia, quoniam *pretiosa* est *in conspectu Domini mors sanctorum eius.* Dormit sane in gloria cuius dormitioni assistunt angeli, occurrunt sancti, et concivi suo praebentes auxilium et impertientes solatium, hostibus se opponunt, obsistentes repellunt, refellunt accusantes et sic usque ad sinum Abrahae sanctam animam comitantes in loco pacis collocant et quietis.

5   *Non sic, impii, non sic,* quos de corpore quasi de foetenti sepulchro, pessimi spiritus, cum instrumentis infernalibus extrahentes, pollutos libidine, obvolutos cupiditate, iniciunt ignibus exurendos, tradunt vermibus lacerandos, aeternis foetoribus deputant suffocandos. Vere expectatio iustorum laetitia, spes autem impiorum peribit.

6   Sane qualis sit illa requies, quae pax illa, quae iucunditas in sinu Abrahae, quae illic quiescentibus promittitur et expectatur, quia experientia non docuit, stilus explicare non poterit. Expectant felices donec impleatur numerus fratrum

blessedness, so that at the approach of death, faith overcomes natural fear, hope tempers it, confident conscience drives it away.

And see how death is the beginning of blessedness, the 4 end of labors, the destroyer of vices. So it is written: "*Blessed are the dead who die in the Lord. Henceforth, says the Spirit, let them rest from their labors.*" And so the prophet, distinguishing the death of the wicked from the death of the elect, says, "*All kings have slept in glory, each man in his house, but you were thrown out of your tomb like a worthless root, rotten and twisted.*" They indeed sleep in glory whose death good conscience commends, for *the death of saints* is *precious in the sight of the Lord.* Truly he sleeps in glory whom the angels stand by as he falls asleep, whom the saints, giving comfort and offering aid to their fellow citizen, run to meet. Aligning themselves against his enemies, repelling those who resist, refuting those who accuse, and in this way escorting the holy soul all the way to the bosom of Abraham, they lay it to rest in a place of peace and quiet.

Not so the wicked, not so. The most evil spirits, using hell's 5 instruments to drag them from their bodies as if from a stinking tomb, throw them, rotted with lust and twisted with greed, to be burned in fire, they hand them over to be mangled by worms, they condemn them to be suffocated by eternal stench. Truly the expectation of the just is happiness, but the hope of the wicked will perish.

Of course because experience has not taught it, a pen 6 cannot describe what kind of rest that is, what peace, what delight in the bosom of Abraham, or what is promised to and awaited by those resting there. They wait happily until the number of their brothers is completed, so that on the

suorum ut in die resurrectionis duplicis stolae induti gloria, corporis pariter et animae perpetua felicitate fruantur.

7   Iam nunc diei illius intuere terrorem, quando virtutes caelorum movebuntur, elementa ignis calore solventur, patebunt inferi, occulta omnia nudabuntur. Veniet desuper Iudex iratus, ardens furor eius, et ut tempestas currus, ut reddat in ira vindictam et vastationem in flamma ignis. Beatus qui paratus est occurrere illi. Quid tunc miseris animi erit quos nunc luxuria foedat, avaritia dissipat, extollit superbia? Exibunt angeli et separabunt malos de medio iustorum, istos a dextris, illos a sinistris statuentes.

8   Cogita nunc te ante Christi tribunal inter utramque hanc societatem assistere et necdum in partem alteram separatam. Deflecte nunc oculos ad sinistram Iudicis et miseram illam multitudinem contemplare. Qualis ibi horror, quis foetor, quis timor, quis dolor! Stant miseri et infelices stridentes dentibus, nudo latere palpitantes, aspecto horribiles, vultu deformes, deiecti prae pudore, prae corporis turpitudine et nuditate confusi. Latere volunt et non datur, fugere tentant, nec permittuntur. Si levant oculos, desuper Iudicis imminet furor. Si deponunt, infernales putei eis ingeritur horror. Non suppetit criminum excusatio, nec de iniquo iudicio aliqua poterit esse causatio, cum quidquid decretum fuerit, iustum esse ipsam eorum conscientiam non latebit.

9   Cerne nunc quam amandus tibi sit qui te ab hac damnata societate praedestinando discrevit, vocando separavit, iustificando purgavit. Retorque nunc ad dexteram oculos et

day of resurrection, dressed in the glory of the double cloak, they may enjoy perpetual joy of body and soul alike.

Now then, gaze at the terror of that day when the powers 7 of heaven will be moved, the elements will be dissolved in fire's heat, hell will lie open, all secrets will be laid bare. The angry Judge will come from above, burning with rage, his chariot like a storm, to take vengeance in his wrath and wreak devastation with fiery flame. Blessed is he who is ready to meet him. In what state of mind will the wretched be then, those whom lust fouls, greed destroys, and pride exalts now? The angels will go forth and they will separate the wicked from the midst of the just, the latter standing on the right, the former on the left.

Now imagine that you are present before Christ's judg- 8 ment seat between each group, not yet assigned to either one. Turn your eyes now to the Judge's left and contemplate that miserable crowd. What horror there, what stench, what fear, what anguish! The wretched and unhappy stand gnashing their teeth, bare bodies trembling, horrible to look at, their faces distorted, downcast in their shame, abashed by the filth and nakedness of their bodies. They want to hide and it is not allowed, they try to flee and it is not permitted. If they lift their eyes, the wrath of the Judge bears down from above; if they lower them, the horror of hell's pit is forced on them. They have no excuse for their crimes, nor will there be any appeal against unjust judgment since whatever decision is handed down, it will not escape their own conscience that the judgment is just.

Now understand how much you should love him who set 9 you apart from that company of the damned by predestination, separated you by calling you, cleansed you by justification. Now turn your eyes to the right and your attention to

quibus te glorificando sit inserturus adverte. Quis ibi decor, quis honor, quae felicitas, quae securitas! Alii iudiciaria sede sublimes, alii martyrii corona splendentes, alii virginitatis flore candidi, alii eleemosynarum largitione fecundi, alii doctrina et eruditione praeclari, uno caritatis foedere copulantur. Lucet eis vultus Iesu, non terribilis sed amabilis, non amarus sed dulcis, non terrens sed blandiens.

10   Sta nunc quasi in medio, nesciens quibus te Iudicis sententia deputabit. O dura expectatio! *Timor et tremor venerunt super me et contexerunt me tenebrae.* Si me sinistris sociaverit, non causabor iniustum; si dextris adscripserit, gratiae eius hoc, non meis meritis imputandum. Vere, Domine, vita in voluntate tua.

11   Vides ergo quantum in eius amore tuus extendi debeat animus, qui—cum iuste posset in impios prolatam in te quoque retorquere sententiam—iustis te maluit ac salvandis inserere.

12   Iam te puta sanctae illi societati coniunctam, vocis illius audite decretum, *"Venite benedicti patris mei, percipite regnum quod vobis paratum est ab origine mundi,"* miseris audientibus verbum durum plenum irae et furoris, *"Discedite a me, maledicti, in ignem aeternum. Tunc ibunt hi,"* inquit, *"in supplicium aeternum, iusti in vitam aeternam."* O dura separatio, O miserabilis conditio!

13   Sublatis vero impiis ne videant gloriam Dei, iustis quoque singulis secundum gradum suum et meritum angelicis ordinibus insertis, fiet illa gloriosa processio, Christo praecedente capite nostro, omnibus suis membris sequentibus et

those among whom he will place you, glorifying you. What beauty is there, what honor, what happiness, what security! Some high on the seats of judges, others resplendent in the martyr's crown, others shining white with the blossom of virginity, others abounding in the generosity of their alms-giving, others renowned for their teaching and erudition— all are joined by the bond of love. Jesus's face shines upon them, not terrifying but lovable, not bitter but sweet, not frightening but inviting.

Now stand as if in the middle, not knowing to which 10 group the Judge's sentence will allot you. What harsh sus-pense! *Fear and trembling came over me, and shadows enveloped me.* If he joins me to those on the left I will not complain of injustice; if he assigns me to those on the right, it should be attributed to his grace, not my merits. Truly, Lord, my life is in your hands.

You see, therefore, how much your spirit should be 11 stretched out in love for the one who—although he could have justly sentenced you, too, as he did the wicked—pre-ferred to place you among the just and the saved.

Now imagine yourself, joined to that holy company, hear-12 ing his voice's decree, *"Come, blessed ones of my father, take the kingdom prepared for you from the beginning of the world,"* while the wretched hear the harsh pronouncement, full of anger and fury, *"Depart from me, cursed ones, into the eternal fire. Then,"* he says, *"they will go to eternal punishment, but the just to eternal life."* O harsh parting, O miserable fate!

But once the wicked are taken away so they do not see 13 the glory of God, and the just placed one by one in the or-ders of angels according to rank and merit, that glorious procession will take place, with Christ our head leading us, all his members following, and the kingdom will be given to

tradetur regnum Deo et Patri ut ipse regnet in ipsis et ipsi regnent cum ipso, illud percipientes regnum quod paratum est illis ab origine mundi.   .

14   Cuius regni status nec cogitari quidem potest a nobis, multo minus dici vel scribi. Hoc scio, quod omnino nihil aberit quod velis adesse, nec quidquam aderit quod velis abesse. Nullus igitur ibi luctus, fletus nullus, non dolor, non timor, non tristitia, non discordia, non invidia, non tribulatio, non tentatio, non aeris mutatio vel corruptio, non suspicio, non ambitio, non adulatio, non detractio, non aegritudo, non senectus, non mors, non paupertas neque tenebrae, non edendi, non bibendi, vel dormiendi ulla necessitas, fatigatio nulla, nulla defectio.

15   Quid ergo boni ibi est? Ubi neque luctus neque fletus, neque dolor est neque tristitia, quid potest esse nisi perfecta laetitia? Ubi nulla tribulatio vel tentatio, nulla temporum mutatio vel aeris corruptio, nec aestus vehementior nec hiems asperior, quid potest esse nisi summa quaedam rerum temperies et mentis et carnis vera ac summa tranquillitas? Ubi nihil est quod timeas, quid potest esse nisi summa securitas? Ubi nulla discordia, nulla invidia, nulla suspicio nec ulla ambitio, nulla adulatio nec ulla detractio, quid potest esse nisi summa et vera dilectio? Ubi nulla paupertas nec ulla cupiditas, quid potest esse nisi bonorum omnium plenitudo? Ubi nulla deformitas, quid potest esse nisi vera pulchritudo? Ubi nullus labor vel defectio, quid erit nisi summa requies et fortitudo? Ubi nihil est quod gravet vel oneret, quid est nisi summa facilitas? Ubi nec senectus expectatur nec morbus timetur, quid potest esse nisi vera sanitas? Ubi

God the Father so he may reign over them, and they reign with him, receiving the kingdom that was prepared for them from the beginning of the world.

The nature of that kingdom cannot, to be sure, be imag- 14 ined by us, much less spoken or written of. This I know: nothing that you would wish to be present will be absent, nor anything present that you would wish to be absent. So there will be no sorrow, no weeping, no pain, no fear, no sadness, no discord, no envy, no tribulation, no temptation, no change of weather or contaminated air, no suspicion, no ambition, no flattery, no slander, no sickness, no old age, no death, no poverty, no darkness, no need to eat, or drink, or sleep, no tiredness, no weakness.

Then what good will be there? Where there is no sorrow 15 or weeping, neither pain nor sadness, what can there be except perfect happiness? Where there is no tribulation or temptation, no change of weather or contaminated air, neither intense heat nor harsh winter, what can there be except perfect balance in all matters, true and complete calmness of mind and body? Where there is nothing to fear, what can there be except complete security? Where there is no discord, no envy, no suspicion nor any ambition, no flattery nor any slander, what can there be except true and supreme love? Where there is no poverty or greed, what can there be except abundance of all good things? Where there is no deformity, what can there be except true beauty? Where there is no work or weakness, what will there be except complete rest and strength? Where there is nothing that weighs down or burdens, what is there except supreme ease? Where there is no expectation of old age, nor fear of disease, what can there be but true health? Where there is neither night nor

neque nox neque tenebrae, quid erit nisi lux perfecta? Ubi mors et mortalitas omnis absorpta est, quid erit nisi vita aeterna?

16   Quid est ultra quod quaeramus? Certe quod his omnibus excellit, id est visio, cognitio, dilectio creatoris. Videbitur in se, videbitur in omnibus creaturis suis, regens omnia sine sollicitudine, sustinens omnia sine labore, impertiens se et quodammodo dispertiens singulis pro sua capacitate sine sui diminitione vel divisione. Videbitur ille vultus amabilis et desiderabilis in quem desiderant angeli prospicere. De cuius pulchritudine, de cuius lumine, de cuius sauvitate, quis dicet? Videbitur Pater in Filio, Filius in Patre, Spiritus Sanctus in utroque. Videbitur non *per speculum in aenigmate,* sed *facie ad faciem.* Videbitur enim sicuti est, impleta illa promissione qua dicit: "*Qui diligit me diligetur a patre meo et ego diligam eum et manifestabo ei meipsum.*" Ex hac visione illa procedet cognitio de qua ipse ait, "*Haec est vita aeterna ut cognoscant te unum Deum et quem misisti Iesum Christum.*"

17   Ex his tanta nascitur dilectio, tantus ardor pii amoris, tanta dulcedo caritatis, tanta fruendi copia, tanta desiderii vehementia, ut nec satietas desiderium minuat nec desiderium satietatem impediat. Quid est hoc? Certe quod *oculus non videt, nec auris audivit, nec in cor hominis ascendit, quae praeparavit Deus diligentibus se.*

18   Haec tibi, soror, de praeteritorum beneficiorum Christi memoria, de praesentium experientia, de expectatione futurorum quaedam meditationum spiritualium semina praeseminare curavi, ex quibus divini amoris fructus uberior

darkness, what will there be except perfect light? Where all death and mortality have been swallowed up, what will there be except eternal life?

What more is there for us to seek? Surely what surpasses 16 all this, namely the sight, knowledge, and love of the creator. He will be seen in himself, he will be seen in all his creatures, ruling everything without anxiety, sustaining everything without effort, sharing himself and distributing himself, so to speak, to each according to his ability, without reduction or division of himself. That lovable and desirable face, on which the angels desire to gaze, will be visible. Who will speak of its beauty, its light, its sweetness? The Father will be seen in the Son, the Son in the Father, the Holy Spirit in each. He will be seen *not through a mirror in obscurity,* but *face to face.* For he will be seen just as he is, having fulfilled that promise he spoke: "*He who loves me will be loved by my father, and I will love him and show myself to him.*" From this vision will come knowledge, about which he said, "*This is eternal life, that they know you, the one God, and Jesus Christ, whom you sent.*"

From all this is born such affection, such ardent and pi- 17 ous love, such sweet tenderness, such wealth of pleasure, such passionate desire, that neither does fullness lessen desire, nor desire hinder fullness. What is this? It is surely *what the eye did not see, the ear did not hear, nor did it rise into the hearts of men what God has prepared for those who love him.*

These, sister, are some seeds of spiritual meditations on 18 the memory of Christ's past favors, the experience of them in the present, and the expectation of those to come that I have taken upon myself to sow for you. May a richer harvest of divine love arise and grow from them, so that meditation

oriatur et crescat, ut meditatio affectum excitet, affectus desiderium pariat, lacrymas desiderium excitet, ut sint tibi lacrymae tuae panis die ac nocte donec appareas in conspectu eius et suscipiaris ab amplexibus eius dicasque illud quod in Canticis scriptum est: *"Dilectus meus mihi et ego illi."*

19 Habes nunc sicut petisti, corporales institutiones quibus inclusa exterioris hominis mores componat. Habes formam praescriptam qua interiorem hominem vel purges a vitiis vel virtutibus ornes. Habes in triplici meditatione quomodo in te Dei dilectionem excites, nutrias, et accendas.

20 Si qua igitur in huius libelli lectione profecerit, hanc labori meo vel studio vicem impendat, ut apud Salvatorem meum quem exspecto, apud Iudicem meum quem timeo, pro peccatis meis intercedat.

EXPLICIT LIBER DE
INSTITUTIS INCLUSARUM.

may arouse affection, affection give birth to desire, and desire arouse tears, so your tears may be your bread day and night until you appear in his sight and you are taken into his embrace and you say what is written in the Song of Songs: *"My beloved is mine and I am his."*

You now have what you asked for, teachings on bodily observance with which a recluse may put in order the behavior of the outer self. You have a prescribed guide for purging the inner self of vices and adorning it with virtues. You have in a threefold meditation the way to arouse, nurture, and feed the fire of the love of God in yourself. 19

If anyone profits from reading this little book, she should make this return on my work and zeal: before my Savior whom I await, before my Judge whom I fear, she should intercede for my sins. 20

HERE ENDS THE BOOK OF
TEACHINGS FOR RECLUSES.

Note on the Texts

My edition of all Latin texts is based in each case on my transcription of a single manuscript. *A Pastoral Prayer (Oratio pastoralis)* and *A Certain Marvelous Miracle (De quodam miraculo mirabili)* survive in only one copy each. My text of *Spiritual Friendship (De spiritali amicitia),* which has a broader transmission, is based on one of the earliest available manuscripts, and that of *Teachings for Recluses (De institutis reclusarum)* on the earliest complete manuscript. The very small number of adjustments to the texts of *A Pastoral Prayer* and *A Certain Marvelous Miracle* either correct obvious scribal errors or adopt emendations that have been proposed previously by other scholars. In *Spiritual Friendship* and *Teachings for Recluses,* departures from the readings of the base manuscripts I have transcribed are all drawn from variants reported in others' critical editions: I have made no conjectures.

In keeping with the Dumbarton Oaks Medieval Library's goal of accessibility, the medieval orthography of the manuscripts has been adjusted to the norms of classical Latin.

A Pastoral Prayer

The unique surviving manuscript text is Cambridge, Jesus College, MS 34, fols. 97r–99r (late twelfth or early thirteenth

century). The text offered here is based on it, but I have sometimes adopted readings proposed by the Corpus Christianorum *Opera omnia* of Aelred's writings. The manuscript does not divide the prayer into sections; I duplicate the section numbering of the Corpus Christianorum edition.

SPIRITUAL FRIENDSHIP

The text is based on New York, Columbia University MS X878.L43, fols. 76v–93v (late twelfth century), one of four pre-1200 manuscripts. I have sometimes adopted readings proposed by the Corpus Christianorum *Opera omnia* of Aelred's writings, which for its edition collated thirteen complete copies dating from the twelfth through the fifteenth centuries. I duplicate the section numbering of the Corpus Christianorum edition, although paragraphing is somewhat different.

A CERTAIN MARVELOUS MIRACLE

The unique surviving manuscript text is Cambridge, Corpus Christi College, MS 139, fols. 147r–49v (late twelfth century), reproduced in Parker Library on the Web (parker. stanford.edu). I have sometimes adopted emendations proposed by the Corpus Christianorum *Opera omnia* of Aelred's writings. The manuscript marks with large capitals only the prologue, beginning *Miracula Domini,* and the main text, beginning *Inter monasteria.* I duplicate the section numbering of the Corpus Christianorum edition, although paragraphing is somewhat different.

TEACHINGS FOR RECLUSES

The text is based on London, British Library, MS Cotton Nero A III, fols. 2r–43v (early thirteenth century), the oldest complete version. I have sometimes adopted readings proposed by the Corpus Christianorum *Opera omnia* of Aelred's writings, which for its edition collated ten medieval manuscripts. The beginnings of sections in the London manuscript are marked by large capital letters. I duplicate the section numbering of the Corpus Christianorum edition, although paragraphing is somewhat different.

SIGLA

C = Cambridge, Corpus Christi College, MS 139, fols. 147r–49v

J = Cambridge, Jesus College, MS 34, fols. 97r–99r

L = London, British Library, MS Cotton Nero A III, fols. 2r–43v

N = New York, Columbia University MS X878.L43, fols. 76v–93v

Hoste = A. Hoste, ed., *De spiritali amicitia*, in *Aelredi Rievallensis opera omnia*, vol. 1, *Opera ascetica*, ed. A. Hoste and C. H. Talbot, Corpus Christianorum Continuatio Mediaevalis 1 (Turnhout, 1971), 279–350

Pezzini = Domenico Pezzini, ed., *De quodam miraculo mirabili*, in *Aelredi Rievallensis opera omnia*, vol. 6, *Opera historica et hagiographica*, ed. Domenico Pezzini, Corpus Christianorum Continuatio Mediaevalis 3 (Turnhout, 2017), 137–46

Talbot = C. H. Talbot, ed., *De institutione reclusarum*, in *Aelredi Rievallensis opera omnia*, vol. 1, pp. 635–82

Wilmart = A. Wilmart, ed., *Oratio pastoralis*, in *Aelredi Rievallensis opera omnia*, vol. 1, pp. 755–63

Notes to the Texts

1.1 ovium *Wilmart*: omnium *J*
     Ad *Wilmart*: At *J*
3.1 Jesus *Wilmart*: Jesu *J*
     meis peccatis orare *Wilmart*: meis peccatis eis orare *J*
5.3 regnent *Wilmart*: regnet *J*
6.2 beneplacitum *Wilmart*: bonum placitum *J*

Spiritual Friendship

Prol.4 dulcesceret *Hoste*: dulcesceret *N*
Prol.5 dulcissimi nominis Jesu *Hoste*: dulcissimi Jesu *L*
        scripturarum *Hoste*: scripturam *N*
1.2   vitiis *Hoste*: divitiis *N*
      interciperetur *Hoste*: inciperetur *N*
1.3   et utinam *Hoste*: ut utinam *N*
1.4   doceas *Hoste*: dicas *N*
1.5   his *Hoste*: hi *N*
      ad *Hoste*: ab *N*
1.6   et quasdam *Hoste*: ut quasdam *N*
1.10 videatur *Hoste*: videtur *N*
1.11 et caritate *Hoste*: in caritate *N*
1.16 et ethnicis *Hoste*: in ethnicis *N*
1.17 utcumque *Hoste*: utrumque *N*
1.18 sufficiant nisi ipsius *Hoste*: sufficiant ipsius *N*
1.19 quod satis cognitum *Hoste*: quod cognitum *N*
1.20 mutui *Hoste*: intuit *N*

curet *Hoste*: cure N

1.25   temporibus *Hoste*: temporalibus N

1.26   credendus sit profecisse *Hoste*: credendus profecisse N

1.28   fingunt *Hoste*: fugiunt N

secundum *Hoste*: secundam N

1.32   enim plures gremio *Hoste*: enim gremio N

1.33   quibuslibet *Hoste*: cuiuslibet N

1.34   sit tibi molestam *Hoste*: sit molestam N

1.35   coniventia *Hoste*: conviventia N

1.36   suavitatis illa quae quanto honestior est tanto est et securior quanto castior, tanto et iucundior *Hoste*: suavitatis illa quae quanto castior tanto et iucundior N

1.37   nuncupentur *Hoste*: nuncupantur N

1.38   studiorumque similitudo conglutinat *Hoste*: studiorumque conglutinat N

1.39   voluptuosarum *Hoste*: voluptuarum N

1.43   fortuna tenet dulcis *Hoste*: fortuna dulcis N

1.44   nullo modo *Hoste*: nulla N

1.48   sincerius *Hoste*: severius N

1.53   unitatis vestigium *Hoste*: unitatis est vestigium N

1.60   appeteretur *Hoste*: appeterentur N

1.61   proinde est amicitiam *Hoste*: proinde amicitiam N

1.63   utitur qui *Hoste*: utitur et qui N

1.65   quae licet a se *Hoste*: quae a se N

1.67   Obstupesco fateor, nec facile id mihi persuaderi posse existimo *Hoste*: Obstupesco teor nec facile mihi persuaderi istimo N *in margin, partially lost to trimming*

2.3   species *Hoste*: specias N

2.4   quoque stilo tradideris *Hoste*: quoque tradideris

2.5   continuus *Hoste*: continus N

licet ex humanis *Hoste*: licet humanis N

arrident *Hoste*: arridunt N

2.8   quid sit amicitia *Hoste*: quid amicitia N

disputatum quid cultoribus *Hoste*: disputatum quibus cultoribus N

visus es comprobasse *Hoste*: visus comprobasse N

2.10   condit *Hoste*: condidit N

2.11   At quae *Hoste*: Atque N
          nulla iactantia *Hoste*: in illa iactantia N
2.16   nunc hic *Hoste*: hinc tunc N
          avidus *Hoste*: avidius N
2.19   sentiuntur *Hoste*: secuntur N
          voluntarieque *Hoste*: voluntarie N
2.22   sine aere ne *Hoste*: sine aere natura ne N
          haurimus *Hoste*: hauriamus N
2.24   impressione fit labiorum *Hoste*: impressione labiorum N
2.25   satellitium *Hoste*: satellitum N
          abutuntur *Hoste*: obutuntur N
2.26   attactu *Hoste*: attractu N
          immitente *Hoste*: immittentes N
2.30   etiam in inhonestis *Hoste*: etiam inhonestis N
2.43   a *Hoste*: ac N
2.49   quia *Hoste*: qua N
2.50   rogo *Hoste*: ergo N
2.51   corrumperentur *Hoste*: corrumperetur N
          formidant *Hoste*: formidavit N
2.53   concesserim *Hoste*: consueverim N
          solis *Hoste*: soliis N
2.55   pervidere *Hoste*: praevidere N
2.56   quid *Hoste*: qua N
2.57   afficit arctius stringit *Hoste*: afficit stringit N
          regat *Hoste*: reget N
2.58   impuris *Hoste*: in puerilibus N
2.60   qui cum nihil *Hoste*: qui nihil N
2.63   multum *Hoste*: multumque N
2.67   turpe et illud *Hoste*: turpe illito N
3.1   arguere *Hoste*: argue N
          promissi tui *Hoste*: promissum N
3.2   ex solo affectu aut *Hoste*: ex solo aufectu aut N
3.6   consors sit animi *Hoste*: consors animi N
3.7   spiritalibus ut nulla sit *Hoste*: spiritalibus nulla sit N
3.13   seipso *Hoste*: ipso N
3.17   temperare *Hoste*: temptare N
          soliti sunt passionem *Hoste*: soliti passionum N

id *Hoste*: ad *N*

3.18 cui *Hoste*: cur *N*

3.20 a me receptus in amicitiam a me numquam *Hoste*: a me numquam *N*

 concurrebat *Hoste*: concurreba *N*

3.21 iam in fata concesserit *Hoste*: iam concesserit *N*

 licet *Hoste*: licet licet *N*

3.22 sese *Hoste*: esse *N*

3.23 regressus *Hoste*: concordia *N*

3.24 confessionis *Hoste*: confessessionis *N*

3.25 desperatio est animae *Hoste*: desperatio animae *N*

3.27 effectui *Hoste*: affectui *N*

3.29 continuos ei *Hoste*: continuous eos ei *N*

 praebuerit *Hoste*: praebuit *N*

3.30 vides *Hoste*: videns *N*

3.35 iracundum *Hoste*: iracundiam *N*

3.36 audisti *Hoste*: audistis *N*

3.37 iracundum magis excitet *Hoste*: iracundiam excitet *N*

3.38 eius aliquando *Hoste*: eius ut aliquando *N*

 suam meae praeferam *Hoste*: suam praeferam *N*

3.39 mihi velim enuclees *Hoste*: mihi enuclees *N*

3.40 electione *Hoste*: elatione *N*

3.44 is *Hoste*: his *N*

3.46 detractionum *Hoste*: retractionum *N*

3.51 sive tristia de omnibus quae cogitantur sive nociva sint sive
 utilia de omnibus *Hoste*: sive tristia de omnibus *N*

3.52 Subtrahitur *Hoste*: Subtrahatur *N*

3.53 ut eorum *Hoste*: ut summa eorum *N*

3.54 utrum ei convenient *Hoste*: utrum convenient *N*

3.59 de illis esse de quibus *Hoste*: de illis de quibus *N*

 vel aliquid superducat *Hoste*: vel superducat *N*

3.61 expectet *Hoste*: expectes *N*

 id *Hoste*: his *N*

 ignoret *Hoste*: ignores *N*

3.62 in adversis et prosperis *Hoste*: in adversis et in prosperis *N*

3.65 est et in multo *Hoste*: est in multo *N*

nostra sunt committenda secreta *Hoste*: nostra sunt committenda sunt secreta *N*

celeretur an nudentur *Hoste*: celeretur ac nudentur *N*

3.66 cuiusquam *Hoste*: quisquam *N*

3.68 propter Deum et se expetenda *Hoste*: propter Deum exspectanda *N*

3.71 sit quod appetitur *Hoste*: sit appetitur *N*

3.74 dilectione vel electione rèsilias *Hoste*: dilectione resilias *N*

probandis taedeat *Hoste*: probandis non taedeat *N*

3.75 certaque *Hoste*: ceteraque *N*

desint indicia dementiae *Hoste*: desunt dementiae *N*

sane est quidam *Hoste*: sane quidam *N*

qui *Hoste*: quae *N*

3.76 vivere tutius arbitrantur *Hoste*: vivere arbitrantur *N*

3.77 volucres caeli et *Hoste*: volucres et *N*

semitas maris. Dic, rogo nunc, utrum sine socio omnia tibi haec possent esse iucunda? Minime *Hoste*: semita maris. Minime *N*

3.80 quam *Hoste*: ac *N*

3.81 videres *Hoste*: videris *N*

iudicares *Hoste*: iudicaremus *N*

qui in eorum *Hoste*: qui eorum *N*

3.82 et a quibus sic diligeris te *Hoste*: et te *N*

3.87 gravitate et spiritalium *Hoste*: gravitate spiritalium *N*

3.88 iisdem *Hoste*: eisdem *N*

fidelitatem *Hoste*: salutem *N*

3.89 huc *Hoste*: huic *N*

facilitatemque *Hoste*: facultatemque *N*

3.92 spondent *Hoste*: spondet *N*

praebendum in tanta *Hoste*: praebendum tanta *N*

3.93 ipse posuit animam *Hoste*: ipse animam *N*

3.95 anteponat *Hoste*: anteponant *N*

3.101 firmitatem *Hoste*: fraternitatem *N*

invicem orent pro invicem erubescant *Hoste*: invicem erubescant *N*

3.102 his *Hoste*: is *N*

3.103   indecens *Hoste*: incedens *N*

3.105   nutrix *Hoste*: adiutrix *N*

3.108   animi *Hoste*: amici *N*

         proprie *Hoste*: quippe *N*

         libere *Hoste*: liberum *N*

3.111   sensum prophetae nostri *Hoste*: sensum pro sensu nostro *N*

3.112   obiurgandus est sed dissumulandum pro loco *Hoste*: obiurgan-
         dus est pro loco *N*

3.115   putent *Hoste*: putant *N*

         causentur *Hoste*: causantur *N*

3.117   interrogat *Hoste*: interrogavit *N*

3.119   primum in initiis *Hoste*: primum initiis *N*

         partem *Hoste*: parte *N*

3.120   imperfectio mecum ascendit *Hoste*: in perfectionem ascendit *N*

         nulli *Hoste*: illi *N*

3.123   coepit me et ipse *Hoste*: coepit et ipse *N*

         mihi eius libertas *Hoste*: mihi libertas *N*

3.124   quibusdam quasi conviciis *Hoste*: quibusdam conviciis *N*

         suspicione *Hoste*: suspicatione *N*

3.125   fucatum *Hoste*: fuscatum *N*

3.126   ei *Hoste*: enim *N*

3.130   impendat *Hoste*: impendant *N*

3.131   assentationem *Hoste*: assentionem *N*

3.132   studia mutuo patefacere *Hoste*: studia patefacere *N*

3.134   pro invicem metuimus et solliciti sumus, omni adversitate de-
         pulsa, quam oportet nunc ut pro invicem sustineamus *Hoste*:
         pro invicem sustineamus *N*

A CERTAIN MARVELOUS MIRACLE

2.1   habitu *Pezzini*: habitui *C*

2.3   impiissimus *Pezzini*: impissimus *C*

4.1   Heu egreditur *Pezzini*: Heu egeditur *C*

10.2   intempestae *Pezzini*: intempestatae *C*

12.1   veracissimis *Pezzini*: verascissimis *C*

Teachings for Recluses

2.1	vel ut liberius *Talbot*: vel liberius *L*
2.3	invenies *Talbot*: invenias *L*
	misera *Talbot*: viscera *L*
3.1	quod *Talbot*: quo *L*
5.1	De silentio inclusarum *title by main text scribe at head of section L, omitted Venarde*
6.1	indicere non possumus *Talbot*: indicere possumus *L*
6.2	exilitate *Talbot*: exillaritate *L*
7.3	nullo *Talbot*: ullo *L*
7.5	lacessenti *Talbot*: lascessenti *L*
7.6	advertas *Talbot*: avertas *L*
8.1	Quibus debet loqui *title by main text scribe at head of section L, omitted Venarde*
9.4	pellas *Talbot*: pelles *L*
11.4	debemus *Talbot*: deberemus *L*
11.5	expressius *Talbot*: expressus *L*
11.6	insistat *Talbot*: insistet *L*
14.3	portes *Talbot*: portas *L*
15.1	si *Talbot*: sed *L*
15.3	iudicaverit aut ratio dictaverit cum dolore *Talbot*: iudicaverit cum dolore *L*
15.4	deserendam *Talbot*: deserandam *L*
16.1	crudior si potu *Talbot*: crudior potu *L*
16.2	mentem *Talbot*: mente *L*
	Agnetem *Talbot*: Agnam *L*
18.1	fricabat *Talbot*: fricat *L*
19.1	effectum *Talbot*: affectum *L*
	saepius *Talbot*: sopitos *L*
20	accipitris *Talbot*: ancipitris *L*
	qui *Talbot*: quae qui *L*
	lascivas *Talbot*: lacivas *L*
21.2	odoramos *Talbot*: oderamus *L*
24.2	divitum *Talbot*: divinitum *L*

24.4	comparant in quo delectantur *Talbot*: comparant *L*
25.2	Adde fortitudini modestiam *Talbot*: Adde modestiam *L*
26.1	peccatis concepit *Talbot*: peccatis meis concepit *L*
26.3	cogites *Talbot*: cogitet *L*
	consolatio desperatorum erectio peccatorum reconciliatio postremo *Talbot*: consolatio postremo *L*
26.4	His *Talbot*: Hinc *L*
28.5	Cum igitur *Talbot*: Cui igitur *L*
28.8	studuerunt *Talbot*: studuerint *L*
29.1	circa *Talbot*: cura *L*
29.4	inebriabaris *Talbot*: inebriaris *L*
	ventre tantae maiestatis *Talbot*: ventre maiestatis *L*
29.6	suavem *Talbot*: suave *L*
30.1	autem nihil *Talbot*: autem quid nihil *L*
31.2	invitata *Talbot*: initiata *L*
31.5	perfunderis *Talbot*: perfundis *L*
	exaudies: exaudis *L*
31.7	pinguescat *Talbot*: pingescat *L*
	animavit *Talbot*: amavit *L*
31.8	praemisisse *Talbot*: praemisse *L*
31.9	interpretabatur *Talbot*: interpretatur *L*
31.22	tondente se non *Talbot*: tondente sic non *L*
31.30	vitta *Talbot*: victa *L*
32.3	In me *Talbot*: Immo *L*
32.4	coacervavi *Talbot*: quo acervavi *L*
32.6	abrupta *Talbot*: abruta *L*
	diffluebam *Talbot*: diffluebar *L*
32.7	scito *Talbot*: scio *L*
32.11	nolo *Talbot*: volo *L*

Notes to the Translations

A Pastoral Prayer

3.1   *is this not your household . . . under one roof*: That is, the flock has been led out of the secular world into the monastic one, which Aelred likens to Moses leading his people out of Egypt to the Promised Land.

3.3   *a wise man might not boast . . . strength*: Jeremiah 9:23.
       Give glory not to us . . . your name: Psalms 113:9(115:1).

4.1   *I do not lay . . . your many mercies*: See Daniel 9:18.

4.2   *So let your eyes . . . prayers*: See Psalms 33:16(34:15).

5.1   *and reaches all the way . . . spirit*: Hebrews 4:12.

5.4   *of all filth of flesh and spirit*: 2 Corinthians 7:1.
       increase of faith, hope, and love: See 1 Corinthians 13:13.

6.1   *to help rather than rule*: Aelred uses the language of the Rule of Saint Benedict 64.8 *(prodesse magis quam praeesse),* a phrase he repeats in section 8.1.
       One of the ancients . . . wonderful love to your people: The reference is to Solomon: see 2 Chronicles 1:7–12. For Aelred, Solomon made his plea to the God who had not yet appeared on earth as the god-man Jesus.

6.2   *you know my foolishness . . . from you*: Psalms 68:6(69:5).
       the throne of your greatness . . . labor with me: Wisdom 9:10.

7.2   *be weak . . . gain them all*: See 1 Corinthians 9:22 and 2 Corinthians 11:29.

8.4   *spiritual weariness*: *Acedia,* a kind of spiritual, even existential ennui, was on the list of evil thoughts or temptations dating to the fourth century that eventually became the familiar Seven Deadly Sins.

Spiritual Friendship

Prol.1   *still a boy . . . to be loved and to love*: Aelred's language echoes Augustine's account of his youth in the *Confessions: adhuc puer* (1.11.17) and *amare et amari* (2.2.2 and 3.1.1).

Prol.3   *worldly prospects abandoned*: Augustine, *Confessions* 6.11.19.

Prol.8   *the misfortune of the preoccupation*: The lament that an abbot's responsibilities distract his attention from more meaningful pursuits is a leitmotif in Aelred's writing.

1.3   *however often you visit your sons here*: Ivo is a monk in a house at which Aelred is staying.

1.11   *Friendship is agreement . . . goodwill and love*: Cicero, *On Friendship* 20.

1.19   *As I see it . . . derives from "friend"*: Cicero, *On Friendship* 26, says that "friendship" *(amicitia)* is derived from "love" *(amor);* Aelred has added the intermediate "friend" *(amicus).*

1.21   *one is made from many*: See Cicero, *On Friendship* 81 and 92.
   He is a friend who loves at all times: Proverbs 17:17.

1.24   *Friendship that can end was never true friendship*: Jerome, *Letters* 3.6.

1.25   *Tradition going back . . . pairs of friends*: See Cicero, *On Friendship* 15.

1.26   *Striving for great achievements is itself great*: A proverbial expression that Aelred perhaps remembered from a fifth-century version: Julianus Pomerius, *The Contemplative Life* 1 Prol. 2.

1.27   *Ask and you will receive*: John 16:24.
   The Lord of virtues is the king of glory himself: Psalms 23(24):10.

1.28   *Pylades and Orestes*: In Greek mythology, Orestes was the son of King Agamemnon, and Pylades was a cousin with whom he had been raised and with whom he shared a close bond. The two worked together to avenge Agamemnon's death by killing his murderer, Orestes's own mother, Clytemnestra. When Orestes faced execution for Clytemnestra's death, Pylades plotted with him to escape, in some versions offering his life in exchange for Orestes's pardon: see Cicero, *On Friendship* 24, and Augustine, *Confessions* 4.6.11.
   There was one heart . . . all things in common: Acts 4:32.

1.29   *complete agreement about matters . . . goodwill and love*: Again Aelred quotes Cicero, *On Friendship* 20, although he adds "complete" (*summa*).

        the girl of Antioch: The reference is to Theodora of Alexandria, who was martyred along with her protector Didymus in 304 CE. Theodora was consigned to the brothel after refusing to sacrifice to pagan gods. Fellow Christian Didymus (who was pretending to be a Roman soldier) exchanged clothes with Theodora so she could escape with her virginity intact. His trick discovered, Didymus was sentenced to death, which Theodora insisted on sharing. Aelred apparently wrote Antioch rather than Alexandria, remembering the same slip in Ambrose, *On Virgins* 2.4.

1.30   *They multiplied beyond number*: Psalms 39:6(40:5).

        No man . . . his life for his friends: John 15:13.

1.32   *not only our friends but also our enemies*: See Matthew 5:44.

1.35   *he who loves wickedness . . . hates it*: See Psalms 10:6(11:5).

1.39   *follows its whoring eyes and ears this way and that*: See Numbers 15:39.

        spreading her legs for all who pass by: See Ezekiel 16:25.

1.40   *wishing and not wishing the same things*: Sallust, *Catiline* 20.4.

1.43   *He is a friend . . . hard times*: Sirach 6:8.

        He is a not a friend . . . drives away: The author of this elegiac couplet is unknown. Ovid wrote in the same meter on the theme of friendship in *Ex Ponto* 2.3, which discusses false friendship in terms similar to Aelred's.

1.46   *I have proposed that you go forth and bear fruit*: John 15:16.

        that you love one another: John 13:34.

        agreement along with goodwill and love: Cicero, *On Friendship* 20.

1.48   *wishing and not wishing the same things*: Sallust, *Catiline* 20.4.

1.52   *You are my God . . . my goods*: Psalms 15(16):2.

1.57   *It is not good for man . . . like himself*: Genesis 2:18.

        the second human . . . "collateral," as it were: See Genesis 2:21–22 for the creation of Eve from Adam's rib, so from one side (*latus*), the root meaning of collateral.

1.63   *He who pleases himself . . . is a fool*: Augustine, *Sermons* 47.9.13.

1.68 *He is a friend who loves at all times*: Proverbs 17:17.

Friendship that can end was never true friendship: Jerome, *Letters* 3.6.

1.69 *what Jesus's friend John said of love*: See 1 John 4:16, where John says God is love.

1.70 *He who abides in love abides in God, and God in him*: 1 John 4:16.

2.2 *overseers of Pharaoh*: See Exodus 5:14.

2.5 *the pages on which I had written down his questions*: This preliminary version of Book One has survived in two manuscripts, which A. Hoste edited along with his critical edition of *Spiritual Friendship*, as *Schedula*, in *Aelredi Rievallensis opera omnia*, vol. 1, pp. 354–634.

2.8 *Here I am*: Some time has passed since Aelred gave Walter his notes, and Walter is now eager to take up the discussion.

2.9 *this life now as well as the next*: See 1 Timothy 4:8.

2.11 *Woe to the solitary man . . . he falls*: Ecclesiastes 4:10.

2.12 *A friend is medicine for life*: Sirach 6:16.

they bear each other's burdens shoulder to shoulder: See Galatians 6:2.

2.13 *friendship makes good times . . . sharing them*: Cicero, *On Friendship* 22.

We do not use water . . . use a friend: Cicero, *On Friendship* 22.

are present for one when absent . . . when dead: Cicero, *On Friendship* 23.

2.14 *Such great honor . . . accompany friends*: See Cicero, *On Friendship* 23.

From now on I will call you not servants but my friends: John 15:15.

2.16 *to be loved and to love*: The same words as in the first sentence of the prologue, recalling Augustine, *Confessions* 2.2.2 and 3.1.1.

false friendship for true . . . for spiritual: That is, Gratian falls into some of the traps discussed in Book One.

2.18 *In friendship . . . willing and true*: See Cicero, *On Friendship* 26.

2.21 *one heart and one soul*: Acts 4:32.

Let him kiss me with the kiss of his mouth: Song of Songs 1:1.

2.26 *the spiritual kiss*: In this section and the next few, Aelred plays on the two meanings of *spiritus*, "breath" and "spirit," in ways that are impossible to replicate in English.

See how good and pleasant . . . in unity: Psalms 132(133):1.

2.27 *Let him kiss me with the kiss of his mouth*: Song of Songs 1:1.

His left hand . . . embrace me: Song of Songs 2:6.

2.31 *in accordance with his name*: The name Gratian (Gratianus) comes from the adjective *gratus*, meaning "pleasant" or "gracious."

2.33 *No man has greater love . . . his friends*: John 15:13.

2.40 *enjoying what was forbidden*: See Genesis 3:6.

King Saul's servants . . . sacrilegious hands: Saul commanded his attendants to kill priests who had allied with the exiled David. They refused, but Doeg single-handedly killed eighty-five priests (1 Samuel 22:17–18).

Jonadab's friend . . . what he wanted: King David's son Ammon fell for his half sister Tamar and conspired with his wily cousin Jonadab to be alone with her. Failing to seduce Tamar, Ammon raped her (2 Samuel 13:1–14).

2.41 *Absalom's friends . . . their fatherland*: King David's son Absalom, after having Ammon killed to avenge the rape of Tamar, worked to gain the loyalty of the Israelites, many of whom joined him in rebellion against his father (2 Samuel 13:23–28 and 15:1–13).

Coming to our own times . . . in such a schism: On the death of Pope Hadrian IV in 1159, the cardinals elected papal chancellor Rolando of Siena as Pope Alexander III, but a minority faction chose Octavian of Monticelli as Victor IV; the cardinal priest John of Crema endorsed Octavian as pope. When the latter died in 1164, Cardinal Otto supported Guido of Crene as pope under the name Pascal III, but Aelred's remark implies he reversed himself.

2.43 *I do not . . . to the quick*: See Cicero, *On Friendship* 18.

soberly, justly, and piously in this life: Titus 2:12.

2.49 *Those who remove friendship . . . more delightful*: Cicero, *On Friendship* 47. Cicero wrote not *a Deo* (from God), but *a dis immortalibus* (from the immortal gods).

2.50 *Was it foolish . . . burned with the scandalized*: See 1 Corinthians 13:13 and 2 Corinthians 11:28–29.

But he had both . . . according to the flesh: see Romans 9:2–3.

2.52   *Hushai the Archite*: Hushai proved his loyalty to his friend King David during the rebellion of David's son Absalom. Hushai feigned loyalty to Absalom and became a spy in his camp, sending word of the rebel army's plans to David. David's troops made an evasive maneuver and soon after defeated Absalom's in a pitched battle (2 Samuel 15:32–35, 16:15–18, 17:5–18:8).

2.57   *It spreads its legs for all who pass by*: See Ezekiel 16:25.

2.58   *We call that . . . carnal desires*: See Augustine, *Confessions* 3.1.1.

2.62   *Barzillai the Gileadite*: During Absalom's rebellion against King David, the wealthy Barzillai was among those who supplied David's army in the desert. After Absalom's death, David invited the aged Barzillai to come live at his side at Jerusalem, an offer Barzillai refused in fear he would be a burden to the king (2 Samuel 17:27–29 and 19:31–37).

2.63   *David and Jonathan*: Jonathan, King Saul's son, made a pact of friendship with the warrior David (1 Samuel 18:1–4) and later shielded David from Saul's murderous rage (1 Samuel 19–20). Later, as king, David restored Saul's estates to Mephibosheth, Jonathan's only surviving son, and made Mephibosheth his table companion in Jerusalem (2 Samuel 9:1–13).

2.67   *one heart and one soul*: Acts 4:32.

2.69   *laying down . . . divine authority decreed*: See John 15:13.

3.2   *command imposed by precept*: Jesus instructed his listeners in the Sermon on the Mount to love their enemies (Matthew 5:44).

3.6   *Since your friend is the partner of your soul*: This section and the next echo ideas in Ambrose, *On Duties* 3.128 and 3.134, sometimes in identical language. Ambrose in turn drew on Cicero, *On Friendship*.

3.8   *agreement about . . . goodwill*: Cicero, *On Friendship* 20, with Aelred's addition of "a certain" *(quadam)*.

3.11   *to wish and not wish the same things*: Sallust, *Catiline* 20.4.

3.15   *There are friends . . . taunting*: Sirach 6:9.

         Do not be the friend . . . into your soul: Proverbs 22:24–25.

         Anger rests in the breast of a fool: Ecclesiastes 7:10.

3.17   *five ways . . . friendship is dissolved and destroyed*: See below, 3.21–25.

3.22   *He who abuses a friend . . . fear not*: Sirach 22:25–27.

3.23 *There can be . . . the friend will flee*: Sirach 22:26–27.

3.25 *He who betrays a friend's secrets will lose his loyalty*: Sirach 27:17.

To betray a friend's confidences . . . unhappy soul: Sirach 27:24.

If a serpent bites . . . no better: Ecclesiastes 10:11.

3.26 *Shimei assaulted holy David . . . with abuse*: As King David's troops relocated during Absalom's rebellion against his father, Shimei pelted David with rocks and curses, continuing as the army moved by (2 Samuel 16:5–13).

Among the words . . . Shimei should be killed: See 1 Kings 2:8–9. Three years later, David's son and heir Solomon had Shimei killed (1 Kings 2:46).

The wretched Nabal of Carmel . . . killed by the Lord: See 1 Samuel 25:10–11, 37–38.

3.27 *When David . . . his people and cities*: See 2 Samuel 10:1–4, 11:1, 12:26–31.

Hence the most impious Ahithophel . . . a traitor: See 2 Samuel 16:15–17:23 for the story of Ahithophel, master strategist to Absalom as he rebelled against his father, King David.

3.28 *the act . . . for six days*: For sharp criticism of her brother Moses, Miriam was punished with temporary disfigurement and banishment (Numbers 12).

3.29 *He is never at rest*: See the Rule of Saint Benedict 64.16.

3.30 *a talkative man will not be justified*: See Job 11:2.

Do you see a man eager . . . than he does: See Proverbs 20:29.

There can be . . . the other: Ambrose, *On Duties* 3.133.

3.40 *Those are worthy . . . should be loved*: Cicero, *On Friendship* 79.

vices often erupt . . . their friends: Cicero, *On Friendship* 76.

3.41 *Instead the friendship . . . happen immediately*: See Cicero, *On Friendship* 76.

3.42 *from which quarrels, curses, and abuse arise*: See Cicero, *On Friendship* 78.

It is exceedingly shameful . . . intimate terms: See Cicero, *On Friendship* 77.

3.44 *should be endured . . . take the blame*: Cicero, *On Friendship* 78.

he who is a friend loves at all times: Proverbs 17:17.

3.47 *King Ahasuerus . . . deceitful plotting*: Ahasuerus, known to his-

tory as the mighty Persian king Xerxes, heaped honors on the courtier Haman. But Haman, nursing a murderous rage against Jews, including Ahasuerus's wife, Esther, ordered their destruction in the king's name. Esther informed her husband of the plot, and Ahasuerus had Haman executed (Esther 3–7).

Jael, Heber the Kenite's wife . . . hammer and nail: Sisera, commander of the army of the Canaanites, cruelly oppressed the tribes of Israel for twenty years. The prophetess Deborah plotted the destruction of Sisera's army, and he fled. Welcomed into the camp of the Israelite Heber the Kenite by his wife Jael, the exhausted Sisera was received with feigned goodwill by Jael, who then killed him (Judges 4:1–22).

The holy prophet David . . . for punishment: God instructed King David to make amends to the Gibeonites, whom David's predecessor King Saul had slaughtered, to end the famine. David handed over seven of Saul's descendants, and therefore relatives of Jonathan, to be sacrificed (2 Samuel 21:1–9).

3.48   *friendship that can end was never true friendship*: Jerome, *Letters* 3.6.

3.56   *slander, shaming . . . treacherous blow*: Sirach 22:27.

3.63   *A friend is tested in necessity*: See Ambrose, *On Duties* 3.130.
        A rich man has many friends: See Proverbs 14:20.
        He who is a friend . . . in adversity: Proverbs 17:17.
        He who pins . . . a weary foot: Proverbs 25:19.

3.65   *He who is loyal . . . a great one*: See Luke 16:10.

3.69   *You will love your neighbor as yourself*: Matthew 22:39.

3.70   *For . . . competition in goodwill*: Ambrose, *On Duties* 3.134.
        friendships among the poor . . . the rich: See Ambrose, *On Duties* 3.135.

3.72   *Some people . . . cannot be*: See Cicero, *On Friendship* 82.

3.74   *medicine for life . . . for immortality*: See Sirach 6:16.

3.77   *all the sheep and cattle . . . the paths of the sea*: Psalms 8:8–9(7–8).

3.82   *loving circle of brothers*: Literally, "crown," *corona*.
        See how good and pleasant . . . in unity: Psalms 132(133):1.

3.83   *Now I will call you not servants but my friends*: See John 15:14–15.
        Because everything that I have heard . . . to you: John 15:15.

You are my friends if you do what I command you: John 15:14.

He gave us a model . . . his father's mysteries: Ambrose, *On Duties* 3.136; there are very minor deviations from Ambrose's exact words.

3.85 *The one your Augustine describes*: Augustine recalls a youthful friendship in *Confessions* 4.8.13–4.9.14. In this paragraph, Aelred (through Walter) uses language similar to and sometimes identical with Augustine's.

3.88 *The foundation of stability . . . stable or loyal*: See Cicero, *On Friendship* 65, for this section.

3.89 *To those should be added . . . frivolity or dissipation*: See Cicero, *On Friendship* 66, for these sentences.

3.91 *He who had much . . . too little*: 2 Corinthians 8:15.

3.92–94 On the friendship of David and Jonathan, the son and heir apparent of King Saul, and Jonathan's protection of David from his father's wrath, see 1 Samuel 18–23. For Jonathan's promise to give up his title to the throne of Israel and serve David, see 1 Samuel 23:17, and for the abuse and threats Saul hurls at Jonathan, see 1 Samuel 20:30–31.

3.95 *Cicero says . . . ahead of his own*: See Cicero, *On Friendship* 63.

3.96 *go and do likewise*: Luke 10:37.

3.97 *Defer to your friend . . . no pride*: Ambrose, *On Duties* 3.129.
A loyal friend is medicine . . . the next: See Sirach 6:16.
Let this law . . . enthusiasm: See Cicero, *On Friendship* 44.

3.98 *Lose money for a friend*: See Sirach 29:13.
the eyes of a wise man are in his head: Ecclesiastes 2:14.
My eyes are always on the Lord: Psalms 24(25):15.
If someone lacks wisdom . . . does not scold: James 1:5.

3.99 *one heart and one soul*: Acts 4:32.

3.100 *When Boaz had noted the poverty of Ruth the Moabite*: For the kindness Boaz showed to the poor foreigner Ruth, see Ruth 2:8–16.
give and receive nothing: Walter refers to the monastic vow to possess nothing individually.

3.101 *Men would lead . . . their midst*: See Pseudo-Seneca, *Monita* 97.

3.102 *he who deprives friendship . . . adornment*: Cicero, *On Friendship* 82.

3.104   *Flattery breeds friends and truth breeds hatred*: Terence, *Andria* 68;
        Aelred probably knew these lines from the quotation of Ter-
        ence in Cicero, *On Friendship* 89.

        still much more harmful . . . flattery and indulgence: See Cicero, *On
        Friendship* 89.

        Not that we should not indulge . . . flatter them: Aelred uses the same
        language here to allow the indulgence and flattery he has con-
        demned in the previous sentence. That is, the argument is in-
        consistent.

3.105   *But sycophancy . . . from a friend*: See Cicero, *On Friendship* 89–90.

3.106   *If you perceive some vice . . . correct an erring friend*: Ambrose, *On
        Duties* 2.128.

3.108   *Therefore, just as it is a characteristic . . . not the truth*: A close para-
        phrase of Cicero, *On Friendship* 91.

3.109   *the truth . . . has no meaning*: Cicero, *On Friendship* 92.

        The just man . . . my head: Psalms 140(141):5.

        My people . . . path of your steps: Isaiah 3:12.

        A hypocrite deceives his friend with his mouth: Proverbs 11:9.

3.110   *God is said . . . faults of sinners*: See Wisdom 11:24.

        wanting not the death . . . and live: See Ezekiel 33:11.

3.111   *Someone says . . . agree with me*: Terence, *Eunuchus* 252–53; Aelred
        probably knew this text through its quotation in Cicero, *On
        Friendship* 93.

        See vain things . . . please us: See Isaiah 30:10.

        The prophets . . . such things: Jeremiah 5:31.

3.113   *When King David . . . verdict against himself*: King David seduced
        and impregnated Bathsheba, the wife of Uriah the Hittite,
        and proceeded to have Uriah killed before taking Bathsheba
        as his wife. God sent Nathan to David to tell him a story of a
        rich man who steals a poor man's lamb. David was outraged
        at the injustice, and Nathan pointed out that the king had
        done something similar. David then admitted his sin (2 Samuel
        12:1–13).

3.117   *He commended . . . Jesus's breast*: See, respectively, John 21:15–17
        (Jesus tells Peter three times to "feed my sheep"), John 19:26–
        27 (from the cross, Jesus tells Mary that John is her son and

tells John that Mary is his mother), Matthew 16:19 (Jesus gives Peter the keys), and John 13:23 (John rests against Jesus after the Last Supper).

One of you will betray me: John 13:21.

at a nod from Peter asked who it was: See John 13:24.

I want him to remain so until I come: John 21:22.

He gave us an example so that we too should do likewise: See John 13:15.

3.119   *are nevertheless alive for me and will always be alive*: See Cicero, *On Friendship* 102.

3.121   *as if deaf . . . his mouth*: See Psalms 37(38):14.

3.122   *subprior's office*: That is, the office of third superior in an abbey, after the abbot and prior.

3.124   *one heart and one soul*: Acts 4:32.

           wishing and not wishing the same things: Sallust, *Catiline* 20.4.

3.126   *the staff of my old age*: Tobit 5:23.

3.131   *how good and pleasant it is for brothers to live in unity*: Psalms 132(133):1.

3.133   *to taste how sweet and sense how delightful Christ is*: See Psalms 33:9(34:8) and 99(100):5.

3.134   *God will be all in all*: See 1 Corinthians 15:28.

A CERTAIN MARVELOUS MIRACLE

1.1   *the father and priest Gilbert*: Gilbert of Sempringham (ca. 1083–1189), the son of a knight, was educated in his native England and in France. In the 1120s he served the bishop of Lincoln but resolved on voluntary poverty and returned home to Sempringham as a parish priest. He established a small community of religious women in 1131. In the following decades he fostered the creation of the Gilbertines, the only monastic order of English origin. Eventually the order counted ten religious communities that included nuns, canons, and lay brothers and sisters, these last mostly of poor backgrounds who supported the community with manual labor. Although he directed the order, it was not until late in life that Gilbert formally pro-

fessed as a canon. Extreme old age forced him to hand over authority to others, and he died in 1189 at the approximate age of 105. He was canonized in 1202.

different provinces of England: Watton was the sole Gilbertine monastery in Yorkshire. In the 1160s, there were eight in Lincolnshire and one in Bedfordshire.

the venerable priest Bede: Bede (ca. 672–735) wrote on a variety of subjects, including history, theology, and chronology. His best-known work is the *Ecclesiastical History of the English People,* completed in about 731.

the holy bishop John: John of Beverley (d. 721), eventually archbishop of York, had ordained Bede, who related the story of a young nun's miraculous healing in *Ecclesiastical History* 5.3. Bloodletting was a regular feature of monastic life, thought to be good for body and spirit.

1.2   *renewing ancient religious practice in that place*: The early medieval community of nuns at Watton, in East Yorkshire, disappeared during the Danish invasions of England in the ninth and tenth centuries. It was refounded as a Gilbertine monastery in 1150, not long before the events described here.

Here indeed the handmaids . . . choirs of angels: In one sentence, Aelred describes the central features of monastic life—manual labor; the cycle of communal prayer, in which the entire book of Psalms is said or sung every week; other collective and individual prayers; and religious learning and contemplation—as well as some of the mystical experiences associated with religious life in community.

her punishment or her glory: That is, whether she had gone to heaven or to hell.

1.3   *the saving Host was made ready*: Special Masses were held on the anniversary of the death of members of monastic communities.

2.1   *Henry of holy and pious memory*: Henry Murdac was abbot of the Cistercian house of Fountains in Yorkshire (1144–1147) and archbishop of York (1147–1153). The girl was an oblate, that is, a child raised in a monastery in the expectation that he or she

would join the religious community. By the thirteenth century, nobody under the age of fifteen could join a Gilbertine house, but there was more flexibility in the early years of the order. Aelred provides no information about the child's background.

no concern for order: Aelred probably also means "for the [Gilbertine] Order."

2.2　　*the brothers of the monastery*: The laborers were probably lay brothers. Although Aelred's text is not specific, "exterior matters" *(exteriora)* here is probably literal, that is, it refers to outdoor maintenance and repair of buildings in the women's portion of the monastic compound.

3.1　　*unless the Lord guards . . . in vain*: Psalms 126(127):1.

No one can correct whom God has despised: Ecclesiastes 7:14.

3.2　　*Balaam*: Balaam, in Numbers 22–24, was a seer who refused to curse the people of Israel. But in Revelation 2:14, he is blamed for tricking the Israelites into adultery and eating food sacrificed to idols.

Babylon: In the late seventh and early sixth centuries BCE, Assyrian kings fought and finally defeated the kings of Judah, many of whose inhabitants were deported to the Assyrian capital of Babylon. The Hebrew Bible portrays this "Babylonian Captivity" as punishment for disobedience to God. Here Aelred foreshadows the nun's punishment.

4.1　　*adulteress*: In Latin, "adultery" can be used to denote unchaste behavior in general.

like a deluded, heartless dove: Hosea 7:11.

4.2　　*noise they heard repeatedly*: The suspicious noise is the stones falling on the wall and roof.

5.3　　*Let it be done according to heavenly will*: See Matthew 6:10.

6.1　　*what was being done with her*: Literally, "with his," the noun left for the reader to supply. The young man, the nuns, and Aelred might all have had different appellations.

like a horse or mule without understanding: Psalms 31(32):9.

6.2　　*not according to knowledge*: Romans 10:2.

7.1　　*Behold the sword of Levi*: In Genesis 34, Dinah, daughter of Jacob, is raped by Shechem, son of the local leader, Hamor. Shechem

wanted to marry Dinah. Jacob demanded that Hamor and Shechem and their men be circumcised as a condition of the marriage. Once the pact was struck, the men were all circumcised.
But Dinah's brothers Levi and Simeon took matters into their
own hands, killing not only Hamor and Shechem but all their
men.

Behold the zeal of the priest Phineas: In the time of Moses, some
Israelites married women who worshiped the Baal of Peor.
God sent a plague as punishment. The priest Phineas skew-
ered one of these couples with his spear, and God, ending the
plague, made a covenant of peace with him, guaranteeing that
all his descendants would be priests (Numbers 25).

the wisdom of Solomon: In old age, King David had as a bed companion, but not mistress, a beautiful woman named Abishag.
When he died, the kingdom went to his son Solomon, in accordance with David's will and a covenant with God, but Solomon's older brother Adonijah plotted to usurp the throne.
When Adonijah asked to marry Abishag, Solomon ordered
him killed immediately: 1 Kings 1–2.

8.1　　*for where sin flowed, grace too overflowed*: Romans 5:20.

9.1　　*you who show your omnipotence . . . take pity*: From a liturgical
prayer sometimes attributed to Gregory the Great, which begins *Deus, qui omnipotentiam* and was part of the Cistercian
breviary.

　　　　all treasures . . . repose: See Colossians 2:3.

　　　　and exult in the sight of God and delight in happiness: Psalms
67:4(68:3).

10.2　　*she saw standing next to her the bishop*: Henry Murdac had been
dead for about a decade when the events recounted here took
place. The pallium is a stole or vestment worn by the pope and
archbishops who have papal permission to do so.

　　　　But see that you confess . . . every day: The archbishop lays out a
partial monastic program for the prisoner. The nuns at Watton
followed the Benedictine Rule, which meant they chanted all
the psalms every week and were obliged to confess their sins.

11.1　　*the father*: That is, Gilbert of Sempringham.

12.1　　*he asked that I not deny my presence to Christ's handmaids*: Gilbert,

then, went in person to Rievaulx to ask Aelred to come to Watton, some forty miles away, to investigate and advise.

13.1　*the Lord is pleased . . . in his mercy*: Psalms 146(147):11. The memorable matters discussed likely included the story of the dead nun who appears in a sunbeam told at the beginning of this account.

praising and glorifying the Lord for everything: Luke 2:20.

13.2　*What God has cleansed you should not call common*: Acts 10:15. On binding and loosing, see Matthew 16:19.

Teachings for Recluses

1.1　*various teachings . . . where it seems useful*: "The fathers"—called "ancients" in the next paragraph—are men who wrote and practiced monastic and eremitic (hermits') life in the fourth century and later. In this text, Aelred cites or echoes authorities, including Jerome, Ambrose, Cassian, Augustine, Benedict, and Gregory the Great.

2.1　*shut in and confined to a small cell with its exit blocked*: Here Aelred champions the monastic ideal of *stabilitas,* staying in one place in the permanent commitment to religious life emphasized in the Rule of Saint Benedict.

2.3　*the old woman with food*: For the appropriate distribution of spare food, see section 4.5.

3.2　*First seek the kingdom . . . given to you*: Matthew 6:33 and Luke 12:31.

4.1　*illness or youth*: Aelred imagines two scenarios that would prevent a recluse from earning her keep: sickness that makes work impossible, or youthful inexperience with handiwork like spinning, weaving, knitting, or embroidery that could raise money for necessities.

before she is enclosed: That is, carries out her plan to be an *inclusa,* one enclosed, which by the twelfth century was often a formal liturgical process.

4.5　*the recluse is instructed*: Possibly a reference to a guide for male recluses written around 900 CE. See Grimlaicus, *Rule for Solitaries,* trans. Andrew Thornton (Collegeville, MN, 2011), 118.

4.6　*your nakedness and your chosen way of life*: Aelred echoes the an-

cient expression *nudus nudum Christum sequi,* "naked to follow the naked Christ," a frequent trope in medieval monastic
writing.

4.7   *if illness necessitates, prepare more nourishing food*: The Rule of Saint
Benedict 36.9 allows sick brothers meat to aid their recovery.

5.1   *silence is the cultivation of justice*: Isaiah 32:17.
It is good to wait in silence for God's salvation: Lamentations 3:26.
It is good for a man . . . be silent: Lamentations 3:27–28.
Hear, O Israel, and be silent: See Deuteronomy 27:9.
I have said . . . my mouth: Psalms 38:2(39:1).
no man can overcome: James 3:8.
she is not alone when she is alone: The notion of company in solitude is an ancient monastic trope with roots in pagan philos-
ophy.

6.1   *Blessed is she . . . Saint Martin*: According to a story about the her-
mit, monk, and bishop Saint Martin of Tours (316–397 CE),
a devout recluse refused an audience with even this distinguished figure, because he was a man: Sulpicius Severus, *Dialogues* 2.12.

7.5   *For it matters little to me that I should be judged by you*: 1 Corinthians 4:3.
his place was made in peace: Psalms 75:3(76:2).
On whom . . . my words?: See Isaiah 66:2.

8.1   *times for speaking and times for keeping silent*: See Ecclesiastes 3:7.

8.2   *give orders to her servants as she pleases*: See section 4. Aelred as-
sumes the recluse will have multiple servants or agents.
The people sat down . . . to play: Exodus 32:6.

8.4   *Once Vespers are finished . . . until collation*: Aelred instructs his sister to fulfill the daily prayer cycle of monks and nuns—Vigils,
Matins, Prime, Terce, Sext, None, Vespers, and Compline—
prescribed in the Rule of Saint Benedict 16. Benedict sets out
times for silence in chapter 42. "Collation" is a light meal or
snack eaten in the evening, so called because it took place
during readings from John Cassian's *Conferences (Collationes),* a
guide to monastic spirituality. This section and the five that
follow draw heavily on the Rule.

9.1   *handiwork*: *Opus manuum* is usually translated as "manual labor,"

hard physical work. But see note to section 4.1 on the work Aelred probably has in mind.

9.2   *Idleness is indeed the enemy of the soul*: See Rule of Saint Benedict 48.1.

     spiritual weariness: See *A Pastoral Prayer* 8.4.

9.4   *liturgy owed to the honor . . . the saints*: In the twelfth century, Cistercians like Aelred performed these prayers to the Virgin Mary and the saints, which are not prescribed in the Rule of Saint Benedict. See also *A Certain Marvelous Miracle* 3.2.

9.6   *any psalms she knows*: Interestingly, Aelred makes room among recluses for those less educated—and perhaps far less privileged—than his sister.

11.1   *Moses . . . ministered to him*: On Moses, see Exodus 34:28; on Elijah, see 1 Kings 19:5–18; on Jesus, see Matthew 4:1–11.

11.2   *This kind of demon . . . fasting and prayer*: Matthew 17:20 and Mark 9:28.

11.3   *the last day . . . earthly exile*: Judgment Day, described in Revelation.

11.4   *You are dust, and to dust you will return*: Genesis 3:19.

     Blessed are those . . . praise you forever: Psalms 83:5(84:4).

12.2   *Saint Benedict allows . . . anything intoxicating*: See the Rule of Saint Benedict 39.4 and 40.3.

14.1   *But now let each one . . . renouncing the world*: The language here is very close to that of the prologue to the Rule of Saint Benedict.

14.2   *A virgin . . . body and spirit*: See 1 Corinthians 7:32, 34.

     Let him who can understand this do so: Matthew 19:12.

14.4   *the nard oil of your virginity*: Nard, or spikenard, is a precious perfume widely known in ancient Eurasia. See Song of Songs 1:11 for language close to Aelred's here; the unguent with which Mary anointed Jesus at Bethany, discussed below at 31.9–12, was nard oil.

     beautiful in form beyond all the sons of men: Psalms 44:3(45:2).

     His breath is sweeter . . . the honeycomb: Sirach 24:27.

     The length of days . . . in his left: Proverbs 3:16.

14.5   *he who is not tested is not proven*: See Sirach 34:9.

15.1   *the most blessed Miriam . . . her timbrel*: Here Aelred modifies the

349

description of a procession of women led by Miriam, the sister of Moses, in Exodus 15:20–21.

These are the ones who were not defiled . . . virgins: Revelation 14:4.

16.2   *blessed Agnes*: Agnes was a young girl of good family tried for being a Christian during the last major persecution, at the beginning of the fourth century CE. When a judge ordered her to be dragged naked to a brothel, she escaped threats to her chastity through miraculous interventions. At last condemned to death, the pyre on which she was to be burned would not light, and she was executed by the sword. The abuse and humiliation of Agnes are typical of the accounts of early Christian martyrs.

16.3   *hearts and innards*: Literally, hearts and kidneys, using the words of Psalms 7:10(9).

I have as my lover an angel of God, who guards my body with great zeal: This statement has been attributed to Saint Cecilia, who was martyred in the late second or early third century CE, since the early Middle Ages. As a young woman, Cecilia, forced to wed despite a vow of virginity, told her husband that an angel watching over her would punish him if he tried to consummate the marriage. The sentence is part of the Cistercian liturgy for Saint Cecilia's Day (November 22).

17.1   *foul humors*: Here Aelred, who frequently uses medical metaphors, refers to ancient Mediterranean medical understanding handed down to medieval Europe, according to which the human body is composed of four humors: yellow bile, black bile, phlegm, and blood. Illness was understood as an imbalance of humors. This "humoral theory" prevailed in Western medicine until the nineteenth century.

in banquets and drunkenness: Romans 13:13.

18.1   *I know a monk*: The monk is in all likelihood Aelred himself: see *Mirror of Charity* 1.28 for an explicitly autobiographical account of Aelred's struggles.

destructive force of bad habit: See Augustine, *Confessions* 8.15.12.

he rubbed his body with nettles: Saint Benedict is reported to have rolled in nettles to ward off lust: Gregory the Great, *Dialogues* 2.2.

18.2　*and I will not release you until you bless me*: So Jacob speaks to the angel who has been wrestling him all night: Genesis 32:26.

20.1　*Hold your fragility suspect*: See Rule of Saint Benedict 64.13.

21.2　*We scent distant war*: See Job 39:25.

22.1　*I saw a man*: This is probably Aelred's friend whom he recalls in *Spiritual Friendship* 3.119–27.

23.1　*mother and nurse of all virtues*: See Rule of Saint Benedict 64.19.

24.3　*who became poor although he was rich*: See 2 Corinthians 8:9.

25.1　*all the glory . . . is within*: Psalms 44:14–15(45:13–14).

　　　Listen, daughter, and see, and incline your ear: Psalms 44:11(45:10), which Benedict adapted as the first sentence of the Rule as "Listen carefully, my son, to the teachings of the master, and incline the ear of your heart."

25.2　*Love . . . the end of law*: 1 Timothy 1:5.

26.1　*I was conceived . . . conceived me*: Psalms 50:7(51:5).

26.2　*First, the flax is plunged . . . waters of baptism*: See Romans 6:3–4 for burial in baptism. Aelred now launches into an extended comparison of the soul's progress with the manufacture of soft, smooth linen from the rough fibers of the flax plant. The analogy is particularly appropriate for addressing a woman, since clothmaking was "women's work" par excellence in medieval Europe, and women often had a legal monopoly on it. Aelred's familiarity with the process has given rise to speculation that cloth was manufactured at Rievaulx in his time, although no documentary or archeological evidence supports this conclusion. Perhaps Aelred had visited linen workshops owned by his monastery. *Linum* means both "linen" and "flax"; it is translated depending on context.

　　　illicit humors: See 17.1 and note.

26.3　*with his breasts bared . . . for your comfort*: Maternal images of Christ are characteristic of Cistercian writers of the twelfth century.

　　　he entrusted her to the disciple . . . a son: See John 19:26–27. The portrayal of John as a virgin, also stressed below, is not biblical; it dates to the fourth or fifth century CE.

26.4　*only one thing is necessary*: See Luke 10:42.

in whom there is no alteration, no shadow of change: James 1:17.

oneness that is always the same . . . never end: See Psalms 101:28(102:27).

27.2   *What you do not want . . . do to another*: See Tobit 4:16 and Luke 6:31.

Everything you want . . . do for them: Matthew 7:12.

28.1   *Martha and Mary*: The story of the sisters in Luke 10:38–42 and John 12:1–8 often serves as a metaphor contrasting the active and contemplative lives. See Giles Constable, "The Interpretation of Mary and Martha," in *Three Studies in Medieval Religious and Social Thought* (Cambridge, 1995), 1–141, for a survey from late antiquity to the seventeenth century. Aelred takes up the account again in 31.9–12.

28.3   *guests, pilgrims, and the poor*: In many medieval monasteries there was an almoner, who oversaw charitable giving. No such office is mentioned in the Rule of Saint Benedict, so in keeping with their close adherence to it, Cistercian abbeys like Aelred's Rievaulx did not have one. Instead, the porter was responsible for both gatekeeping and giving alms.

28.4   *cloistered monks*: By *claustrales*, "cloistered monks," Aelred means ordinary monks, who hold no office in the monastery like abbot, prior, porter, or cellarer. In Matthew 6:31–34, Jesus cautions his follower not to worry about food, drink, or the morrow.

Let the despicable ones . . . with saffron have embraced dung: This passage is densely packed with biblical allusions: "Set them who are despicable in the church to judge" (1 Corinthians 6:4); "The sluggard is pelted with ox manure" (Sirach 22:2); "Our soul is sickened at this very meager food" (Numbers 21:5, where the Israelites ask Moses why he brought them from Egypt to die in the desert); and the quotation "Those who were nourished with saffron have embraced dung" (Lamentations 4:5).

28.6   *Nothing is more precious than goodwill*: Gregory the Great, *Homilies on the Gospels* 1.5.3, says that "indeed nothing offered to God is more precious than goodwill" *(nihil quippe offertur Deo ditius voluntate bona)*.

28.8   *holy men ... to long for it*: Gregory the Great, *Homilies on the Gospels* 1.5.4.

29.3.   *Therefore ... to the past*: The remainder of section 29 and sections 30 and 31 recount the incidents from the life, death, and resurrection of Jesus as told in the gospels.

     Hail, full of grace ... among women: Luke 1:28.

     the Word was made flesh ... grace and truth: John 1:14.

29.6.   *Now then, climb into the mountains*: Aelred directs the recluse to join in the so-called Visitation, described in Luke 1:39–56. Mary visits her cousin Elizabeth, who is pregnant with John the Baptist ("the herald of the Lord"). Recognizing the presence of Jesus, John quickened in his mother's womb.

29.7   *A child is born to us, a son is given to us*: Isaiah 6:9.

     Glory to God in the highest ... goodwill: Luke 2:14.

30.1   *Do you not fear God ... He did nothing wrong*: Luke 23:40–41.

     Remember me when you come into your kingdom: Luke 23:42.

     I think it useful ... affirmation of its truth: The story that the thief who would eventually be crucified alongside Jesus first met him as a child is not in the canonical New Testament established in the fifth century. It appears in the Syriac or Arabic Infancy Gospel, one of many texts that contain additional accounts of Jesus's life and teaching. Aelred is careful to offer the story as useful for meditation rather than as historically certain.

31.1   *Son, why did you do this ... in anguish*: Luke 2:48.

31.4   *He among you who is without sin ... stone at her*: John 8:7.

     Has no one condemned you ... condemn you either: John 8:10–11.

     Go, and sin no more: John 8:11.

31.5   *that most blessed sinner*: Luke 7:36–38 recounts the incident. The sinning women was understood in the Middle Ages to have been Mary Magdalene.

     insist fittingly, unfittingly: 2 Timothy 4:2.

     How long will you turn your face from me?: Psalms 12(13):1.

     How long will I cry out without your listening?: Habakkuk 1:2.

     give me back the joy of your salvation: Psalms 50:14(51:12).

     my heart said to you ... I will seek: Psalms 26(27):8.

31.6 *But you will not fail to stop at that house*: For accounts of the paralytic's healing, see Matthew 9:2–7, Mark 2:3–12, and Luke 5:18–25. Such a crowd surrounded Jesus on this occasion that the men bringing the sick man had to lift him onto the roof and let him down from above.

  My son . . . your sins are forgiven: Mark 2:5.

31.7 *Is your eye evil because he is good?*: See Matthew 20:15.

31.8 *Your sins are forgiven*: Mark 2:5.

31.9 *See how he loved him*: John 11:36.

31.10 *having broken open the box . . . Jesus's head*: Mark 14:3. Here and in the next several sentences, Aelred refers to the feast at Bethany (see 28.1–2, above), including the versions in Matthew 26:6–12 and Mark 14:3–9 that do not mention Mary and Martha by name.

31.11 *Why such waste . . . to the poor*: Matthew 26:8–9. "The betrayer" asking this question is Judas, although according to Matthew, all the disciples joined in the complaint; Judas is alone in his objection in John 12:4–6.

  Let her alone . . . good work for me: Mark 14:6. The two sentences that follow are Aelred's invention.

31.13 *Hosanna to the son of David . . . the name of the Lord*: Matthew 21:9.

31.14 *banquet of salvation*: The Last Supper.

31.16 *his name is John*: Luke 1:63.

  all the treasures of wisdom and knowledge: Colossians 2:3.

31.17 *Father, keep them in your name*: John 17:11.

  I want that they, too, may be with me where I am: John 17:24.

31.18 *My soul is sad unto death*: Matthew 26:38.

  your sweat became like drops of blood trickling on the ground: Luke 22:44.

31.19 *Could you not thus stay awake with me for one hour?*: Matthew 26:40.

31.22 *for he is led . . . his mouth*: See Isaiah 53:7.

31.23 *Behold the man*: John 19:5.

31.24 *the woman*: Pilate's wife; see Matthew 27:19. Aelred sees her intervention as a ploy of Satan's to prevent Jesus's death.

  princely power is on his shoulder: Isaiah 9:6.

31.27   *Father, forgive them*: Luke 23:34.

31.29   *Woman, behold your son . . . your mother*: John 19:26, 27.

31.30   *eat the honeycomb . . . with your milk*: See Song of Songs 5:1.

31.31   *that noble counselor*: Joseph of Arimathea, named in all four gospels.

       My beloved is to me . . . between my breasts: Song of Songs 1:12.

31.33   *Do not touch me*: John 20:17.

32.1   *our parents' evil*: Aelred refers here to the fact that his father was a married priest, or to the general sinfulness of human conception through sex in Augustinian thought, perhaps both.

32.3   *a wanderer and a fugitive, and whoever met me killed me*: See Genesis 4:14; Aelred speaks of himself in the language of Cain's lament.

32.5   *Consider, if you please, those foul deeds*: See Augustine, *Confessions* 2.2.2.

       No one can correct whom God has despised: Ecclesiastes 7:14.

32.6   *fog of lust . . . gushing torrent*: A close paraphrase of Augustine, *Confessions* 2.2.2.

       the words of the wicked prevailed over me: Psalms 64:4(65:3).

       my still-weak youth . . . abyss of degradation: A close paraphrase of Augustine, *Confessions* 2.2.2.

       I went further . . . yet you kept silent: Augustine, *Confessions* 2.2.2.

32.8   *wanting not the death . . . converted and live*: See Ezekiel 33:11.

32.13   *Where your treasure is . . . too*: Matthew 6:21.

33.4   *Blessed are the dead . . . their labors*: Revelation 14:13.

       All kings have slept . . . rotten and twisted: Isaiah 14:18–19.

       the death of saints is precious in the sight of the Lord: Psalms 115(116):15.

       the bosom of Abraham: The resting-place of the beggar Lazarus in Luke 16:22.

33.5   *Not so the wicked, not so*: Psalms 1:4.

33.6   *double cloak*: See Revelation 6:11.

33.10   *Fear and trembling . . . enveloped me*: Psalms 54:6(55:5).

33.12   *Come, blessed . . . the world*: Matthew 25:34.

       Depart from me, cursed ones . . . eternal life: Matthew 25:41, 46.

33.13   *the kingdom will be given to God the Father*: See 1 Corinthians 15:24.

33.16 *not through a mirror in obscurity, but face to face*: 1 Corinthians 13:12.

He who loves me . . . show myself to him: John 14:21.

This is eternal life . . . whom you sent: John 17:3.

33.17 *what the eye . . . those who love him*: 1 Corinthians 2:9.

33.18 *My beloved is mine and I am his*: Song of Songs 1:16.

Bibliography

Editions and English Translations

A Pastoral Prayer

Dutton, Marsha L., ed. *For Your Own People: Aelred of Rievaulx's Pastoral Prayer.* Translated by Mark DelCogliano. Kalamazoo, MI, 2008.

Lawson, R. Penelope, trans. "The Pastoral Prayer." In *Treatises; The Pastoral Prayer,* by Aelred of Rievaulx, 103–18. Spencer, MA, 1971.

Wilmart, A., ed. "L'oraison pastorale de l'abbé Aelred." *Revue Benedictine* 37 (1925): 263–73. Reprinted in *Aelredi Rievallensis opera omnia,* vol. 1, *Opera ascetica,* edited by A. Hoste and C. H. Talbot, Corpus Christianorum Continuatio Mediaevalis 1, pp. 755–63. Turnhout, 1971.

Spiritual Friendship

Braceland, Lawrence, trans. *Spiritual Friendship.* Collegeville, MN, 2010.

Hoste, A., ed. *De spiritali amicitia.* In *Aelredi Rievallensis opera omnia,* vol. 1, *Opera ascetica,* edited by A. Hoste and C. H. Talbot, Corpus Christianorum Continuatio Mediaevalis 1, pp. 279–350. Turnhout, 1971.

Laker, Mary Eugenia, trans. *On Spiritual Friendship.* Washington, DC, 1974.

Williams, Mark F., trans. *Aelred of Rievaulx's "Spiritual Friendship": A New Translation.* Scranton, PA, 1994.

A Certain Marvelous Miracle

Freeland, Jane Patricia, trans. *A Certain Wonderful Miracle.* In *The Lives of the Northern Saints,* by Aelred of Rievaulx, edited by Marsha L. Dutton, 109–22. Kalamazoo, MI, 2006.

McNamara, JoAnn, trans. "The Nun of Watton." *Magistra: A Journal of Women's Spirituality in History* 1 (1995): 122–38.

Pezzini, Domenico, ed. *De quodam miraculo mirabili.* In *Aelredi Rievallensis opera omnia,* vol. 6, *Opera historica et hagiographica,* edited by Domenico Pezzini, Corpus Christianorum Continuatio Mediaevalis 3, pp. 137–46. Turnhout, 2017.

Teachings for Recluses

Macpherson, Mary Paul, trans. "A Rule of Life for a Recluse." In *Treatises; The Pastoral Prayer,* by Aelred of Rievaulx, 41–102. Spencer, MA, 1971.
Talbot, C. H., ed. *De institutione reclusarum.* In *Aelredi Rievallensis opera omnia,* vol. 1, *Opera ascetica,* edited by A. Hoste and C. H. Talbot, Corpus Christianorum Continuatio Mediaevalis 1, pp. 635–82. Turnhout, 1971.

FURTHER READING

Burton, Pierre-André. *Aelred de Rievaulx (1110–1167): Essai de biographie existentielle et spirituelle.* Paris, 2010. Translated by Christopher Coski as *Aelred of Rievaulx (1110–1167): An Existential and Spiritual Biography.* Collegeville, MN, 2020.
Dutton, Marsha L., ed. *A Companion to Aelred of Rievaulx (1110–1167).* Leiden, 2017.
———. "Introduction." In *The Life of Aelred of Rievaulx and the Letter to Maurice,* by Walter Daniel, 7–88. Kalamazoo, MI, 1994.
Fergusson, Peter, and Stuart Harrison. *Rievaulx Abbey: Community, Architecture, Memory.* New Haven, CT, 2000.
Jamroziak, Emilia. *Rievaulx Abbey and Its Social Context, 1132–1300: Memory, Locality, and Networks.* Turnhout, 2005.
Knowles, David. "Ailred of Rievaulx." Chap. 6 in *Saints and Scholars: Twenty-Five Medieval Portraits.* Cambridge, 1962.
Licence, Tom. *Hermits and Recluses in English Society, 950–1200.* Oxford, 2011.
McGuire, Brian Patrick. *Brother and Lover: Aelred of Rievaulx.* New York, 1994.
Sommerfeldt, John R. *Aelred of Rievaulx: Pursuing Perfect Happiness.* New York, 2005.
Truax, Jean. *Aelred the Peacemaker: The Public Life of a Cistercian Abbot.* Collegeville, MN, 2017.

Index